ecpr PRESS

Series Editors:
Dario Castiglione (University of Exeter) and
Vincent Hoffmann-Martinot (Sciences Po Bordeaux)

urban foreign policy and domestic dilemmas

insights from Swiss and EU city-regions

Nico van der Heiden

ecpr PRESS

This thesis was accepted as a doctoral dissertation by the
Faculty of Arts of the University of Zurich in the spring semester 2009
on the recommendation of Prof. Dr. Daniel Kübler
and Prof. PhD Julie-Anne Boudreau

First published by the ECPR Press in 2010

The ECPR Press is the publishing imprint of the European Consortium for Political Research
(ECPR), a scholarly association, which supports and encourages the training, research
and cross-national cooperation of political scientists in institutions throughout Europe and
beyond. The ECPR's Central Services are located at the University of Essex, Wivenhoe Park,
Colchester, CO4 3SQ, UK

Typeset by the ECPR Press
Printed and bound by Lightning Source

British Library Cataloguing in Publication Data
A catalogue record for this book is available from the British Library

Paperback ISBN: 978-1-9073010-7-0

www.ecprnet.eu/ecprpress

Publications from the ECPR Press

ACKNOWLEDGMENTS

I would like to thank Daniel Kübler for his never-ending support of my work. He always believed that I would finish the thesis. Without his support and without our discussions of almost every aspect of this thesis, I could not have completed this project.

The Institute for Political Science at the University of Zurich provided an environment in which my scientific interest flourished for more than four years. I would especially like to mention Katrin Rindlisbacher, who not only helped me with every possible administrative struggle but also encouraged me with her positive attitude in general. Additionally, my opportunity to attend the NCCR doctoral school both provided professional training and facilitated an in-depth discussion of my project. There, I profited from the comments of other doctoral students, especially Laurent Bernhard, Andrea Iff, Philippe Koch, and Urs Scheuss.

Jean-Pierre Collin accepted me as a guest researcher for one year at the Institut National de Recherche Scientifique 'Urbanisation, Culture et Société' at the Université de Québec à Montréal. The friendly and stimulating atmosphere in Montréal allowed me to complete my thesis. I would like to thank Mélanie Gauthier, Vincent Guillon, Marie-Ève Lafortune, Stephanie Poirier, and Mélanie Robertson for their help during my year abroad. Julie-Anne Boudreau, from the same institute, kindly accepted the responsibility of being the second supervisor for my thesis.

Upon my return to Switzerland, I found a new stimulating workplace at the University of Lucerne. Joachim Blatter gave me the necessary freedom to finish my thesis, which I highly appreciated.

Sandra Egli supported me through the usual dissertation periods of despondency. I am very grateful that she calmed me down in the middle of the night when I awoke from a nightmare about rescaling. I would also like to thank my parents, who showed interest in my thesis even when its subject matter was not entirely clear to them, or to me, or to any of us.

This project would not have been possible without funding from two institutions. First, the State Secretary for Research financed the participation in the COST action A26, which examined city-regions' competitiveness and social cohesion. This allowed me to conduct the fieldwork for the seven city-regions under scrutiny. Both the work within the COST action and the work within another network funded by the European Science Foundation (CITTA) facilitated a profound test of my analytical framework. During that period, I profited from the comments of Ernesto d'Albergo, Neil Brenner, Ian Gordon, Alan Harding, Bernard Jouve, Christian Lefèvre, Willem Salet, Alan Scott, Peter Terhorst, and many others. Second, the Swiss National Science Foundation supported me with a scholarship for young researchers for my final Ph.D. year in Montréal.

I would like to thank all the interview partners who collaborated with me on the project. They showed interest in my project, and they were extremely generous with their time.

Finalising the thesis would not have been possible without the help of the following people, who dedicated endless hours to proofreading and commenting on this thesis: Luzia Vetterli, Sabina Uffer, Swen Hutter, Laura Kopp, Sandra Egli as well as Jacque Woolley and Mark Kench from ECPR Press. I apologise for reducing their life expectancies.

CONTENTS

| list of figures and tables

Figures

Tables

| list of abbreviations

ADERLY	Agence pour le Développement Economique de la Région Lyonnaise (Agency for the Economic Development of the Lyon region)
AIMF	Association Internationale des Maires Francophones (International Association of French-speaking Mayors)
CCI	Chambre de Commerce et d'Industrie (Chamber of Commerce and Industry)
CDU	Christlich Demokratische Union (Christian Democratic Union)
CEMR	Council of European Municipalities and Regions
CLIP	Cities for Local Integration Policy of Migrants
CVA	Communauté des Villes Ariane (Community of Ariane Cities)
DELICE	Réseau des Villes Gourmandes du Monde (Network of the Gourmet Cities of the World)
DEZA	Direktion für Entwicklung und Zusammenarbeit (Swiss Agency for Development and Cooperation)
ECAD	European Cities Against Drugs
ECDP	European Cities on Drug Policy
EMTA	European Metropolitan Transport Authorities
EU	European Union
EURADA	European Association of Development Agencies
FIPOI	Fondation des Immeubles pour les Organisations Internationales (Building Foundation for International Organisations)
GCD	Global Cities Dialogue
GDS	Global Digital Solidarity
GDP	Gross Domestic Product
GGS	Gemeinden Gemeinsam Schweiz (Swiss Communities Together)
GTZ	Deutsche Gesellschaft für Technische Zusammenarbeit (German Organisation for Technical Cooperation)
IAEC	International Association of Educating Cities
IAPMC	International Association of Peace Messenger Cities
ICLEI	International Council for Local Environmental Initiatives
IFGRA	International Federation of Green Regions Association
IGO	International Governmental Organisation
IOC	International Olympic Committee
IRE	Innovative Regions in Europe
IULA	International Union of Local Authorities
KBSS	Klimabündnisstädte Schweiz (Swiss Climate Alliance Cities)
LUCI	Lighting Urban Community International
NGO	Non-Governmental Organisation
OWHC	Organisation of World Heritage Cities
PPP	Public-Private Partnership

R&D	Research and Development
RZU	Regionalplanung Zürich und Umland (Greater Zurich Regional Planning Association)
SEGRE	Service des Études Générales et des Relations Extérieures (Service for General Studies and External Relations)
SYTRAL	Syndicat mixte des Transports pour le Rhône et l'Agglomération Lyonnaise (Mixed syndicate of Transport for the Rhône region and the agglomeration of Lyon)
SVP	Schweizerische Volkspartei (Swiss People's Party)
UCLG	United Cities and Local Governments
UCP	United Cities against Poverty
UN	United Nations
UNESCO	United Nations Educational, Scientific and Cultural Organisation
UTO	United Towns Association
UMVO	Union Mondiale des Villes Olympiques (World Union of Olympic Cities)
WHC	World Historical Cities
WHO	World Health Organisation
WTO	World Trade Organisation

1 introduction

NETWORKING CITY-REGIONS IN THE
NEW SCALAR ORDER

The scalar question of politics is increasingly and intensively discussed by scholars of urban geography and urban political science (Harvey 1992; Leitner and Sheppard 2003). The common understanding of a traditional scalar hierarchy, in which the national state is dominant and the regions and cities are subordinated, must be replaced by a more complex scalar redefinition of politics (Wood 2005: 205). I argue that this redefinition must include three lines of argument: first, the increased importance of city-regions as nodal points in economic processes; second, globalisation as a deterministic structuring of politics in urban areas; and third, the new phenomenon of city-regions' international activities.

Current state rescaling processes are shaped by globalisation as an economic reshuffling of the traditional processes of place and production (Brenner 1999: 447). In the medieval age, the city-region was the dominant scale as the nodal point of both economic and political processes in Europe (Le Galès 2002, see also Saunier 2002: 515; Taylor 2007: 3). This was transformed from the seventeenth century onwards as the rise of the national states led to an international system of sovereign states that interacted only through their autonomous foreign policies. For decades, far into the twentieth century, city-regions were tightly controlled at the national level. Sutcliffe (1983: 263, quoted in Ewen and Hebbert 2007: 328) aptly summarised this period as one in which 'the State took over the city, the city disappeared.' In the wake of globalisation, which is seen as a hollowing out (Jessop 2004) and a perforation of national sovereignty (Duchacek 1984),[1] Le Galès (2003) assumes a 'retour des villes'.

Scholars point to attractive patterns for city-regions in the age of globalisation; truly global city-regions, such as London, Tokyo, or New York, gain enormous power due to globalisation (Knox 1995; Massey 2007; Sassen 1991). Within these cities, capital accumulates and the global flow of trade is managed. Such cities are nodal points of globalisation (Scott 1996; Storper 1997); through their importance in economic processes, they gain political power (Friedmann 2001: 122).[2] This raises an important question: is the city-regions' increased importance in economic processes followed by an increased political connectivity of city-regions across national borders?

---

1   This aspect, which has, of course, been challenged, is further addressed on page 5ff.

2   The most astonishing example of this might be London's role in the English economy and thereby in the British national state (Syrett and Baldock 2003; Thornley 2003). Of course, not all cities are winners of globalisation. Many of the city-regions that predominantly relied on blue-collar jobs have suffered tremendous losses of both workplaces and inhabitants (Gestring *et al.* 2005).

The linkages between large city-regions are numerous. Primarily, these links are economically oriented. In earlier days, city-regions were places of trade; now, this function has been disfavoured by a new centrality of the management of the flows of goods in globalised city-regions (Castells 1994, 1996). Through new communication methods, geographical distance has become almost virtual for the transfer of capital and knowledge (Moss and Townsend 2004). Still, urban areas connect national economies to the global scale,[3] and the competitiveness of city-regions is increasingly determined by their connectivity to other major metropolitan centres (Castells 1994: 29). Whereas the hinterland traditionally produces for the respective city-region and the rural areas produce for the local or national market,[4] international firms that are oriented towards the global market settle within city-regions. On the city-region's scale, transport chains join together, and global trade is managed and conducted (Keeling 1995; Tussie 2006).

The goal is to investigate whether the global economic connectivity of urban regions is followed by a corresponding connectivity of politics. Although political linkages between city-regions are not a new phenomenon, there has been an astonishing increase of these networking activities since the 1980s (Benington and Harvey 1999a, 1999b; Kunzmann 2002).[5] Traditionally, city partnerships constituted the main form of such activities. Some of them can be traced back to the Middle Ages, and there was a boost of new city partnerships after the Second World War. However, city networking is a new phenomenon that has spread over Europe throughout the last twenty-five years. The international activities of one community[6] are defined as a city's engagement in transnational cooperation schemes that involve at least one partner city in another country.[7] Networking thus allows city-regions to 'leapfrog over space, connecting spatially separated territorial units as members of a network of interaction and exchange' (Leitner *et al.* 2002: 297). This blurs the traditional concepts of global, local, foreign, and domestic, and it leads to a transcendence of the formal realities of international affairs (Kirby *et al.* 1995: 267f.).

The analysis focuses on formally established partnerships and networks (see also Taylor *et al.* 2007b).[8] This restriction allows a serious understanding of an (a priori assumed) comprehensive policy area in which politics controls the established international relations. Perhaps the best-known example of a political link between city-regions is the Eurocities network (Heinelt and Niederhafner 2008), which was established in 1986 with an original orientation as a lobby organisation of secondary cities. Since then, the network has been steadily growing; it now

---

3   This aspect will be addressed further on pages 5ff and 28ff.

4   This aspect will be addressed further on pages 27ff.

5   For a general overview of the literature on the network society, see Castells (1996), which also contains an interesting analysis of the increasing importance of non-state actors' networking.

6   I use the term 'community' to refer to the local political scale.

7   See Perkmann (2003: 156) for a definition of cross-border cooperation in general. See Lefèvre and d'Albergo (2007: 319) for a more empirical definition of urban foreign policy.

8   For a discussion of informal and/or private networks, see Taylor *et al.* (2007a).

covers more than 130 member cities in thirty countries. Eurocities has become the cities' most influential lobby organisation towards the European Union (EU), and its members cooperate within numerous policy fields. As transborder cooperation has increased simultaneously with the rise of the EU, the two processes' connection can be fruitfully analysed by comparing city-regions from EU member states with Swiss city-regions.

RESEARCH QUESTIONS

To tackle the phenomenon of city-regions' international activities, the research question, the following theoretical section, and the empirical analysis will each be divided into two steps. In the first step, international activities of city-regions are treated as the dependent variable and the determinants of city-regions' foreign policies will be examined. In the second step, international activities of city-regions will be treated as the independent variable. These two steps will reveal what changed after city-regions begin participating in international activities.

Why do city-regions go global?

As will be explained in the empirical section, particularly in the case study section, the differences among the city-regions under scrutiny are astonishing. The city-regions differ not only in intensity but also in the content of their international activities (see Giezen 2005; Lefèvre and d'Albergo 2007). Therefore, the first goal of this research is to determine *which factors account for the intensity and the orientation of the international activities of city-regions.*

The goal is to find elements that explain why a city-region follows a certain path within its international activities. Therefore, explanatory factors will be observed on the macro level and the meso level to understand 'which networks [city-regions] join, whether to join them as co-leaders or regular members, and when to enter or leave networks' (Leitner and Sheppard 1999: 240), since these decisions are important factors for the future (economic) prospects of city-regions. In this analysis, a distinction will be drawn between the intensity of international activities, which means the extent to which a city-region is involved in international activities, and the content of international activities, which means the orientation that is followed within the chosen activities.

What is changed by city-regions' international activities?

Here, international activities are the driving force of changes in policy-making at the city-region scale and beyond. The internationalisation of certain policy areas through international networking should alter the traditional method of policy-making at the city-region scale. Additionally, city-regions' pursuit of their own international activities places pressure on the traditional multi-level governance setting. Governance mechanisms, both on the horizontal axe (representing the interplay between different communities within a city-region) and on the vertical axe (representing the city-region's relation towards upper-level governments), are expected to change. However, it is still unclear how and to what extent this occurs.

Therefore, the second research question, which addresses this issue, asks *whether the international activities of city-regions transform the intrascalar and interscalar policy-making process.*

Of course, not only the latter two arguments, which concern changes caused by city-regions' new international activities, but also the two research questions are interlinked. Figure I.1 shows the double analytical logic of my model of city-regions' international activities.

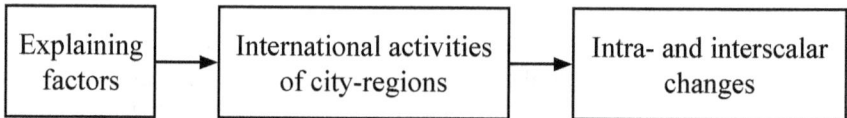

Figure I.1: A first basic overview of the model of international activities of city-regions

CHAPTER OUTLINE

As stated previously, both the theoretical and the empirical parts of this book follow the distinction outlined in the discussion of the research question above. The theoretical discussion will start by explaining city-regions' international activities with the rescaling theory. The rescaling theory provides a broader theoretical framework of scalar changes in a post-Fordist era. This macro-theoretical approach will be combined with the varieties of capitalism approach, on the meso level, to provide a more encompassing framework that theoretically explains the intensity and the orientation of city-regions' international activities. Treating international activities as an independent variable, I turn to three scales or interscalar relations by using different strands of the rescaling theory. In the first step, changes in the policy-making process at the city-region scale will be examined. In the second step, I will consider questions of horizontal and vertical governance and summarise the theoretical argument and present a model of city-regions' international activities. Readers less interested in the theoretical model of urban foreign policy can find an overview of the model at the end of Chapter One.

The empirical part is divided into two sub-parts. It begins in Chapter Two with an examination of the seven city-regions under scrutiny in order to provide insights into every city-region. The case studies explain the mechanisms of the international activities of the respective city-regions. Readers less interested in the details from the city-regions can find a summary at the end of each case study. Thereafter, the empirical analysis is guided by the theoretical argument outlined in Chapter Two, and it is based on a comparative analysis of the seven city-regions. The argument is divided again in Chapter Three, which explains the diversity of international activities, and Chapter Four, which discusses the changes caused by the city-regions' international activities. Some summary findings, especially on the links between the two research questions, are provided in the Conclusion.

chapter one | a theory of urban foreign policy

As discussed previously, the theoretical approach is divided into two sections. The first section highlights factors that explain the astonishing variety of city-regions' international activities. The second section addresses theoretical assumptions about changes caused by the new urban foreign policy.

The rescaling theory provides a broader theoretical framework that will guide the following analysis, on both the theoretical and the empirical levels. The rescaling approach analyses scalar shifts of political steering capacity in an era of a globalised economy. Although it seems intuitively plausible to analyse urban foreign policy as a scalar shift of political steering capacity, this idea, as will be argued, needs further refinement because proponents of the rescaling approach oversimplify the patterns that city-regions follow within their international activities. Thus, the second step turns to the varieties of capitalism approach. This meso-level approach, although closely linked to the rescaling theory, provides alternative explanations for the different patterns followed by city-regions within their international activities. It will be argued that the rescaling theory predicts no general logical reason for a city-region to act on the international scale. Instead, the explanation here relies on the economic specificities of each city-region.

Next, the second research question will be investigated by setting international activities as the independent variable and reflecting on the changes caused by these newly emerging activities. I propose three scalar levels of reflection. First, the city-region itself will be examined and the question will be asked whether urban policy-making has changed, and, if so, how it has changed. The interplay between politics, the administration, and the public in a rescaled statehood will also be examined. Second, horizontal governance will be scrutinised and will focus on whether the interplay between the core city and the surrounding communities has changed through international activities of the local scale. The literature on metropolitan governance in a rescaled statehood will guide the respective analysis. Third, elements of vertical governance will be explored. In this context, the question will be asked whether traditional intergovernmental relations have changed because of the international activities of city-regions. Questions of multi-level governance in a rescaled statehood will also be examined.

WHY DO CITY-REGIONS GO GLOBAL?

Globalisation and the rescaling of the state: a macro approach

Analysing transformations of statehood using the rescaling approach primarily means looking at politics spatially.[1] Place, as a variable, has been neglected in political science for a long time. According to the rescaling approach, this leads to a deceptive and incomplete analysis of the current trends and challenges of politics (Brenner *et al.* 2003). Agnew (1999) argues that neglecting the scalar question leads to the territorial trap of political science, and Beck (1997) coined the term 'methodological nationalism'. The primary question of a scale-sensitive approach to politics regards how the interplay between different governmental levels has changed.

By analysing the transition from a Fordist to a post-Fordist regime of state regulation,[2] the scalar transformation of statehood in contemporary capitalism is at the heart of this research strand. The transformation from a Fordist state regulation system towards a system of 'entrepreneurial urban governance' (Harvey 1989) will be traced by following the three phases of this transformation, as described in Brenner (2004).

1. This examination starts with the Fordist era and its scalar-economic redistribution mechanisms;

2. next, the transition of statehood that followed the economic restructuring of the 1970s will be discussed;

3. in the last step, current scalar trends in the era of global economic competitiveness will be shown, which will allow for the derivation of hypotheses for the international activities of city-regions.

In this context, it will be shown that these activities are part of urban policy-making in an era of rescaled statehood in contemporary capitalism.

Fordism and the dominance of the national scale

The years between the end of the Second World War and the early 1970s are usually described as the Fordist era. This period of economic growth generated consistent revenues for the state.[3] The national scale was pre-eminent for both

---

1   One might add that this is a spatial (neo-) Marxist perspective of urban politics. I will not deal with the neo-Marxist basis of the rescaling theory here. See Giddens (1981) for the introduction of space in the Marxist analysis of politics, and see Harvey (1985) for the adaptation of this logic to urban politics.

2   Although much of the research on the Fordist regime of accumulation, the transformation towards urban entrepreneurialism (see below), and the rescaling approach to statehood is based on the regulation theory (see Brenner 2000b), I do not explain the details of this approach. For recent overviews of regulation theory, see Jones and Ward (2004), or Uitermark (2005). For the origins of the regulation school, see Liepitz (1977), Boyer (1986), Lefebvre (1974), and Jessop (1990, 1994).

3   Jessop (1992a) defines four elements of the Fordist mode of regulation: the labour process, the regime of accumulation, the mode of regulation, and the mode of societalisation (see also Goodwin and Painter 1996).

conflicts and solutions in economic management (Jessop 2002: 25; MacLeod and Goodwin 1999: 710). Because of the cold war, foreign policy decision-making concentrated on the national scale, which controlled security policies and the army. National borders served as important economic barriers (Jessop 1994: 253; 2002: 26; Peck and Tickell 1994: 290) because the taxation of imports was one instrument used to protect the domestic market. The revenues from that taxation led to even more increased profit for the national state. Therefore, companies largely produced for their home market and relied on national market regulations (Leitner and Sheppard 1998: 285).[4] The scalar interplay between the national and local level, like the global interplay between largely separated economies, was relatively straightforward. The national state managed foreign relations and the well-being of the domestic economy but redistributed the collected revenues to lower scalar levels, which allowed it to maintain large redistribution programmes (Jessop 1994: 254ff.).

This was accomplished in two ways. On the one hand, the national state distributed large amounts of money to the local entities in order to provide general social welfare programmes. This diminished the social inequalities among individual citizens.[5] As most citizens, especially those in need of state social programmes, lived in urban areas, those areas profited most from the welfare redistribution programmes. Hence, the cities were under the tight control of the national state (Heeg *et al.* 2003: 140).[6] The hierarchical interplay between the national, the regional, and the local scale was straightforward and was oriented towards social cohesion (Jessop 2002: 71).[7] On the other hand, the national scale was also occupied with the question of regional and thus spatial inequalities (Keating 2001: 372). National governments spent large amounts of money on programmes that provided access to infrastructure and that supported the establishment of businesses in rural areas. The goal of the national policy was an equalisation of spatial inequalities between urban and rural areas. 'The task of state spatial intervention, under these conditions, was to mould the geography of capital investment into a more balanced, cohesive, and integrated locational pattern throughout the national territory' (Brenner 2004: 16), or, even more precisely, 'one nation geographically as well as socially' (Goodwin and Painter 1996: 646).

Thus, although there were problems concerning the institutional organisation of large metropolitan areas (Ostrom 1972; see also Kübler 2003), the tight fit between urban dynamism and national economic growth (Sassen 1991; Taylor 1995)

---

4 However, this argument is certainly less valid for small, open economies (like Switzerland; see Katzenstein 1985, 2003).

5 Hence, the Fordist era is also labelled as Keynesian statehood (Keil 2003; Peck and Tickell 1994: 283).

6 It remains an open question whether this straightforward hierarchical interplay was true in national contexts other than the Anglo-American one in which this theory was developed.

7 Leitner and Sheppard (1998: 285) correctly note that a social-cohesion-oriented policy was not known in American urban politics (see also Peterson 1981). Still, economic security in a stable hierarchical government scheme was common for both European and American urban politics.

was unquestioned as long as gross domestic product (GDP) growth rates allowed for large scalar redistribution programmes. City governments could concentrate on city management and the distribution of public goods. Questions of metropolitan governance predominantly addressed administrative efficiency, local service provisions, and regional planning (Brenner 2003: 299). Nevertheless, the national scale was the primary scale of political-economic regulation (Boyer 1996: 45; Brenner 2004: 3), controlling both the interplay with other national states across borders as well as the sub-national state scales within its own territory.

The crisis of the 1970s and the transformation of the scalar interplay
The oil crisis of 1973 was the starting point of a worldwide recession, which altered not only the economic system but also the state spatial interplay.[8] The breakdown of the Bretton Woods monetary system of stable currency exchange rates ended the national states' ability to treat their economies as autarchic spaces (Altvater 1992: 37; Jessop 2002; Peck and Tickell 1994: 291) and created an opportunity for global competitiveness (Dicken 1994: 122ff.). Supply and demand of one national economy are thus no longer necessarily linked. This has decreased the ability of national states to tax imports and financial products while simultaneously increasing international competition between national economies (Gill 1995: 417).

Fiscal retrenchments on the national scale also altered the Fordist redistribution mechanisms between the national and local scales. Decreasing national state revenue no longer allows for large transfers from the national to the local scale, especially in times of economic recession (Harvey 1989: 4; Mayer 1994: 320). Consequently, intergovernmental conflicts concerning interscalar redistribution programmes have increased (Peck and Tickell 1994: 306). The Fordist local social policies are undermined due to the reduction of financial transfers from the national state. 'The availability of public funds for redistributive spatial policies was thus severely constrained, and traditional forms of compensatory regional policy, like other forms of social policy, were scaled back' (Brenner 2004: 169).[9] Hence, at the post-Fordist transition, the 'pyramid shaped model of territorial organization' (Brenner 2004: 168) had not yet been altered. Due to the increased competitiveness of national economies, however, the fiscal redistribution possibilities towards the local scale were reduced dramatically. As discussed in the next section, the scalar system of state spatial organisation also changed in the era of globalisation.

---

8   This section does not examine the changes in the mode of production from Fordist mass production to a mode of flexible specialisation; rather, it focuses on spatial political changes. For an analysis of the changes in the production system that occurred from the 1950s to the 1980s, see Hirst and Zeitlin (1997).

9   The redistribution's ability to reduce inequalities between individuals decreased as well. However, the rescaling approach focuses on spatial inequalities.

The post-Fordist state and globalisation: the end of place?
Throughout the 1980s, economic globalisation continued and led to a steadily increasing competition between places.[10] Capital became easily transferable and, therefore, place became relatively unimportant for economic processes (Cox 1993: 437, 1997; Cox and Mair 1991: 202; Parkinson and Harding 1995: 56). Or, as Castells (1996: 407ff.) argues, 'spaces of flows' will triumph over 'spaces of place' in the making and shaping of the new global order of centrality. The state consistently loses ground on controlling market activities (Hirst and Thompson 1996, 1997; Lash and Urry 1987). In a global competing market, only national states that offer low taxes, unrestrictive zoning laws, large subsidies, and consequent low or non-tariff policies will be able to provide attractive workplaces.[11] Therefore, the possibilities for redistribution policies, both interpersonal and interscalar, are further reduced (Marston 2000: 225). Instead, the state changes its focus; no longer a passive respondent to globalisation pressures, it becomes a competitive state (Dicken 1994; Porter 1990) that proactively tries to position its territory on the global scale (Brenner 2004: 172f.). The goal is to increase or stabilise economic wealth by acquiring the highest possible share of global investments. The main concern of national states in the post-Fordist era is thus one of global competitiveness, as economic growth is not as easily achievable as it was under the Fordist system of production and is only possible through gaining a better position in the world market.

Simultaneously, but not contradictorily, the national state loses its control of the market activities within its own territory (Simeon 1991: 49). Thereby, the financial basis of tax and tariff income is further reduced, and it is not replaced by other income possibilities. Jessop (1994) summarises this logic of the national state, which tries to enhance its competitiveness by undermining its own financial basis, as a hollowing out of the national state.[12] Undermining thereby means that the national state, in order to guarantee economic growth within its territory, reduces its grip on economic activities. Therefore, the national scale has become less important in the age of globalisation. The rescaling literature now addresses whether the losses on the national scale can be compensated on other scales and, if so, which scales can accomplish that task.

---

10   Here, I will focus on the transformation of the state towards post-Fordism. For an overview of the changing economic production processes in post-Fordism, see Elam (1994).

11   Liepitz (1994b) links this development to the broader concept of individualism, which, in his point of view, has gained new importance among the Western intelligentsia since the early 1980s. Liepitz (1994b: 344) subsumes the idea of 'liberal-productivism' and the implications for economic processes rather ironically: 'We must be competitive! And to that end the initiative of entrepreneurs must be freed. And if the social consequences are unfavourable? Too bad. We must be competitive! To what end? Because free enterprise dictates that we be competitive. And so the story unfolded.'

12   Jessop changes his view on the hollowing out of the national state in his later works (see Jessop 2004) and relativises his hollowing-out thesis for a multi-scalar analysis of statehood.

Entrepreneurial city-regions in a 'glocalised' world

Collinge (1999) disagrees with the general hypothesis of a hollowing out of state-hood (see also Brenner 2004: 45); conversely, Collinge speaks of a relativisation of state spatial scales instead of a complete descaling of statehood. The reshuffling of the hierarchy of spaces (Liepitz 1994a) leads to a system in which city-regions are the new primary actors in global competitiveness (Castells 1994: 23, see also Peck 2002) because they are nodal points of globalisation (Friedmann 2001: 122; Scott 1996; Storper 1997). City-regions' strategic position as territories in which capital and knowledge are concentrated and in which transportation links come together makes them the primary scale of international competition (Scott *et al.* 2001: 15ff.).[13] Additionally, although capital is supposedly completely mobile nowadays (Lash and Urry 1993), companies still need infrastructure to operate, and this infrastructure is rather immobile in most cases; production processes are still locally bound (Cox 1993: 434; 9; Cox and Mair 1991: 199; Hubbard 2007: 192).[14] However, these local embeddings of economic processes are increasingly concentrated in urban areas rather than spread over larger territories since the national state is no longer capable of regulating the dispersion of economic growth throughout the country. Instead, the market logic of concentration now dominates the spatial questions of distribution and imminently leads to a concentration of capital in large city-regions.

The scalar orientation of competition has thus changed from national states to city-regions,[15] or, as Harding (1997: 295) states, 'localities have something to play for and something to compete with.' Finding themselves directly competing with other city-regions, localities adapt to their new settings by introducing their own mechanisms of neo-liberal adjustment. This results in increased locational poli-cies[16] instead of policies aimed at social cohesion (Begg 1999: 805; Gill 1995: 417; Pickvance and Preteceille 1991). The goal of such policies is clearly to position the city on the global scale of capital circulation by enhancing and presenting its attributes that are considered to be most competitive (Brenner 2004: 207; Gordon 1999: 1002; Ohmae 2001). Harding (1997: 297) summarises what is expected from the new neo-liberal politics of production at the city scale: a 'greater concern with the state of the local economy; the fortunes of locally based businesses [and] the potential for attracting new companies and/or promoting growth within indigenous firms' (see also Moulaert *et al.* 2003a; Swyngedouw *et al.* 2002). This leads to a system of entrepreneurial urban governance (Harvey 1989) in which the economic well-being of a city-region no longer primarily depends on its position

---

13   For a critical review of globalisation as a motor of urban competition, see Budd (1998).

14   Cox (1993: 437) provides a detailed analysis of this 'nonsubstitutability of local social relations' in economic cooperation schemes.

15   For a discussion of the concept of cities in competition, see Begg (1999). For the application of the competitiveness concept to political entities, see Krugman (1996); for a critical discussion of this approach, see Porter (1990).

16   Locational politics can be defined as politics that intends to bring economic gains to specific spatial areas (see Brenner 2000a). It refers to the German term Standortpolitik.

within a national urban scalar hierarchy but rather depends on its position in a global hierarchy of large city-regions.[17]

There is thus a double logic within the post-Fordist capital system. On the one hand, competition becomes increasingly global and ignores national borders. On the other hand, competition shifts downwards to the city-region scale since city-regions are the main competitors and since the economic performances of city-regions become increasingly disentangled from those of their national states (Lever 1999: 1035ff.). Both tendencies show an increasing scalar complexity of state action; at the same time, however, both tendencies show a weakening of the national scale (Jessop 1994; Peck and Tickell 1994).

Swyngedouw (1992, 1997, 2000b) coined the term 'glocalisation' for this double process, meaning that although globalisation leads to heavier competition and to the erosion of political steering capacity at the national scale, economic processes are still rooted in local places, especially city-regions.[18] 'Glocalisation' is 'a double movement of globalisation on the one hand and evolution, decentralisation or localisation on the other' (Swyngedouw 1992: 40; see also Castells 1994: 31). City-regions are nodal points for globalisation processes because they link the national economy to the international marketplace (Savitch and Kantor 2002; Scott 1996: 263). In sum, the rescaling literature's general argument posits that supranational and sub-national units have gained increased importance in economic processes due to the logic of 'glocalisation' (Harding 1997: 294).

> The postwar project of national territorial equalization and sociospatial redistribution has thus been superseded by qualitatively new national, regional, and local state strategies to position major urban economies optimally within global and supranational circuits of capital.
>
> *(Brenner 2004: 3)*

The question then is how and to what extent does the state employ scalar strategies to react to the changed logic of global economic competition? As stated before, the starting point of the rescaling theory is not the hollowing out of statehood but rather the relativisation of the importance of the national scale in policy-making and the scalar shifts of statehood that follow thereafter. Thus, the question does not ask whether some scales have become unimportant in the age of globalisation (i.e. deterritorialisation); rather, it asks which territories are the ones in which political decision-making is still possible (i.e. reterritorialisation; Brenner 1998: 3, 1999: 435f.). The literature examined here also states that space is not unimportant in the era of global competition; city-regions do not need to be 'leaves in the wind of globalisation' (Savitch and Kantor 2002: 346). But the notion that the world can be simply divided into different 'black-boxed' national states in the age of globalisation leads to a territorial trap (Brenner *et al.* 2003: 2). Geo-economic logics have

---

17   The approach of the 'entrepreneurial city' (Hall and Hubbart 1996, 1998) is certainly close to the approach of the 'urban growth machine' (Logan and Molotch 1987, 2002) and the regime theory (Stone 1993).

18   See Robertson (1998) for a critical analysis of the use of the term 'glocalisation'.

thus led to increased importance for both the supranational and the sub-national scale of statehood. The next step is to examine how the state, as a multi-layered political entity, has reacted to the new logic of 'glocalisation'.

State responses: upscaling and downscaling
The first possible way to compensate for the loss of decision-making possibilities on the national scale is to adjust the political decision-making process to the level of global economic processes by shifting decision-making processes upwards towards the supranational level (i.e. upscaling) (Jessop 1994: 270f.). There are numerous examples of this trend; the process of European integration or international trade organisations like the World Trade Organisation (WTO) are the most prominent. National states are increasingly intertwined; they can no longer autonomously make decisions in many policy areas because international regulations, supranational laws, and complex systems of bilateral agreements between countries restrict them. The second possibility is downscaling, which is the shift of decision-making capabilities to lower sub-national levels of the state (Goodwin *et al.* 2006) and especially to city-regions. It is an open question whether the strengthened position of city-regions in economic processes coincides with the growing importance of political steering possibilities.

Rescaling as a process can thus be defined as both upscaling and downscaling; it is the decentralisation of the national scale of state regulation in favour of new sub-national and supranational territorial configurations (Amin 1994: 28; Brenner 1999: 435). Or, as Jessop (1994: 264) states: 'This loss of autonomy [on the national level] creates in turn both the need for supranational coordination and the space for sub-national resurgence.'[19]

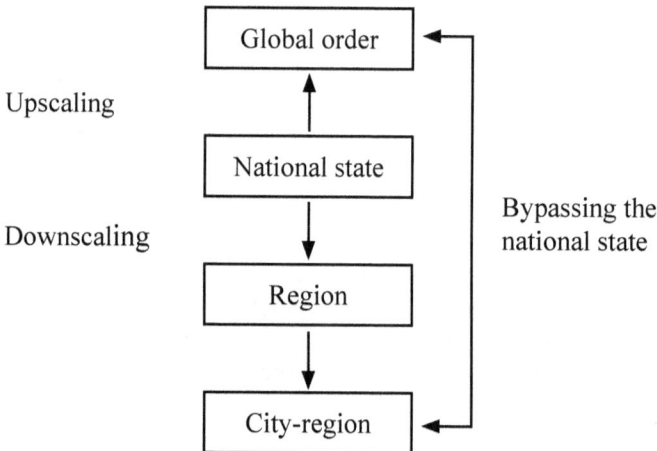

Figure 1.1: Bypassing the national state

---

19 Jessop (2002: 235, quoted in Goodwin *et al.* 2006: 424) also explicitly points to cross-national alliances as part of the rescaling process. The powers of national states 'are delegated upwards to supraregional or international bodies, downwards to regional or local states, or outwards to [...] cross-national alliances.'

Figure 1.1 summarises the argument concerning multi-level governance's appearance in the age of global competition between large city-regions. As the national state loses control towards the global order (upscaling) and towards the city-regions (downscaling), city-regions themselves start to bypass the national state and to participate directly in the global order[20] as main actors in the global economic competition (Jessop 1994: 264). In a traditional understanding of multi-level governance, city-regions were subordinated under the regional and national scale; now, city-regions 'jump scales' (Smith 1995, see also Collinge 1999: 568).

The foreign policies of city-regions in a rescaled statehood
The arguments presented so far have shown that the traditional understanding of statehood and international relations is insufficient for the analysis of modern political processes. In earlier days, it was clear that only the national state operated on the international level and that city-regions, as subordinates of the national state, followed the directives given by the national state and hence never intervened on the international level. The most significant new element is that city-regions have begun to enter international and foreign policy-making processes and have become actors on the international level (Heeg *et al.* 2003: 141). This leads to a bypassing of the national state (Jessop 1992b: 32), which now can only control the foreign activities of city-regions indirectly. 'Some state capacities [...] are being usurped by emerging horizontal networks of power – local and regional – which bypass central states and connect localities or regions in several nations' (Jessop 1994: 264). Cities are thereby capable of achieving a bargaining capacity in the face of market forces (Savitch and Kantor 2002).

These arguments lead to the rejection of Liepitz's (1994a: 38) notion that the national state reserves the administration of external relations in the post-Fordist era. Instead, 'interurban networks not only hinge upon, but are also part of the transformation of extant state power and the complex rescaling of political power that are currently unfolding in the EU and its member states' (Leitner and Sheppard 2002: 164).

Thus, city-regions' international activities can be perceived as the state's response to a 'glocalised' economy because they connect the city-regions as nodal points of globalisation within the global scale where competition takes place. Bypassing the national state is thus the political response of city-regions through which they connect themselves to the global competitive market (Collinge 1999: 568; Harding 1997: 295). Through international activities, city-regions form their own transnational connections on the European and global scale by maximising the possibilities of the downscaling process, which were described above. Observing the international activities of city-regions thus enables an analysis of those rescaling processes.

Therefore, competitive city-regions are almost forced to pursue political activities on the global level, independent from the national foreign policy. They 'jump scales' (Smith 1995) in order to construct transversal linkages within the suprana-

---

20   See also Perkmann (2003: 153).

tional scalar order (Brenner 2003: 310), and thus they develop cross-border relationships according to their need to stay competitive. Or, as Kincaid (1989: 225) highlights, '[Cities] will have to become international.' The rescaling theory offers this general proposition concerning the international activities of city-regions:

> City-regions intensify their international activities by responding to globalisation challenges.

Thus, the basic argument of the rescaling theory posits that the national state loses political steering capacity due to the post-Fordist transformation; as city-regions become nodal points of globalisation, they gain political steering capacity due to downscaling processes. City-regions should thus be able to increase their international contacts. The next question to be examined is the content of city-regions' international activities, as described by the rescaling approach.

The foreign policy of city-regions and urban locational politics
Early contributions have analysed international activities of city-regions as 'a new policy option [...] which has the potential to overcome the negative effects of urban competition' (Heeg et al. 2003: 139). As argued above, a rescaled statehood tends towards an increase of urban locational politics as part of newly emerging competition strategies for promoting city-regions on the global scale. This increase is caused by a scalar shift of competition towards the city-regions as nodal points of these processes. A possible counter-trend against the neo-liberal shift towards urban entrepreneurialism could emerge at the city-region scale (Moulaert et al. 2007: 196; Pendras 2002).[21] Ideally, city-regions can use their new strength, which has resulted from the downscaling processes of statehood, and their international activities

> as a new and promising attempt to overcome negative effects of deregulation at the level of national states, of increasing flexibility of companies with respect to location choices and of the limited reach of urban actors in a globalised economy. [...] Metropolitan cooperation can provide a way for political re-regulation in fields which have faced dramatic changes due to neo-liberal transformation processes. Considering the debate on urban competition and its negative implication for urban society, metropolitan cooperation also opens a new window of opportunity to counteract disempowering processes. Though it is no guarantee for an overall improvement of urban development, cooperation can be used as an instrument to strengthen social cohesion in cities.
>
> *(Heeg et al. 2003: 151f.)*

Swyngedouw (1997) agrees by stating that cities might be nodal points for a counter-trend formed by political movements of standing against the neo-liberal orientation of politics in general (see also Bulkeley 2005: 889; Harvey 1989: 5; Keil 2003; Leitner and Sheppard 1999: 233; Smith 2002). International activities

---

21 See Peck and Tickell (1994: 311) for the rare argument that 'solutions to the crisis of uneven development in after-Fordism are unlikely to come from the bottom – through local competition – but instead must begin with action from above – through national and global coordination.'

are thereby perceived as a means to overcome the competition among city-regions. Interurban networks are seen as opportunities to form a monopoly of major economic areas in which cooperation should prevail over competition. City-regions that cooperate with each other through urban networking should stop their race to the bottom and will start cooperating and stop competing (Castells 1994: 31), or that they would at least cooperate on the European scale in order to face competition from other continents (Nijkamp 1993).[22]

This view has been challenged by a more critical view of rescaling processes (Peck 2002: 333). Jones and MacLeod (1999, see also MacLeod 1999) argue that the downscaling processes, which shift political decision-making power towards city-regions, do indeed open up new possibilities for statehood at the local level but that the content of such increased policy-making is anything but clear. The authors challenge the view that the scale of the city-region can take up the national state's losses of decision-making power. Rather, the same logic that led to the decrease of steering capacity at the national scale is reproduced at the city-region's scale as well; politics is losing control over market processes, only focusing on providing the best options for attracting businesses by lowering taxes and reducing social welfare expenditures.

As city-regions compete with each other on a global scale and as they become increasingly involved in economic development, they cannot afford to engage in international activities that counteract the inherent logic of global competition. Instead, the contrary might occur. International activities are even used by the entrepreneurial city as an important element of locational politics (John 2000: 877; Leitner and Sheppard 2002: 158; Phelps et al. 2002: 214f.). Therefore, it is expected that most international activities of city-regions will focus on marketing activities (Church and Reid 1996: 1310). As the scale of economic competition has shifted from an intra- to an international level, the global scale is thus also perceived to be the best scale for promoting the city-region and its economic advantages. Thus, within interurban networking platforms, locational politics of city-regions can be conducted. City-regions' international activities thus do not pose a counter-trend against the neo-liberal turn in urban policy-making; rather, they are an integral part of such a strategy (Aldecoa and Keating 1999: V).

What does this mean for the content of city-regions' international activities? Savitch and Kantor (2002: 48f.) introduce a distinction between an orientation toward social cohesion and an orientation toward economic competitiveness in urban policy-making (see also Ache et al. 2008; Buck et al. 2005). Savitch and Kantor differentiate between a political strategy, which primarily endeavours to equalise the inequalities among the citizens, and an economic strategy, which primarily endeavours to increase international competitiveness. The authors argue that cities which faced severe economic restructuring processes in the post-Fordist era now favour a competitiveness-oriented strategy. City-regions, which did not

---

22   Peck and Tickell (1994: 292) view the international activities of city-regions as part of a more general search for a new institutional fix and posit that 'neo-liberalism is part of the problem, not part of the solution.'

undergo such a harsh economic decline and which hold a better position in the international marketplace, possess the ability to focus on social aspects.

The same distinction between social and economic orientation can be applied to urban foreign policy-making (Lefèvre and d'Albergo 2007); on the international level, city-regions choose between a strategy that aims at social and ecological goals and one that aims at internationally promoting the city-region economically. My theoretical argument, as developed before, favours the critical analysis of urban policy-making, which states that city-regions become more and more entrepreneurial. It is therefore argued that city-regions, which face the challenges of a global market, will focus primarily on questions of economic well-being rather than on questions of social cohesion through their strategy of international activities. This is the first hypothesis.

Hypothesis 1:   Globalisation pressures lead city-regions to develop a coherent economic-oriented strategy for their international activities.

This hypothesis thus aligns with the more critical analyses of transformations of urban policy-making in the age of globalisation, such as the example presented by Leitner and Sheppard:

Cooperative networks between cities are potentially an effective means of increasing the economic and political leverage of cities in an increasingly flexible global economy. [...] If networks simply elevate the economic-growth-at-any-cost approach and competitiveness ideology of elite politics from the urban to the network scale, reductions in social and spatial inequalities are unlikely.[23]

(Leitner and Sheppard 1999: 242)

Church and Reid (1996: 1300) agree with this understanding of interurban networking, stating that 'cross-border cooperation is usually developed to improve the comparative economic advantage of regions involved' (with reference to Cappellin 1992). Since most of the rescaling debate addresses the negative effects of globalisation and the possible dangers that accompany the scalar blurring of political steering capacity, this strand of the rescaling approach is followed too.

This topic is also essential to the understanding of the relation between interurban networking and the scalar orientation of competition. It is assumed that city networks might change the scalar order towards a competition of city networks instead of a competition of city-regions themselves (Leitner and Sheppard 1999; Phelps *et al.* 2002). Still, this would not alter the neo-liberal tendencies followed in interurban cooperation schemes. Or, to use terms from the business world, interurban cooperation does not lead to a monopoly of large city-regions but only to some mergers and strategic alliances, which then compete with each other (Leitner and Sheppard 1999: 233). Cooperation will thus remain exploited by the logic of competitiveness (Church and Reid 1996: 1315; Cremer *et al.* 2001: 383; Leitner and Sheppard 1999: 240).

---

23   For a discussion of the distinction between social cohesion and competitiveness in interurban networking, see Leitner and Sheppard (2002: 151).

In conclusion, the two general arguments of the rescaling theory are summarised:

1. It is argued that due to the systemic logic of the transformation of the capitalist reproduction system and due to the increased global competition of city-regions as the new scales of international competition, city-regions intensify their international activities.

2. Moreover, they do so in order to increase their competitive positions, not to foster social cohesion.

Varieties of city-regions' capitalisms: a meso approach

The rescaling approach emphasises general trends when looking at the transformation of statehood in the era of global competitiveness. Although the rescaling approach does not explicitly neglect different trajectories of specific territories, it also does not emphasise divergent trajectories or eventual empirical mismatches (except in Brenner 2004). It is therefore possible to disagree with Brenner's (2004: 19) notion that the rescaling theory is a meso-level approach and rather to argue that the rescaling theory is a macro approach to statehood that provides broad overviews of current general scalar trends and of shifts in multi-level governance settings. Using the rescaling theory to explain differences between the international activities of city-regions is therefore hardly possible.

The second step is to use a meso-level analysis to explain the diversity of city-regions' international activities. This approach, as will be shown, is complementary rather than contradictory to the rescaling theory. The varieties of capitalism approach does not contradict the downscaling hypothesis of the rescaling approach. However, it argues from a more empirical standpoint and does not develop general conclusions for all city-regions but rather argues for a diversity of responses to the 'glocalisation' processes.

The meso-level analysis of city-regions' international activities will be tackled from two different angles. In a first step, the varieties of capitalism approach, which is a neo-Marxist (and neo-institutional) analysis of locally embedded economic production systems, will be utilised.[24] In a second step, a neo-classical economic approach, which is based on Ricardo's theorem, is introduced. This approach leads to the same conclusion as the varieties of capitalism approach; there is logic in diversity rather than uniformity in the case of city-regions' international activities.

---

24 For an overview of the different theoretical outlines that have tackled the idea of varieties of capitalisms, see Coates (2005). For an explanation of the different approaches to capitalism within the varieties of capitalism approach, see Albo (2005). In this study, I will only draw from the neo-institutional branch.

The first logic of diversity: embedded social systems of production[25]
The basic idea of the varieties of capitalism approach proposes a necessary coherence between the economic orientation and the political-institutional setting
within a given territory (Hall and Soskice 2001a; Streeck 1997). Economic actors
do not operate independently from the political-institutional settings into which
they are embedded. Rather, there is a complex interdependency between firms that
follow market logic and state actors (Hall and Soskice 2001a: 5; Keating 2001:
374). Thus, a complementarity of institutions (Amable 2003: 5f.; Aoki 1994) is
constructed through a long, place-dependent process. This close interdependency
makes the institutional forms more efficient (Berger 1996: 21ff.; Hall and Soskice
2001a: 17; Taylor 1995). An intrinsic logic of the complex social configuration
leads single institutions (and firms) to fit automatically within the broader logic
of a certain social system of production (Hollingsworth 1991; Hollingsworth and
Boyer 1997: 2).[26] This leads to monopolies of place, which can be conceptualised
as place-specific assets that are not (or not easily) imitated elsewhere (Boyer 1996:
30; Jessop 1997: 67; Scott 2001: 4). The monopolies of place are not the same
for all places, and they do not need to converge over time under globalisation
(Amable 2003: 66). Although globalisation might place more pressure on city-
regions to focus on economic performance, there is no single best way to achieve
increased economic performance; rather, there are several possible ways (Amable
2003: 23; Boyer and Hollingsworth 1997: 51; Harding 1997: 308).[27] The varieties
of capitalism approach argues that neglecting the place-specific institutional settings will hinder rather than foster economic growth (Hollingsworth and Boyer
1997: 36; Hollingsworth *et al.* 1994: 10; Streeck 1997).

According to this argument, firms that are embedded into such a system are also
constrained by certain characteristics of the system. Thus, against the logic presented in the analysis of globalisation and the rescaled statehood approach, those
firms are not free to play out certain places against others (Camagni 2007: 114).[28]

> Regions can only attain superior levels of long-run economic efficiency and
> performance if competition and markets are brought into play *in combination
> with* formal and informal structures of local regulation (including socio-
> cultural networks which enable trust and collaboration).
>
> *(van der Heiden and Terhorst 2007: 343, original emphasis)*

---

25   In this section, I draw on previous work that I have produced with Pieter Terhorst (see van der
     Heiden and Terhorst 2007). For a recent overview of the development of the varieties of capital-
     ism approach and its relation to spatial geography, see Peck and Theodore (2007).

26   Feldman (1997: 32) speaks of the processes of a social system or the regulations that mutually
     condition each other.

27   For an analysis of market mechanisms and of the varieties of capitalism approach's divergence
     from such a logic of production, see Boyer (1997).

28   Instead, the firms are dependent on their close relations with other firms and state institutions;
     these relationships are based on trust (Gordon 1999: 1005; Hollingsworth and Boyer 1997: 24).

This embeddedness in a specific social system of production (Granovetter 1985) is exactly why economic processes are still place-bound in the era of globalisation; this embeddedness 'keeps the state in the game' of competition (Jessop 1998). Nevertheless, against the logic of a common trajectory of 'glocalisation', as presented above, the varieties of capitalism approach argues that such social systems of production are themselves place-specific.

Transformations of the social systems of production follow a path-dependent logic and are therefore relatively slow and incremental (Hall and Soskice 2001a: 13; Hollingsworth 1997: 277ff.).[29] The specific interdependence of economic and political institutions in a given area creates a place-bound specificity (Hall and Soskice 2001a: 37). Therefore, different social systems of production do not converge (Crouch and Streeck 1997: 2; Hollingsworth and Boyer 1997; Hollingsworth *et al.* 1994: 10ff.; Hollingsworth and Streeck 1994: 282ff.)[30] but rather persist (Crouch and Schmitter 1996). Because of the specificity of such social systems of production, these systems have a competitive advantage over others (Kitschelt *et al.* 1999, see also Feldman 1997: 46; Peck 2002: 332). Hasty alterations of the social system of production would destabilise the long-established political-economic setting within a certain place and would contradict the pattern followed by the setting of political-economic institutions in a given era. Additionally, such alterations will most likely lead to a destabilisation of the whole area. Hence, despite the global logics of adaptation, single places might not need to follow similar tracks. Following a path-dependent track of specialisation is thus economically more stringent.

Although the advocates of the varieties of capitalism thesis reduce their original analysis to comparisons of national states,[31] there is more weight to the argument proposed by Hollingsworth (1998, see also Hancké 2003; Hollingsworth and Boyer 1997; Jonas and Ward 2007: 176) that this approach requires further scalar refinement. The approach was originally blind to multi-level aspects of political-economic settings. Nevertheless, it seems intuitively clear that the national scale is not the only scale of importance in specific settings between the political and the economic sphere. The general scalar blindness of the varieties of capitalism approach causes the problematic fixation on the national scale as the single or at least the predominant scale of analysis. It can be argued that the same mechanisms of institutional entanglement are responsible for a specific economic advantage at the city-region level (Hirst and Zeitlin 1997; Hollingsworth and Boyer 1997; Sabel 1997). Some social systems of production at the city-region level play an important role in managing economic activities for societies as a whole (Hollingsworth 1998: 484).

---

29   On the concept of path-dependency, see Lipset and Rokkan (1967) and Krasner (1988).

30   For a counter-argument, see Strange (1997).

31   See, for example, Amable (2003), Berger and Dore (1996), or Hall and Soskice (2001b).

Occasionally, the national state has been a modest actor in facilitating the emergence and persistence of flexible specialized production systems, but more frequently regional and local governmental authorities have promoted this form of social system.

(Hollingsworth 1998: 493)[32]

Modes of production vary not only among countries but also among city-regions, both within countries and on a more international scale (Krätke 2007: 163ff.). Most of the city-regions are known for their specificity in one (or two) economic domain(s) (Hall 2001: 64). City-regions, both historically and currently, pursue economic specification. It can therefore be argued that a diversified response to globalisation pressures will occur according to the path-dependent political-economic institutional setting of each city-region. But does the logic of a place-specific adaption to globalisation processes truly contrast with the neo-classical economic theory, as predicted by Hollingsworth (1998: 498)? The next section argues that a neo-classical economic explanation leads to the same conclusion of place-specific responses to global economic pressures.

The second logic of diversity: the Ricardo theorem of specialisation
The basic proposition of Ricardo's (1817) theorem is very simple; regions should focus their production on domains in which they are comparatively most competitive (Hall and Soskice 2001a: 36).[33] This holds true even if one region has no absolute advantage in any product. The division of labour and the following specialisation on a product for which the relative advantage is the greatest economically benefits all involved regions. Of course, low transportation costs and no barriers to trade are preconditions for the applicability of the Ricardo theorem. However, both preconditions seem to be less problematic in a globalised economy.[34] Moreover, although this theorem was originally developed for national states, the logic can be adapted to any spatial unit. The logic is even more stringent within national states, in which there are no barriers to trade, whereas national barriers to trade are (or were) restrictions to realising a relative advantage. Thus, following the logic of the neo-classical economic theory, there is a trend toward specialisation, which is inherent in the logic of market forces (Kincaid 1989: 225). Therefore, city-regions should focus their economic activities on the assets for which they possess relative cost advantages over other city-regions.

Competition between city-regions leads to a 'geographical *differentiation* in which individual capitals continually seek out place-specific locational assets and

---

32 Hollingsworth (1998: 494) argues, in accordance with the rescaling approach, that the diversified quality mass production of the Fordist era was embedded in national social systems of production, whereas flexible specialisation systems, which are typically used in the post-Fordist mode of production, are embedded in sub-national socio-political structures.

33 Hence, the theorem of Ricardo is also called the theory of comparative advantage.

34 Unfortunately, however, the theorem is based on a certain immobility of capital. If capital were completely mobile, then it would be economically logical to invest in the place where absolute cost advantages are highest.

territorially specific conditions of production that may enable them to enhance their competitive advantages' (Brenner 2004: 13, original emphasis). This leads to a place-specific form of cooperation among producers to increase external competitiveness (Smith and Dennis 1987: 168), where 'the particular location of a place within the international division of labour under conditions of heightened inter-urban competition thus [...] becomes an asset to be exploited *on the basis of locally-determined priorities*' (Mayer 1992: 263 cited in Peck and Tickell 1994: 303, emphasis from Peck and Tickell).

These place-specific assets are shaped by the long-standing tradition of production in a certain city-region. The accumulation of specific knowledge is both place-bound and path-dependent. It is place-bound because the local interplay between different actors constitutes the relative advantage in know-how. It is path-dependent because the local interplays have been established over longer periods of time. Both elements concretise the scalar speciality of relative economic competitive advantages.

But what is the role of politics in the economic logic of place-specific competitive advantages? It should adapt to this place-specific logic of competitiveness and push political institutions towards the place-specific economic assets of their respective city-regions. This would involve equipping major urban regions with 'customized regulatory arrangements, which [are] increasingly seen as a crucial institutional basis for enhancing global competitive advantages and attracting mobile capital investment' (Brenner 2004: 2f.). Place-specific economic assets are therefore increasingly seen as the motors of local or interscalar political-institutional configurations and changes. These changes, in turn, enhance or sustain international competition of the respective areas. The role of politics is thus to recognise and achieve the gains from the specificities that distinguish its own city-region from others (Begg 1999: 800). Thus, both from a neo-classical economic perspective as well as from the neo-Marxist-inspired approach (varieties of capitalism), it can be argued that there is an inherent logic for place-specific economic specificities and their respective political-administrative institutions. In a third step, this theoretical argument will now be applied to the international activities of city-regions.

Variety of city-regions' international activities
If the international activities of a city-region are viewed as part of a locational policy strategy, then the same logic applies to them as to locational politics in general. A city-region's international activities should align with the specific economic advantages of that city-region (Hubbard 2007: 195; Leitner and Sheppard 1999: 230). This requires a focus on international activities in the domains where the city-region is economically strongest (Leitner and Sheppard 1998: 300). Instead of a general increase due to globalisation, according to the proposition deduced from the rescaling approach, the varieties of capitalism approach accounts for a more place-specific selectivity of these activities and an engagement in the international activities of city-regions according to their specific economic needs.

I argue here that how much a city-region is affected by globalisation is an important factor in explaining the extent of its international activities (Savitch and Kantor 2002). The degree of internationalisation of an industry heavily influences its local system of production. Some economic sectors are highly globalised, whereas others are oriented towards local or national markets. Economic vulnerability is higher in a globalised sector-mix. Because of this, the city-regions that are most vulnerable to global economic pressures are expected to engage most in international activities. International activities of city-regions provide an opportunity for a political system to respond to the needs of its respective economic sector-mix.[35]

If the economy of a city-region is highly globalised and oriented towards international markets, then the politics of the city-region will follow the same logic and turn its scalar attention towards international interurban policy-making. A foreign policy can thus comprise part of a place-specific social system of production, if the respective economic system is globally oriented. In contrast, city-regions that focus on regional or national markets and that thus operate in more closed markets should see policy-makers' respective responses of orienting themselves towards these scales politically and thereby favouring a traditional multi-level governance scheme.

Consequently, the political institutions will adapt to the economic-scalar logic of local business. Because this economic logic is not the same for every local system of production, a place-specific orientation of city-regions' international activities is expected. This is the second hypothesis.

Hypothesis 2: City-regions act on the international level according to their specific economic needs.

The question asks whether transnational 'metropolitan cooperation has up to now been more a fuzzy option of some cities and political actors rather than a planned, conscious activity' (Heeg *et al.* 2003: 143) or whether actors at the city-region level have indeed started to perceive international activities as part of a larger strategy that aligns with their local social system of production.

The goal of the first theoretical section, regarding the international activities of city-regions, was twofold. On the one hand, how the macro logics of adapting to global economic processes trickle down to the micro level of policy-making in the domain of international activities of city-regions was analysed. On the other hand, how the global logics of capital restructuring shape policy-making at the city-region scale was investigated. These are indeed two sides of the same coin, but only the double reflection allows for a full understanding of the underlying interdependencies of the global and local elements that are at the heart of this analysis.

---

35   O'Toole (2001) and Cremer *et al.* (2001), although implicitly, use this approach in their analysis on sister city relationships. They note that political and economic cooperation must align with the place-specific needs of the social system of production in both cities and that economic cooperation is hardly achievable without an in-depth understanding of the two political systems.

FROM EXPLAINING CITY-REGIONS' INTERNATIONAL ACTIVITIES TO INTRASCALAR AND INTERSCALAR CHANGES

The impact of international activities on the policy-making of city-regions is now examined, and the relation of the core cities with the agglomeration communities is also inspected, as well as the relation of the city-region with upper-level governments concerning the international activities of city-regions. The starting point of the following analysis is the hypothesis that urban foreign policy is pursued as a means of urban locational politics. International activities help to position a city-region on the global scale. The capacity to jump scales (Smith 1995) is believed to widen the room for the manoeuvre of urban policy-making (Brenner 2000: 375). In this sense, the extent to which international activities of city-regions can be considered investments in political capital will be examined, which is understood here as a 'concerted effort to modify institutions, structures and practices that will enable cities to bargain more effectively and expand choice' (Savitch and Kantor 2002: 357). According to Savitch and Kantor (2002: 321), there are three scales at which initiatives can be taken to increase such bargaining capacity: the city-community, the region, and the nation-state. This scalar differentiation will be followed in the forthcoming analysis. Therefore, the following theoretical examination analyses the scalar interplays between different levels and the intra-city developments of city-regions' international activities.

CHANGES CAUSED BY CITY-REGIONS' INTERNATIONAL ACTIVITIES

Who governs?
In international relations, the foreign politics of sovereign national states are traditionally seen as the key element of high politics (Taylor 1990: 12), which means that the decisions in this policy field are much more fiercely debated and contested than those in fields of low politics (Hocking 1999: 27, see also Wellmann 1998: 10). The sovereignty of national states is the key element of international relations, and it determines the scalar analysis of international politics, focusing on national states. Existing research has emphasised the internal logic of foreign politics at the national level (see Klöti *et al.* 2005) and the inclusion of sub-national (but only regional, not local) scales in the international policies of the national state (see Ehrenzeller *et al.* 2002; Sturny 1998). However, research has not yet addressed city-regions' international activities' divergence from the logic of national states' international relations. It is still unclear whether the newly-emerging international activities of city-regions are also part of high politics at the respective scale or whether their importance has not reached the same level as it has for the national scale. The rescaling of possibilities in international activities down to the city-regions level is a new and still ongoing process. The analysis of how the international activities of city-regions are actually carried out cannot rely on a well-established grid of analysis, as can analyses of negotiating national states.

A question therefore arises: who is actually involved in the decision-making process regarding international activities at the city-region scale? The rescaling theory places hardly any emphasis on questions of actual decision-making but rather argues from a macro-analytical logic of global adaptation, which states that there is no choice but to adapt to the 'glocalised' logic of urban entrepreneurialism. Globalisation's pressure on city-regions was enforced in a way that did not leave any options for urban policy-makers than to adapt to global competitiveness. As presented in the proposition based on the rescaling theory,[36] this means an increase of city-regions' international activities as part of locational politics.

Only within the critical strand of the rescaling approach is the city-region seen as the scale for a possible counter-trend against the neo-liberal turn in national policy-making (see Harvey 1989; Keil 2003; Leitner and Sheppard 1999; Pendras 2002; Smith 2002; Swyngedouw 1997). This strand of rescaling literature presents the hope that grass roots movements, with the help of local non-governmental organisations (NGOs), will start to question the neo-liberal adjustment, first at the city scale (Liepitz 1994a) and then at higher scales as well.

As previously discussed,[37] the rescaling literature is generally more sceptical about the possibilities of facing the neo-liberal shift in policy-making at the city-region scale. Most rescaling theorists (Brenner 2004; Jones and MacLeod 1999; Peck 2002) predict a trend towards more business-oriented politics and an increasing importance of locational politics at the city-region scale. This, as it will be argued, complements a more top-down method of urban policy-making, which includes:

1. a tendency towards public-private partnerships instead of traditional state policy-making;

2. a trend towards a greater importance of executive politicians, especially the mayor; and

3. an exclusion of the public from this policy field. Hence, the goal is to determine whether the process of rescaling and the accompanying changes in urban policy-making towards locational politics have influenced the interplay among political players in urban policy-making.

Public-Private Partnerships (PPPs)

The literature on the shift from government to governance (Goodwin *et al.* 2005: 424; Harding *et al.* 2000; Le Galès 1998; Lefèvre 1998) discusses the increasing interdependence of public and private actors in (urban) policy-making. Due to the increased complexity of policy-making, including at the city-region level, governmental actors increasingly depend on the experience of private actors (Harding 1997: 301; Harvey 1989: 7; Hubbard 2007: 191). Within locational politics, outsourcing or close cooperation with businesses can be expected (Swyngedouw *et*

---

36   See pages 5ff.

37   See pages 5ff.

al. 2002).[38] Due to its functional logic of attracting business to a specific place, policy-makers working within locational politics collaborate most closely with private actors. Therefore, according to the logics of the rescaling approach, the importance of PPPs at the city-region scale will only increase (Swyngedouw 2000a: 69). PPPs are also an integral part of the turn towards urban entrepreneurialism (Harvey 1989: 7) since entrepreneurial goals are more easy achievable in private or semi-private governance forms. The transfer of steering capacity from the political sphere to a semi-political or private sphere helps in the pursuit of neo-liberal goals with the exclusion of the public from the decision-making process. Thereby,

> the interventionism of the state in the economy is equally rescaled, [...] downwards to the level of the city or to the region where public-private partnerships shape an entrepreneurial practice and ideology needed to successfully engage in an intensified process of interurban competition.
>
> *(Swyngedouw 2000a: 69, with reference to Harvey 1989)*

As hypothesised above, international activities can be seen as part of the turn towards urban entrepreneurialism. They are one of the instruments that can be used to promote the city-region on the global scale as a place for investment and business. Following this logic leads to predicting an increasing importance of PPPs in the international activities of city-regions (Keating 1999: 4). The complexity of international relations for city-region policy-makers will also increase. Because there are no long-standing traditions or well-known best practice rules in urban foreign policy, this complexity increases the chance for a complete outsourcing or at least an inclusion of private actors in the governmental process (Keating 1999: 11). Therefore, the steering capacity is likely to be divided or blurred between public and private actors in the international activities of city-regions.

Elite policy-making and the exclusion of the public
The general concern of democracy within the rescaling approach regards the increased elite-oriented method of urban policy-making. The concern is based on the assumption that the public, understood as the parliament and the citizens, is more critical than policy-makers in the shift to urban entrepreneurialism (Purcell 2007, see also Held 1995).

> Democratic decision-making is seen as slow, messy, inefficient and less likely to produce the kind of tax reductions, infrastructure spending, insurance reforms and business deregulation that attract and keep capital in an increasingly competitive global economy.
>
> *(Purcell 2006, with reference to Hoggett 1987)*

The assumption of a democratic deficit in the rescaled statehood has so far lacked a serious empirical test. Public actors' reactions to 'glocalisation' logics at the scale of the city-region are an important issue. Additionally, the discourse

---

38   See Collinge (1999: 563) for an analysis of PPPs within regulation theory and of their interrelation with the hollowing out of the national state.

concerning neo-liberal policy-making at the city-region level is a top-down oc-
currence (Fainstein 2001b; Harding 1997: 308). Elites are engaged in the turn
towards urban entrepreneurialism because they reflect on the necessity of adapting
to global pressures on city-regions (Hall and Hubbart 1996: 159), whereas citizens
do not.

In their analysis of large urban development projects, Moulaert *et al.* (2003b:
58) conclude that the decision-making process for these projects is conducted
within unelected bodies that try to exclude the public as much as possible. The
hegemonic coalition tries to dictate a growth-oriented policy for the city-region,[39]
whereas the inclusion of the public is seen as hindrance to a quick adaptation
to globalisation logics (Swyngedouw *et al.* 2003, Logan and Molotch 2002).
Therefore, 'a generalized shift towards more autocratic, undemocratic, and authoritarian modes of governance' occurs (Peck 2002: 338, see also Church and
Reid 1996; Leitner and Sheppard 2002: 164). This pessimistic analysis of politics
is shared by Swyngedouw, who sees that

> The double rearticulation of political scales (downwards [... and] upwards
> [...]) leads to political exclusion, a narrowing of democratic control, and,
> consequently, a redefinition (or rather a limitation) of citizenship rights and
> power. In short, the glocalisation or rescaling of institutional forms leads to
> a more autocratic, undemocratic, and authoritarian (quasi-)state apparatuses.

> *(Swyngedouw 2000a: 70, with reference to Morgan and Roberts 1993;*
> *Swyngedouw 1996, 1998)*

The exclusion of the public therefore accompanies the neo-liberal turn in urban policy-making. 'The forms that exclusion takes, with discussions dominated
by networked local elites relying on professionalised governance and decision-
making processes, can facilitate implementation of a neo-liberal agenda of competitiveness and innovation' (Leitner and Sheppard 2002: 165).

International activities are something new and complex, which increases the
possibility of a top-down policy-making process. International contacts are primarily conducted by specialised people from the city administration who possess appropriate knowledge of interscalar complexities (Church and Reid 1996).
Citizens and their political representatives in the parliaments are less aware of this
new instrument in urban policy-making. Additionally, the role of the mayor as
chief-representative of the city-region is also strong. Because the mayor usually
is the focal point for international contacts, an increased importance of the international activities of cities (as proposed by the proposition of the rescaling theory)
would closely attend a strong role of the mayor in general. Martins and Rodriguez
Alvarez (2007) speak of glocal mayors due to the mayors' increased engagement
on the global scale.

Hypothesis 3: The mayor and the bureaucracy play strong roles in the
decision-making process concerning a city-region's international activities.

---

39   Here, my approach partially reflects the urban growth machine theory again.

The legitimisation of this behaviour will be focused on output legitimacy rather than input legitimacy (Risse 2006; Scharpf 1998). Policy-makers will note that, due to globalisation pressures, output legitimacy (i.e. staying competitive) has gained importance over questions of input legitimacy (i.e. democratic deliberation in policy-making).[40] Therefore, the same can be said for international activities. The goal to enter the local territory into the global interurban competition justifies the shorter, top-down decision-making procedure in which a strong mayor and bureaucracy carry out international activities. Public officials can then follow a more competitiveness-oriented logic within these activities (Leitner and Sheppard 2002: 167). Kincaid (1989), in the only study that actually investigates public opinion of cities' international activities, showed that the public was quite sceptical but did not know much about the topic.[41] It is therefore important to analyse the decision-making process of city-regions' international activities.

After examining the changes in policy-making at the city-regions level, the interplay between the core city and the agglomeration communities will now be explored. The next section will provide a theoretical analysis of possible changes in the relations among political entities at the city-region scale.

Horizontal governance: strengthening the core city?

Although some research that examines city-regions' international activities uses the rescaling approach, almost all authors refrain from explicitly dealing with the most important aspect of this strand of research, which is scale itself (see Leitner 2004). Albeit implicitly, researchers use the city as the scale of reference for their analyses of international activities, without further discussing this assumption (for the exception that proves the rule, see Friedmann 2001). This is inherently problematic because it neglects the central concern of critical geography, which is bringing place and scale into the analysis of political processes. It can therefore be argued that an analysis of city-regions' international activities should be scalarly open. The scalar mechanisms must be examined within a city-region instead of assuming certain scalar arrangements to be fixed (Hubbard 2007: 187). Additionally, questions of metropolitan governance (see Lefèvre 1998) within urban foreign policy-making should be examined more carefully. The scalar interplays between the core city and the agglomeration communities will therefore be analysed concerning their international activities, although the discussion on metropolitan governance between metropolitan reformers, public choice, and new regionalism will not be addressed[42]; rather, the discussion will be limited using the rescaling

---

40   Or, it has gained importance over questions of social equality (Fainstein 2001a, b).

41   Cremer *et al.* (2001: 394), although their work is not supported by an empirical investigation, assume that the citizenry is sceptical towards city-regions' international activities for three reasons: first, an unaware or apathetic attitude; second, a choice of partner cities that is not understood; third, a view of partnerships as possibilities for politicians to travel at the taxpayers' expense.

42   See Lefèvre (1998), Kübler (2003), or Heinelt and Kübler (2005) for an overview of the debate, and see Hubbard (2007: 193) for a summary of the interlinkages between the rescaling approach and the new regionalism approach.

approach to metropolitan governance, which focuses on the scalar configuration between the core city and its surrounding communities (see also Boudreau *et al.* 2007; Boudreau and Keil 2001; Brenner 2003).

Intra-regional cooperation for inter-regional competition?
The starting point here is the idea that urban economies and economic linkages go far beyond the territorial borders of the core city (Cheshire 1999; Sassen 2001). Besides the international component, the core city's economy also disperses into the hinterland. Thereby, city-regions form a (more or less) coherent economic network that builds itself around the core city. Additionally, the economic network leads to a place-specific asset for city-regions, an economic specification, and a complex inter-dependence of economic and political institutions at the city-region level[43]. The varieties of capitalism approach argues that economic activities within one city-region should be seen as a complementary process in which diverse enterprises form a place-specific economic cluster.

Although the economic networks are more tightly interwoven in urban areas, there is not necessarily a connection between a city-region's economic scalar density and its political organisation. Even in highly economically interconnected urban regions, the fragmentation of a territory's political organisation can be significant, which makes its political organisation difficult. There is thus a mismatch between the functional and the political spaces in urban areas. Hence, Brenner (2003: 299) states that metropolitan governance is back on the agenda in the era of globalisation. Here, the important issue regards whether the mismatch between an economically integrated and a politically divided territory causes problems. The rescaling approach points to the fact that an internal political-spatial division within urban areas increasingly becomes a problem of international competitiveness (Parkinson and Harding 1995: 73).

Strengthening the core city for inter-regional competition?
There is thus a double logic of competition (Keating 1995: 120; Sager 2002: 64f.). On the one hand, there might be competition among different political territories within a city-region regarding the attractiveness for capital. On the other hand, as presented above, globalisation has led to an increasing competition among large city-regions on a global scale. Although it is unclear to what extent the economic relations within a city-region are characterised by competition, it seems uncontested that the core city is primarily responsible for linking an agglomeration economy to the global market. There seems to be a division of labour in which 'each of these cities has its own hinterland funnelling resources to the center, and it is this center that links the regional into the global economy' (Friedmann 2001: 121).

Accordingly, the core city plays a dominant role in international competition, although there are strong economic ties between the core city and the respective hinterland (Harvey 1989: 8; Jonas and Ward 2007: 171). The competition between the peripheral communities and the core city for capital investment, state subsi-

---

43   See pages 17ff.

dies, and other collective goods restrains global competitiveness (Brenner 1999: 437f.; Parkinson and Harding 1995: 73). Any internal fight over capital investment at the city-region scale hinders an aggressive and coherent entrance into global competition. Cooperation within urban regions, however, can be an institutional springboard for engaging more aggressively in territorial competition against other urban regions (Brenner 2003: 302f.; Ward and Jonas 2004: 2122f.).

The next important question asks whether the economic logic of an intertwined agglomeration, with a dominant core city that links it to the global market, is followed by a similar logic in politics, especially concerning the international activities of city-regions. Following the logic of downscaling in the era of globalisation, this process grants additional steering possibilities to city-regions, and predominantly core cities, since regulation is seen as possible on the scale that is economically most important. As discussed previously, the core city, although dependent on an economic backup with the respective hinterland, is the key scale as the nodal point of globalisation. Consequently, the rescaling literature suggests a strengthened position of the core city towards its hinterland (see MacLeod 2001; Norris 2001).

Hypothesis 4: The core city gains influence against the agglomeration communities through its international activities.

It is therefore crucial to analyse city-regions' international activities in a scale-sensitive manner and to analyse the interplay among the diverse political entities within one economic area, regarding linking the city-region politically to the global scale. The organisation of the political entities' involvement must be analysed, as must the different entities' perceptions of their interplay regarding international activities. The rationale presented above suggests that the core city strategically uses its predominant position in linking the whole city-region to the global scale in order to strengthen its position towards the agglomeration communities.

Vertical governance: strengthening city-regions?
The aim of this section is to incorporate upper-level governments into the spatial analysis of city-regions' international activities. Since the downscaling of political steering capacity necessarily includes a multi-scalar analysis, the inclusion or exclusion of upper-level governments in city-regions' international activities will be investigated,[44] and whether this collaboration is cooperative will be determined (Hocking 1999: 31f.).

Again, the rescaling approach will be followed in analysing the vertical scalar interplay between different layers of government regarding the city-regions' international activities. The main question hereby addresses the changes in the relations between city-regions and upper-level governments. How do the regional and/or national scale react to city-regions' international activities? What is their relation with the EU? Again, the logic of economic determinism will be followed

---

44   See also Ward (1996: 436) for a general argument for the necessary inclusion of upper-level governments in the analysis of urban politics.

in analysing these multi-level governance issues. In other words, an economic logic will be presented initially that guides the analysis of a respective political response.

City-regions as motors of national economies

As presented above, globalisation not only leads to an increased competition among national states and a consequent hollowing out of the national scale in policy-making, it also changes the scalar nature of international competition. Due to an increased concentration of highly globalised economic sectors in urban areas and a decreased ability of the national state to equalise inter-regional economic differences (and to redistribute economic growth from urban to rural areas; Harding 1997: 301; Keating 2001: 374), urban areas gain increased importance in economic competition (Le Galès 2002). Several authors therefore define a post-Fordist era of inter-urban, rather than inter-national, competition (Begg 1999; Budd 1998; Cox 1995; Gordon 1999; Ward and Jonas 2004). Thus, both a downscaling and an upscaling of economic competition have occurred. Does this mean that the national scale has lost all its regulatory competencies in a globalised world? Rather, the rescaling approach argues for a different, multi-scalar conceptualisation of national policy-making possibilities (Uitermark 2005).

The scalar interplay for economic growth changes from a condition of national dominance and dependent city-regions to a condition of dominant city-regions and a possible inclusion of other, upper-level governments in growth strategies at the city-region scale. Instead of a relatively simple downscaling, this change rather leads to a regulatory regime that can be characterised as multi-scalar and in which 'the nation-state will not wither away but instead develop itself more and more as a strategic partner for local actors' (Uitermark 2005: 160, see also Harding 1997: 301). The partnership, following the logics of a rescaled statehood, should focus on the predominant role of city-regions for economic growth (Begg 1999: 804). The national scale should limit its regulatory role to supporting these economic powerhouses (Harding 1995: 295) and should thereby track a new understanding of federalist policy-making. Instead of the Fordist mode of regulation, which distributed economic assets largely and equally over urban and rural eras,[45] a trend in which the national scale turns its efforts from rural areas to urban growth poles will occur (Brenner 1998: 3; MacLeod 2001). 'As of the early 1980s, national states began to introduce new, post-Keynesian spatial policies intended to re-concentrate productive capacities and specialised, high-performance infrastructural investments into the most globally competitive city-regions within their territories' (Brenner 2004: 2).

If Swyngedouw (2000a: 66) is correct that 'virtually each government, at every conceivable scale of governance, has taken measures to align its social and economic policy to the 'exigencies' and 'requirements' of this new competitive world (dis)order' (with reference to Peck and Tickell 1994, 1995), then there will be a shift from a dominant national scale in economic regulation to a support-

---

45   See pages 5ff.

ing national scale for city-regions' international competitiveness (Keating 2001: 374). Again, this logic of systemic structuring, which is presented by the rescaling approach, means that the national scale finds itself in a systemic trap and is forced to change its focus and to concentrate on providing city-regions with the best possible institutional conditions (Brenner 2004: 166). If the national scale does not accept its new primary function of enhancing the competitiveness of its city-regions, then there will be a sanctioning of the globalised capital system by a reduced growth of the respective national economy (Brenner 1999: 302; 447).

Encouraging or hindering city-regions to go global?
How do upper-level governments react to the newly emerging phenomenon of urban foreign policy regarding city-regions' international activities? According to the logic presented above, the national scale should strongly favour and support these activities because they increase the connectivity of nodal points of capital accumulation and thereby create economic growth for the whole country. Due to the decentralisation of policies that are important for the national economic well-being, national states should consequently view the international activities of city-regions as aspects of the new scalar importance of city-regions in global competition (Brenner and Theodore 2002; McGuirk 2004: 1020). Therefore, state governments should not prevent city-regions from pursuing their own international activities.[46]

This analysis of intergovernmental support (Keating 2001: 383; Savitch and Kantor 2002) can be adapted to any political scale above the city-region (Parkinson and Harding 1995: 65). The need to focus on city-regions as motors of economic growth should be perceived by every upper-level government (Leitner and Sheppard 1998: 301, 1999: 231). To compete globally, regions and nations should concentrate their resources and policies on the needs of city-regions and on supporting the city-regions' competitiveness in an increasingly inter-urban global competition (Brenner 2004: 166). If international activities are perceived as a necessary political response to economic processes and as part of a locational policy strategy for fostering economic growth at the city-region level, then city-regions should be able to count on the support of upper-level governments for their international activities (Church and Reid 1996: 1315).[47]

A more critical analysis of city-regions' international activities has challenged this view of intergovernmental support. Some scholars perceive international relations as a zero-sum game among the different political levels, which means that any new activity of sub-national entities must necessarily conflict with those of the national scale. Therefore, 'national governments have tended jealously to guard their control over this process [international activities] and have been prone to exclude other actors' (Rees 1997). Kincaid (1989) (see also Aldecoa and Keating

---

46 Brenner (2004: 260) calls the new scalar setting a 'Rescaled Competition State Regime'.

47 One could argue that this notion of policy-making is very close to the urban growth machine approach. See also McGuirk (2004: 1025) for an analysis of the inclusion of upper-level scales in the neo-liberal discourse at the city scale.

1999; Keating 2001: 386; Kincaid 2002) agrees with the pessimistic analysis of upper-level support for city-regions' international activities. He observes that city-regions usually become active on the international scale when they strongly disagree with a policy on the national level; for example, an increasing number of city partnerships were established between the United States and Nicaragua during the US embargo against Nicaragua in the 1970s (Cremer *et al.* 2001: 382; Kincaid 1989: 241). There is thus a latent conflict between the foreign policy of the national and the sub-national scales, and urban foreign policy is expected to be the most prominent in times of strong disagreement among the different political scales (Church and Reid 1996: 1313; Keating 1999: 5).

Instead of aligning with national or regional strategies of economic growth, city-regions' international activities can be seen as bypassing the national scale (Ward and Williams 1997: 457) and as an empowerment of the local scale vis-à-vis the national scale (Leitner and Sheppard 2002: 163). City-regions follow this strategy to gain more regulatory independence from upper-level governments, and this strategy at the city-region level will therefore conflict with regional or national interests.

Sub-national city-regions and the supranational EU
The double logic of support or competition can be applied not only to the relations between the city-region and the regional or national scale but also to the relation between the city-region and the supranational scale (i.e. the EU). Several scholars note the importance of the EU in interurban networking (see Church and Reid 1996; Friedmann 2001). However, the theoretical understanding of the interscalar relations between the sub-national and the supranational scales is still underdeveloped. EU regulations increasingly influence urban policy-making directly (Marshall 2005). How the supranational and sub-national scale react to this increasing interdependence is, however, less clear. The EU could, on the one hand, view the new phenomenon of city-regions' international activities as a contest with its own efforts to gain power in international relations. On the other hand, the EU could support the new tendency of urban areas to increase their linkages across borders in order to strengthen the overall economic competitiveness of Europe or to undermine the national scale. Marshall (2005, see also Kübler and Piliutyte 2007) pointed to the double logic from the city-region's perspective. On the one hand, city-regions increasingly profit directly from EU funding (Marshall calls this 'downloading Europeanisation'; see also Church and Reid 1996: 1299; Leitner and Sheppard 2002: 159ff.). On the other hand, city-regions try to influence the EU's policies (which Marshall calls 'uploading Europeanisation'; see also Articus 2005). The relevant question for this analysis asks whether city-regions use their international contacts to strengthen their position towards the EU (uploading).

Strengthened city-regions
Following the rescaling approach to multi-level governance, which sees strong ties to upper-level governments as a necessary condition for city-regions to operate powerfully in the global competition of city-regions (Brenner 1999: 444) leads to a logic that strengthens city-regions towards the upper-level scales.

Hypothesis 5: City-regions gain influence against the upper-level governments through their international activities.

Consequently, the inclusion of different scales in city-regions' international activities will be examined.

A MODEL OF CITY-REGIONS' INTERNATIONAL ACTIVITIES

The double analysis of city-regions' international activities started by explaining the amount and orientation of those international activities on two analytical levels (see Figure 1.2). To explain both the intensity and the orientation of city-regions' international activities, the rescaling approach was first used at the macro-level, examining its proposition that city-regions should increase their international activities.

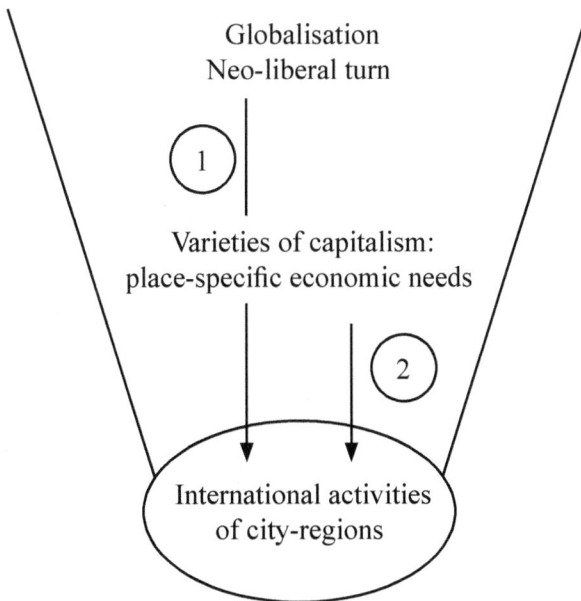

Figure 1.2: Explaining the international activities of city-regions

The rescaling approach is quite clear about the increase of city-regions' international activities; political steering capacity has been downgraded to city-regions due to global economic processes that strengthen the position of city-regions as nodal points of global competition. However, the direction in content is less clear; nevertheless, the more pessimistic branch of the rescaling theory has been utilised, which points to the increased use of the international activities by city-regions for economic purposes. This resulted in the first hypothesis:

> 1: Globalisation pressures lead city-regions to develop a coherent economic-oriented strategy for their international activities.

The varieties of capitalism approach was then utilised, which helped explain the divergent patterns of city-regions' international activities. This approach states that no general trend of city-regions' international activities originates from economic logic. These international political contacts are rather an adjustment to the specific economic needs of the respective city-regions. Therefore, the outline of city-regions' international activities do not necessarily converge. Hence, my second hypothesis:

> 2: City-regions act on the international level according to their specific economic needs.

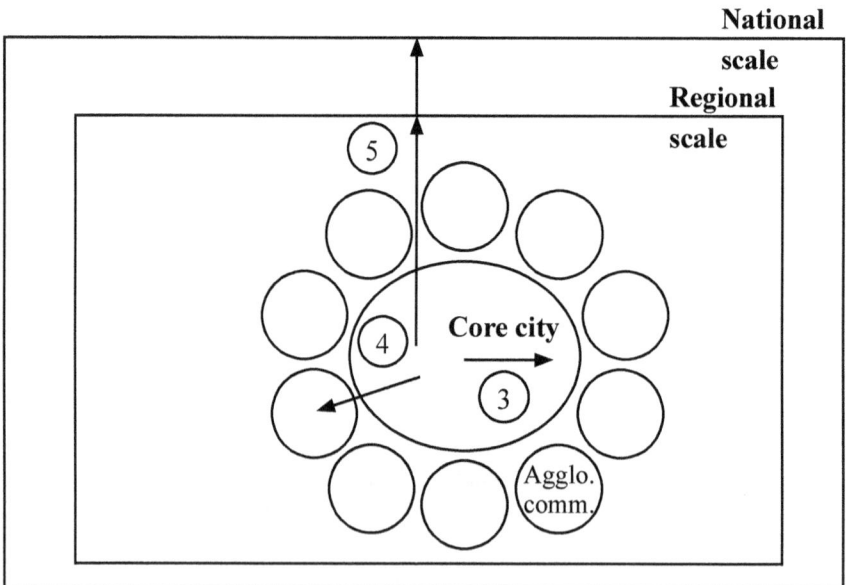

Figure 1.3: Intrascalar and interscalar changes caused by city-regions' international activities

In a second step, the intrascalar and interscalar changes caused by city-regions' international activities were examined (see Figure 1.3). Changes in policy-making at the city-region scale were first observed, and deriving again from the critical strand of the rescaling approach, a top-down method of urban policy-making was proposed. Accordingly, the third hypothesis was formulated:

3: The mayor and the bureaucracy play strong roles in the decision-making process concerning a city-region's international activities (i.e. urban governance).

Next, an investigation of the relation between the core city and the agglomeration communities concerning the city-regions' international activities was presented. The core city's predominant position in international networking should allow it to strengthen its position against the agglomeration communities. The fourth hypothesis, then, argues that:

4: The core city gains influence against the agglomeration communities through its international activities (i.e. horizontal governance).

Finally, the relations between the city-region and upper-level governments were inspected. If international activities are a new instrument in urban policy-making, then they should strengthen the position of the city-region towards the upper-level governments at the regional, national, and supranational levels. Therefore, this is the final hypothesis:

5: City-regions gain influence against the upper-level governments through their international activities (i.e. vertical governance).

chapter two | the seven city-regions under scrutiny

In this section, the seven city-regions will be analysed according to the theoretical guidelines presented above. This analysis will start with the logic behind the case selection and some methodological remarks and then continue with a presentation of the findings from the five Swiss city-regions and from the two EU city-regions.[1] The key characteristics concerning political structuring and number of inhabitants of the five Swiss city-regions and the two EU comparative city-regions are summarised in Table 2.1.

Table 2.1: The seven city-regions under scrutiny

City-region	Inhabitants	Communities	Communities with more than 10,000 inhabitants	Core city inhabitants (and % of city-region)
Stuttgart*	2667,766	179	61	591,550 (22.2%)
Lyon	~1,200,000**	57	19	444,369 (~37%)
Zurich	1,080,728	132	23	363,273 (33.6%)
Geneva	471,314	74	9	177,964 (37.8%)
Berne	349,096	43	7	128,634 (36.8%)
Lausanne	311,441	70	6	124,914 (40.1%)
Lucerne	196,550	17	7	59,496 (30.3%)

Sources: Bundesamt für Statistik (2008), Grand Lyon (2008a), and Verband Region Stuttgart (2007). Figures are for the year 2000 for the Swiss city-regions, 1999 for Lyon, and 2005 for Stuttgart.

* The figures for the agglomerations of Lyon and Stuttgart are not fully comparable with those of the Swiss city-regions because the definition of a city-region is not the same in every country. Still, the differences are not so remarkable that they hinder a cross-national comparison of the respective entities.

** The city-region of Lyon does not publish a more precise figure of its inhabitants.

Each case study will begin with a short overview of the respective city-region, according to its most important political and economic functions. The goal is to

---

1 The order of the case studies is alphabetical. There are no diffusion effects (see Berry and Berry 1990; Braun and Gilardi 2006) between the seven city-regions concerning their international activities. Hence, any order of presentation could have been chosen.

analyse the extent of globalisation of each city-region. An outline of the identified international activities will first be presented, with the focus on the amount and intent of international activities. The orientation that the city-region follows within its different networks and partnerships will be particularly examined to determine whether the macro hypotheses of the rescaling approach, i.e. that international engagements have increased recently and that city-regions are oriented towards increased global competitiveness, are correct for the respective city-region. On the meso level, the analysis will determine whether each city-region's international activities can be linked to its economic situation, as predicted by the varieties of capitalism approach.

Turning then to spatial changes, the policy-making process within international activities will first be outlined to determine who is involved in the policy-making of the city-region's international activities. The relations between the core city and the communities in the agglomeration are then analysed to ascertain whether the core city uses its advantageous position to link its agglomeration economy to the global scale. Next, the relations with upper-level governments will be examined to reveal whether the city-region uses its new political steering capacity, which was gained by its international connectivity, against upper-level governments. Each case study is concluded with a short summary of its most important aspects.

CASE SELECTION

The most important variables for the case selection are presented in Table 2.2. The most important independent variable that explains the amount and direction of a city-region's international activities is the city-region's social-economic system of production. The case selection thus represents a maximal variety of city-regions' economic specific characteristics.[2]

Table 2.2: Characteristics of the seven city-regions

City-region	Economic specificity	Metropolitan government	Federalist country	Part of the EU
Berne	National Administration	No	Yes	No
Geneva	NGOs/IGOs	No	Yes	No
Lausanne	Sports Administration	No	Yes	No
Lucerne	Tourism	No	Yes	No
Zurich	Banking and Insurance	No	Yes	No
Stuttgart	Automobile Industry	Yes	Yes	Yes
Lyon	Diversified	Yes	No	Yes

---

2   Of course, this is only a crude overview of the economic situations of the city-regions. I will further address their respective social systems of production in the respective case studies.

For an analysis of the changes caused by city-regions' international activities, there are three important variables, all of which contain considerable variety. First, examining metropolitan governance is important when looking at both horizontal governance (the interplay between the core city and the agglomeration communities) and vertical governance (the relation between the city-region and upper-level governments). The two city-regions that have metropolitan governments (Lyon and Stuttgart) will be compared with the five Swiss city-regions, which lack such regional institutions.

Second, the state structure is crucial when examining the use of city-regions' international activities against upper-level governments (i.e. vertical governance). Theoretically, there is a difference between city-regions embedded in federalist countries and city-regions in centralistic countries. The comparison of a French city (which has a centralistic state organisation) with city-regions from federalist countries is useful when considering urban foreign policy.

Third, when observing interscalar relations, interurban networking is affected not only by the relations within the respective national states but also by the relations with the supranational EU. Since my respective hypothesis posits that city-regions use their international contacts to strengthen their positions towards upper-level governments, the differences between the two city-regions from EU member states (Lyon and Stuttgart) and the five Swiss city-regions, which do not belong to the EU, will be examined. The case selection therefore allows the possibility to determine whether the EU has an influence on urban foreign policy-making. For the cross-country comparison, Lyon and Stuttgart were chosen because their relative importance within their national states is comparable to most of the Swiss city-regions. I mostly relied on qualitative expert interviews for this project (Kvale 1996; Meuser and Nagel 1991). In total, I conducted eighty-three interviews.[3]

BERNE: A CAPITAL CITY WITH A NATIONAL ORIENTATION

International position and economic orientation
The city-region of Berne contains a total of 349,096 inhabitants, which are spread over forty-three communities (Bundesamt für Statistik 2008a).[4] The city of Berne is included in only one international comparison; it is ranked ninth in Mercer's (2009) study on quality of living. Berne is only the third-best Swiss city in Mercer's study; Zurich and Geneva are first and second.

Berne is the capital city of Switzerland. It serves as the political headquarters of the national parliament and government; this is its most important economic factor. Its function as capital city means that most important national administration services and attached sectors are situated in the region of Berne (Tripartite Arbeitsgruppe Bundesstadtstatus 2003: 3; 6). Hence, both the absolute number and the percentage of jobs in public administration are significantly higher in Berne than in any other Swiss city-region (Bundesamt für Statistik 2008b). Out

---

3   The analysis was conducted in the years 2005-2007. More recent developments could not be
    considered systematically.

4   All figures are according to the census of the year 2000.

of the total of 148,143 jobs in the city of Berne, 23,747 are in public administration (Statistikdienste der Stadt Bern 2007). This comprises 16 per cent of jobs, not counting closely related service sectors such as transportation and telecommunication, which compose another 15,808 or 10.7 per cent of jobs within the city of Berne. Other public sector jobs (e.g., in teaching or health care) make up another 38,811 or 26.2 per cent of jobs in the city of Berne.

The city-region of Berne has not developed any further specialisation in economic terms, although it promotes itself as the Swiss centre of informatics and of the medicinal, health, and service sectors (Wirtschaftsförderung Region Bern 2008). Other sectors, such as banking, tourism, or engineering, play a much smaller role in Berne than in other city-regions (Statistikdienste der Stadt Bern 2007). This leads to a strong focus on the national scale as a point of reference in economic terms since the central functions of Berne are attached to the Swiss political system. The city-region's social system of production is therefore closely linked to the national political-administrative state. To speak of Berne's international position is therefore somewhat misleading because its national position as a capital city is much more important.

International activities

The city partnerships and the networks
The city of Berne has only participated in three international activities, two of which it still pursues (see Table 2.3). Berne has not established any formal city partnership with another city beyond the Swiss borders. Although the city government[5] discussed the possibility of establishing city partnerships in the early 1990s, it decided that a capital city should not privilege any one foreign city with a formally established partnership. This decision has since not been addressed again (see below).

Berne is a member of the Climate Alliance network. It joined the network in 2004, after the other large Swiss cities had already joined, and it focuses on its respective national section, KBSS (Klimabündnisstädte Schweiz, i.e. Swiss Climate Alliance Cities, see also Behringer 2003: 25), rather than on the international Climate Alliance.[6] The city administration did not undertake any effort to become a member of the Climate Alliance; instead, it was forced to do so by a parliamentary motion. This partly explains the city's reluctance to participate in international cooperation on climate issues.

Berne used to be a member of the organisation European Cities on Drug Policy (ECDP). Along with Zurich, Berne struggled with more drug-related problems

---

5   I use the term city government for the executive branch and the term city councillor for the members of the city government.

6   The establishment of this network is somehow particular; it contains national sections of both the climate alliance and the international cooperation scheme (Behringer 2003: 25). Instead of a purely international network, the Climate Alliance is a multi-level network.

Table 2.3: The international activities of the city of Berne[7]

International activity*	Description	Categorisation
Climate Alliance	Cities for a liberal environmental policy	Thematic network**
ECDP	Cities for a liberal drug policy (until 2001)	Thematic network
OWHC	Cities with a world heritage	Thematic network

*   The international activities are ordered first along their categorisations (as partnerships, thematic networks, or lobby networks), second along their policy domains (alphabetically), and third along the names of their networks or partner cities (alphabetically).

**   I grouped the networking activities into two categories: thematic networks and lobby networks. Thematic networks have a clear focus on one specific policy area. Regarding content, these cooperation schemes endeavour to foster cooperation between city-regions in their respective policy areas. Interurban lobby networks have a procedural orientation. City-regions cooperate in these networks to lobby at a specific scale for their own benefit. Clearly, the two forms of interurban networks are intermingled, since most lobby networks provide some sort of cooperation opportunities in certain policy areas as well.

than other Swiss cities (Kübler and Wälti 2001: 42); thus, Berne and Zurich cooperated on a liberal drug policy and joined the ECDP network as founding members in 1990. Berne participated actively in the network's meetings until the end of the 1990s. When the goal of the network, which was to establish a more liberal drug policy on the respective national scales, was accomplished, the policy-makers did not see any need to collaborate further within the ECDP network, although informal contacts remained important.

Berne is also a long-standing member of the Organisation of World Heritage Cities (OWHC); it is the only Swiss member of that network, which brings together cities that have UNESCO- (United Nations Educational, Scientific and Cultural Organisation) classified world heritages. After a national request that the old town of Berne be classified as possessing a world heritage was approved by UNESCO in 1983, Berne joined the organisation as a founding member. The head of the preservation of historical monuments in the city of Berne participates regularly in the bi-annual meeting of the OWHC and uses these contacts to learn about best practice rules in other cities.

---

7   Berne joined the European coalition of cities against racism in 2008. I do not include this network in my analysis because the network was founded only very recently. The city of Berne also joined the new network Cities for Children (set up by Stuttgart; see pages 114ff.) in 2007. Because Berne's engagement within this network is not yet determined at the time of writing, however, I must exclude the network from my analysis.

Organisation of international contacts
The external relations of the city of Berne are affiliated with the service for city development and are one of their five policy domains. The external relations belong to the service for city development only because of an internal reorganisation in 2004, and they focus primarily on relations within the city-region of Berne, with the canton[8] of Berne, with other cantons, and with the federal government. The service for city development does not fulfil any coordination function among the three networks that are carried out on the departmental level because the international contacts are not viewed as an important aspect of city development (see below). The service only coordinates the external relations of the city of Berne within Switzerland. One of the policy-makers who is engaged in an international network has regretted this orientation of the service for city development. He compared the situation of Berne with other Swiss and EU cities, and he missed the support from a specialised organisational unit within the city administration that focuses on international activities:

> In contrast to German cities, we do not have a supportive structure. We do not have someone responsible for international contacts, someone who could have been supportive to us.

(Head of Historic Preservation)

Orientation of international contacts
Berne has not recently increased the intensity of its international contacts, and it does not plan to intensify its international engagement in the near future. Berne is coincidentally engaged in three international networks, and it proactively refuses to engage in a city partnership. This reveals neither an economic nor a social orientation within Berne's rare international activities. The focus on three networks that are unrelated to the city-region's economic orientation is coincidental rather than strategic.

Linking the economic situation with international activities
A comparison of Berne's economic situation and its international activities reveals obvious similarities. Within both the economic and political domains, the national scale is the predominant scale of reference for the city-region of Berne. The economic and political subsystems are closely interlinked because the function of Berne as a capital city is an important economic factor for that city-region (Tripartite Arbeitsgruppe Bundesstadtstatus 2003: 3). To speak of interaction between the economic and political subsystems is therefore a bit misleading, since the two are automatically intertwined. The city-region's dependence on federal governmental services is anchored in the policy-makers' perspectives, and its relations with the federal government are seen as predominantly important for its well-being. The policy-makers in Berne thus have the scalar perception of a national city but not of an international city. Moreover, their reluctance to engage in

---

8   Cantons are the regional level in the three-tier federal structure of Switzerland.

international activities coincides with their focus on national politics. The city of Berne seems to rely on its close relations with the national administration to connect itself to the international level. According to the head of City Development, there is no perceived need to act on the international scale, since that is accomplished by the spatially close national administration:

> We are, of course, privileged because we can profit from the international network of the capital city [...]. If we have a request for a European city, we ask the ambassador and try to establish contact through him. He makes the contacts for us.
>
> *(Head of City Development)*

Accordingly, although the international activities are formally integrated into the service for city development, no such initiatives have yet been presented from the department to increase the international connectivity of the city.

The city's engagement within the OWHC network is partly linked to the city's tourist sector. However, the city of Berne uses its label as an UNESCO world heritage more than its cooperation within the OWHC network to attract tourists (Swissinfo 2008, 13th September). Cooperation within the OWHC is not used to promote the city of Berne on the international scale, since the network is a rather technical cooperation of people who work to preserve the monuments. Unsurprisingly, the respective administrative units did not encourage international cooperation within the Climate Alliance network (as in many other cases). Instead, green politicians forced the city administration to join that international cooperation scheme. The environmental department reacted to this by focusing its attention on the national section of the Climate Alliance (the KBSS). Again, the national scale is seen as the predominant scale of reference in Berne's policies.

The policy-makers who are involved in international activities do not perceive Berne as a highly globalised city. Instead, they view it as a medium-sized city that has a clear focus on the regional and national scale, in both the economic and political domains. In the words of the Head of City Development:

> I think that the awareness here is relatively large that we are a middle-size European city and not a metropolis.
>
> *(Head of City Development)*

The policy-makers do not see Berne as a city that has been or will be severely affected by globalisation. The actors that cooperate(d) within the city networks do not view their engagement linked to globalisation as a structuring process. The city government has strategically decided to focus on its relations with other political entities within the Swiss border, not across it. This decision is rooted in an understanding of Berne as a medium-sized city that is little known beyond Switzerland. The reluctance to engage in international activities is therefore based on the understanding of Berne as a city that is not highly globalised. Therefore, Berne's international activities are congruent with its social system of production. Because the city's economic system focuses on the city's central function of national administration, the city pursues almost no international activities.

Who governs?

The mayor directly controls the service for external relations and he has not undertaken any efforts to increase the city's international contacts. The city-region's few networking activities, which hardly involve politics, are conducted by the city administration. Hence, the involvement of the parliament and the public within the international activities of the city of Berne is very limited. This is not surprising, considering the small number of networking activities that Berne pursues.

In the case of the ECDP network, it is astonishing that the public never really noticed Berne's membership, even though that membership arose in response to questions from the public in at least one other city.[9] The city's membership in the ECDP network was clearly oriented to liberalise the national state's rather restrictive drug policy and to give individual cities more freedom to deal with the problems created by drug users in their urban areas. The network's espoused liberal drug policy raised considerable resistance from right-wing parties. At first, right-wing parties questioned Berne's membership in the ECDP network; after the membership was established, however, there was no debate. The city government also never readdressed its decision. Berne's decision to join the network was a political move, but the city administration carried out that networking activity thereafter. Additionally, no private actors participated in Berne's cooperation within the ECDP network. Although cooperation with private actors was common in drug policy, especially in the 1990s when cities shifted to more liberal policy orientations, Berne did not follow suit in its international networking. Only the city bureaucrats participated in the network reunions, and the information gained from the networking activities was not spread to private actors.

Within the two other networks (Climate Alliance and OWHC), cooperation remained restricted to the city administration. The city government decided to join the networks and then refrained from discussing any aspect of its participation within the networks. Within both networks, no private actors have been involved at any time.

In general, the city-region's international activities are not debated; international connectivity seems to be a non-issue in Berne's political agenda. The city government has only once discussed these activities as a whole in connection with its decision to focus on external relations within Switzerland. No discussion within the city parliament or with the public has addressed the city's (non-)engagement on the international scale. The few international activities of the city of Berne are clearly in the hands of the city administration. Private actors and the public are wholly excluded from Berne's few international activities.

Horizontal governance

An examination of the international activities of the cities in the agglomeration of Berne (see Table 2.4) reveals that four of the six communities that contain more than 10,000 inhabitants each have at least one partner city each and that none of the communities are engaged in networking activities.

---

9   See pages 73ff. for Lucerne's engagement in the ECDP network.

Table 2.4: The international activities of the cities in the agglomeration of Berne

Swiss city	Partner city/cities
Köniz	Prijepolje (Serbia)
Ostermundigen	Trojan (Bulgaria) / Löhnberg (Germany)
Münsingen	Humpolec (Czechoslovakia) / Münsingen (Germany)
Ittigen	Dobrusch (Belarus)

Interestingly, there is no cooperation regarding the cities' respective international activities, neither among the four agglomeration communities nor between any of the four communities and the city of Berne. Both sides seem to intend this non-cooperation. Neither the communities in the agglomeration nor the city of Berne have ever tried to cooperate with each other on international matters. Additionally, none of the involved actors see any profit in potential cooperation. They all perceive their international activities as belonging to their own communities, and they do not predict any possible gains from collaborating with other communities. Meanwhile, there is also no competition among the agglomeration communities and the core city over international activities. None of the activities have been set up as strategies against other communities. Again, possible links within the metropolitan area concerning international activities seem to be a non-issue and are characterised by non-debate.

The policy-makers of the core city of Berne do not seem to be aware of the possibility of using their primary position to connect the city-region to the global scale. This is not surprising since the city of Berne itself is only very reluctantly connected internationally, at least through formal networking. Even within the three networking activities of the city of Berne, there is absolutely no inclusion of the agglomeration community and no attempt to achieve any cooperation. This is surprising in the case of drug policy and the ECDP network since the city of Berne successfully brought the agglomeration communities into its drug-policy-making coordination bodies (Kübler and Wälti 2001: 49). Still, the networking activity within the ECDP network remained completely within the city borders, nor was it used to position the city against the agglomeration communities in this otherwise hotly debated policy area of metropolitan governance.

Two of the partnerships of communities were involved in cooperation schemes beyond the city-region level. The partnership of Köniz was established through Gemeinden Gemeinsam Schweiz, i.e. Swiss Communities Together (GGS[10]), an organisation that assisted communities from ex-Yugoslavia after the war in the early 1990s. The GGS coordinated the humanitarian aid contributed by Swiss communities through several regional coordination committees (Schumacher 1998: 221). Köniz was thereafter the only Swiss community that established a

---

10   Some basic information on GGS and the partnership project with former Yugoslavia can be found in Schumacher (1998).

formal partnership with a community from ex-Yugoslavia (Prijepolje) in 2005, and the cooperation of Köniz within GGS diminished significantly thereafter.[11] The canton of Berne initiated the partnership of Münsingen with Humpolec (see below).

Vertical governance

Relations with the federal state

The analysis of vertical governance schemes is the most interesting element of the case of Berne. Since Berne primarily relies on good relations with the national scale rather than relations at the international scale, a close relationship between the two levels would be expected in Berne's few international activities. Berne's decision not to enter any formal partnership with another city is based on its respect of its role as the capital city of Switzerland. Offering any city exclusive access through a partnership is viewed as inappropriate for a capital city. The city of Berne has avoided any conflict with the national scale by not engaging in such a partnership, although the national state has never formally asked the city of Berne not to enter into such a partnership, according to the involved policy-makers. An anticipatory obedience rather than a formal cooperation between the national and the local scale explains Berne's reluctance to participate on the international scale.

The friendly understanding between the federal state and the city scale has one prominent exception: the cooperation within the ECDP network, since the primary goal of this network was the promotion of a drug policy that was in conflict with the national policy.[12] The ECDP network seems to present a contrasting case to the generally good relations between the city of Berne and the national state. This was the only international activity of Berne that clearly endeavoured to bypass the national scale by linking the city of Berne with other Swiss and European cities that experienced similar problems in drug policy. Berne's engagement was seen as an international backup against the regional and the national drug policy, and it was used to promote awareness that other European cities faced similar problems. The regional and national scales, in the view of the participating cities, were following a too-restrictive drug policy that created severe problems in urban areas. Later, national politics adapted to the new, more liberal drug policy that had been developed by the cities and promoted by the ECDP network.

The city's participation in the OWHC network was facilitated by a national initiative to declare the old town of Berne as a UNESCO world heritage site. Because only national states can apply for sites to become UNESCO world heritages, the national scale needed to promote Berne's candidacy. Although the city of Berne accomplished most of the work required for the application, the national

---

11 Although GGS tried proactively to engage more Swiss communities in a formal partnership, it remained unsuccessful.

12 Cities primarily were in conflict with the position of the national parliament. The federal council and the responsible department already favoured a more moderate drug policy. However, the parliamentary support on the national scale for such a liberal drug policy only occurred later.

state's Department of Culture officially applied for and obtained the label for the old town of Berne. The city officials hoped for support from upper-level governments in sustaining the UNESCO label and help in the international cooperation on these matters. Neither the national state nor the canton of Berne, however, ever supported this international networking, although city officials tried several times to include actors from upper-level governments.

The partnerships of Ostermundigen with Trojan and of Köniz with Prijepolje, profited from a co-financing by the Direktion für Entwicklung und Zusammenarbeit, i.e. Swiss Agency for Development and Cooperation (DEZA). Interestingly, among all the Swiss communities examined in my study, only three profited from such a co-financing by the national scale. Two of those communities[13] are in the city-region of Berne. Ittigen also asked for a co-financing of its development aid for its partner city Dobrusch, in Belarus. Although the DEZA rejected the demand, the communities in the city-region of Berne were clearly better informed, overall, about the possibilities for accessing the national scale for a co-financing of their international activities. No community from any other city-region knew about this possibility. Berne's geographic proximity to the national administration allows for a closer cooperation with and a better knowledge of access points to the national scale. This again highlights the importance of the national administration for the city-region of Berne.

Relations with the canton
Although the canton of Berne has increased its own reflections on its international activities (Regierungsrat des Kantons Bern 2007), it has only once engaged in the international activities of its communities. The canton of Berne initiated partnerships with Czech communities after the fall of the iron curtain (Kanton Bern 1998; *Neue Zürcher Zeitung*, 2008, 11th August: 9). One cantonal councillor wanted to help the countries from Eastern Europe to quickly integrate into Western Europe after the fall of the iron curtain. The canton of Berne therefore initiated and co-ordinated a programme to connect communities from the canton of Berne with communities from South Bohemia in the Czech Republic, and it organised a total of four meetings for interested communities in Berne. Over the years, this led to a total of 111 partnerships between communities of the canton of Berne and partner cities in the Czech Republic (Kanton Bern 2004). Only one such partnership occurred in the city-region of Berne; Münsingen partnered with Humpolec.

The canton of Berne thereafter supported the initiation of the partnerships and organised a conference of all the partner cities after ten years (Kanton Bern 2001, 2002a). Interestingly, although the canton tried to involve the city of Berne in the project, Berne rejected this offer because of its status as the capital city (see previous discussion) and because of its generally difficult relationship with the canton. The person responsible for the programme on the cantonal level and the involved communities regretted the missing engagement of the communities in the city-region of Berne and especially of the city of Berne

13   The third community was the city of Zurich, with its partnership with Kunming; see pages 84ff.

Although the canton of Berne maintained its role as coordinator among the different partnerships and occasionally provided help when a partnership underwent a crisis, it was not involved in the partnerships directly. After the initiation phase, the canton kept its engagement to a minimum and did not invest financial resources in the partnerships (Kanton Bern 2002b). The canton does not keep track of the different partnerships; therefore, it is uncertain how many are still active.[14] Some of the involved communities desired a stronger engagement of the canton. However, the canton increased its own connections to the region of South Bohemia as part of its own international strategy (Justiz- Gemeinde- und Kirchendirektion des Kantons Bern 2004).

Apart from the initiation of these communal partnerships, the communal level has not been involved in the international activities of the canton of Berne, and vice versa. Therefore, the ties between the canton and the communities regarding international activities are rather weak. The communities within the agglomeration of Berne and the core city itself did not want to participate in any coordinated cooperation scheme with the cantonal level. However, this absence of coordination is not rooted in any strategy for using international activities to bypass the regional scale or to improve the position of the city-region towards the canton.

Relations with the EU
In the context of the preservation of cultural heritages (through the OWHC network), the increasing influence of the EU is often mentioned. Several new OWHC support programmes and regulations have originated from the EU, which directly influences policies on cultural heritage at the city level. Berne is absent from the EU's upper-level governmental support and from the respective coordination programme of EU cities. One interview partner mentions Berne's absence from a general trend towards increased networking in urban policy-making and the corresponding problems:

> I recognised that Switzerland is only very reluctantly engaged in networking, if one compares with Germany, and this has a lot to do with the EU. [...] All these German cities with their networks [...] and lots of connections in many policy areas [...]. I realised we are nowhere. It is really an exception if we are connected internationally, if we cooperate internationally. [...] There is also much more money involved through the EU; they support such activities financially. Switzerland is always outside, because it is not part of the EU.
>
> *(Head of Youth Department)*

Although the city-region's absence from the EU was mentioned as a problematic aspect, its relations with the EU are generally not part of the discourse in the international policy-making procedures in the city-region of Berne.

---

14 However, the canton of Berne sent a questionnaire to its involved communities in the preparation phase of the ten year jubilee (Amt für Gemeinden des Kantons Bern 1997). This questionnaire revealed that many of the partnerships had dissolved.

Short summary
The analysis of the city-region of Berne's international activities has shown no in-crease in the intensity of these activities. On the contrary, Berne's engagement on the international level is very modest, which makes it almost impossible to deter-mine the orientation of these contacts. The city-region's reluctance to engage in in-ternational networks can be explained by its specific political-economic situation as the capital city of Switzerland. The city's focus on the federal administration corresponds with its economic orientation towards the national scale. Therefore, the policy actors have decided to focus their external relations towards upper-level governments, neighbouring cantons, and, predominantly, the federal state. Foreign relations are considered unnecessary for a medium-sized capital city.

Berne's few international activities are controlled by the communal adminis-tration because no parliamentarian or public discussion on these matters has ever occurred (except for the parliamentarian decision to join the Climate Alliance net-work). Private actors are not included in any of the networking activities. There is absolutely no coordination between the different international activities of the communities in the agglomeration of Berne and no strategic use of Berne's rare in-ternational contacts towards the agglomeration communities. Concerning Berne's relations with the canton and the federal level, contacts are surprisingly scarce. At the least, however, the communities in the city-region of Berne are better informed about the access points for demands of co-financing their international activities by the national state than communities in other city-regions.

GENEVA: INTERNATIONAL CITY OF PEACE AND SOLIDARITY

International position and economic orientation
The city-region of Geneva contains a total of 471,314 inhabitants with the city of Geneva, containing 177,964 inhabitants, as the core city (Bundesamt für Statistik 2008a). The agglomeration of Geneva is the only city-region under scrutiny that includes foreign communities. However, since this study investigates inter-city-region and not intra-city-region relations, this is of minor importance. The ag-glomeration's transborder composition has no influence on the intensity or the orientation of Geneva's international activities.

Besides Zurich, Geneva is the only Swiss city that is sometimes represented in international city rankings. Beaverstock *et al.* (1999) and Taylor (2004) rank it as a 'gamma world city',[15] mostly because of its role as an international headquarters of international governmental organisations (IGOs) and NGOs. In Mercer's (2009) study on quality of living, Geneva is consistently ranked as one of the top three cities worldwide. In the European Cities Monitor's ranking of business-friendly cities, published by Cushman & Wakefield and Healey & Baker (1990–2009), Geneva is eleventh for 2009 and surpassed Zurich in 2007 for the first time since the rankings were conducted. Geneva is the only Swiss city-region that systemati-

---

15   Beaverstock *et al.* (1999) rank the 'world cities' in five categories: alpha, beta, gamma, strong
      evidence of world city formation, and some evidence of world city formation.

cally uses its international rankings for promotional activities. Whereas other city-regions occasionally use some international comparisons, the canton of Geneva published a systematic report on the international competitiveness of the Geneva area for the fifteenth time in 2008 (Geneva Economic Development Office 2008c).

Geneva owes its international reputation to its role as a city that hosts international peace negotiations. It currently contains twenty-three IGOs and approximately 250 NGOs (Geneva Economic Development Office 2008a; Schweizerischer Bundesrat 2008: 5), and it is among the top four cities that host IGOs in Europe (van der Wusten 2004). Van der Wusten (2007) classifies Geneva as a 'multilateral political world city', and Vaissade (2000: 26) calls it the 'capital city of multilateral negotiation' (author's translation). Geneva's reputation as an international city can be traced back to the Calvin era (van der Wusten 2007: 212), and its more specific reputation as a city of peace dates back to 1846, when Henri Dunant founded the Red Cross in Geneva (Geneva Economic Development Office 2008b). In 1919, after the First World War, the League of Nations (the predecessor of the United Nations [UN]) settled in Geneva (Vaissade 2000: 26). The UN, which was founded in 1945, has always located its European headquarters in Geneva (Vaissade 2000: 26). Geneva is also the seat of several UN-institutions, such as the World Health Organisation (WHO).

The importance of IGOs and NGOs for the Genevan economy becomes clear through an investigation of the political endeavours in this respect. The canton of Geneva, with financial support from the federal state and the city of Geneva, maintains an International Geneva Welcome Centre. The goal of the centre is to support NGOs that wish to settle in the Geneva area and to assist international newcomers with practical issues such as housing (see Geneva Welcome Centre 2008). Geneva also hosts an institution that manages the real estate needs of international organisations (the Fondation des Immeubles pour les Organisations Internationales, i.e. the Building Foundation for International Organisations [FIPOI]). The FIPOI organises the contacts with the federal government that can grant favourable loans to international organisations. Additionally, the canton of Geneva offers land on a favourable leasehold basis through the FIPOI (FIPOI 2008).

Political lobbying for international organisations to settle in the Geneva area was particularly strong amidst the negotiations for a new WTO headquarters (*Neue Zürcher Zeitung* 1994, 20th July: 19, 1995, 6th June: 14).[16] However, in 2006, the WTO announced that it needed more office space. The national council of States first voted in favour of offering a 60 million Swiss Francs interest-free credit for the renovation of the old building (*Neue Zürcher Zeitung* 2007, 20th September: 16). The WTO later increased its claims, and the federal council finally voted for a credit line of 130 million Swiss Francs for the renovation and the densification of the WTO building (*Neue Zürcher Zeitung* 2007, 29th December: 16, 2008, 15th

---

16   In 1995, the Swiss federal state extended an interest-free credit line of 31 million Swiss francs for the new building of the WTO in Geneva. This financial contribution was part of Switzerland's agreement with the WTO to settle in Geneva (*Neue Zürcher Zeitung* 1994, 20th July: 19: 19). The FIPOI manages the credit lines.

September: 16). The federal council has repeatedly mentioned the importance of the WTO, because of its 750 employees' activities in the Genevan economies, in order to defend the relatively high financial engagement (Schweizerischer Bundesrat 2008: 9). The WTO director threatened that the organisation would leave Geneva if Switzerland would not substantially contribute to the costs of the renovation (*Neue Zürcher Zeitung* 2007, 2nd May: 13, 2007, 10th May: 16; *Neue Zürcher Zeitung am Sonntag* 2007, 16th September: 17).

The federal council of Switzerland estimates the annual expenditures of the IGOs in Geneva at approximately 4.5 billion Swiss Francs (Schweizerischer Bundesrat 2008: 6). In addition to IGOs and NGOs, banks are another important economic factor for the Geneva area. Geneva, in addition to Zurich, contains a high concentration of (mostly private) banks. Currently, 140 banks have branches in Geneva, and about 32,000 people work in Geneva's financial sector (Geneva Economic Development Office 2008c).[17] Geneva entitles itself a 'world capital of asset management' (Geneva Economic Development Office 2000). The trading sector is also economically important for Geneva. All these strong economic sectors for the Geneva area share a common international component. IGOs, NGOs, banking, and trading are all highly globalised sectors in which international competition is fierce. The Genevan economy is therefore more vulnerable to global economic changes than other Swiss city-regions, due to its strong dependence on international business sectors (Hitz *et al*. 1994: 172).

International activities

City partnerships and networks
Geneva has no formally established international city partnerships, but it is a member of twelve international networks (see Table 2.5). The rationale behind Geneva's lack of a formal partnership with any particular city is somewhat similar to Berne's arguments (and Lausanne's, as will be discussed later[18]). As a host city of international organisations, many of which are related to the UN, policy-makers view preference of any one city as problematic. Referring to Swiss neutrality in general and the special role of Geneva within that neutral country, policy-makers consistently argue that it would be inappropriate to develop formal partnerships with foreign cities. Such partnerships could be viewed as expressing a preference for certain countries, which would cast doubt on Geneva's ability to provide a neutral place for international negotiations. Policy-makers consider strict neutrality to be a necessary condition for the impartiality of Geneva as a place for international contacts.

---

17   Numbers are for the canton of Geneva. In total, there are approximately 230,000 jobs in the service sector in the canton of Geneva (Geneva Economic Development Office 2008c: 7).

18   See pages 63ff.

However, Geneva has established friendly contacts with fourteen cities world-wide.[19] Often, these contacts were established during international conferences held in Geneva or through certain peace projects within Geneva's international contacts (see the next section).

Table 2.5: The international activities of the city of Geneva[20]

International activity	Description	Categorisation
Les Rencontres	Cities cooperating on cultural policy	Thematic network
GCD/GDS	Cities for digital solidarity	Thematic network
IAEC	Cities cooperating on education policy	Thematic network
Energie-Cités	Cities for a liberal environmental policy	Thematic network
ICLEI	Cities for a liberal environmental policy	Thematic network
IAPMC	Cities for global peace	Thematic network
LUCI	Cities cooperating on lighting policy	Thematic network
UCP	Cities fighting poverty	Thematic network
WHC	Cities with a historical old town	Thematic network
AIMF	Multi-thematic network	Lobby network
Eurocities	Multi-thematic network	Lobby network
UCLG	Multi-thematic network	Lobby network

Geneva is a member of the Les Rencontres network, which organises several meetings per year to discuss the domain of culture. Several members of Geneva's department of culture participated in the networking activities in the early 1990s, but their engagement stopped after a few years. The current head of the Department for Cultural Affairs re-entered the network in 2005 and has participated regularly in the meetings since then. Thanks to the contacts established in this network, Geneva officially supported Lyon in the competition to become the capital of culture in 2013.[21]

---

19   These cities are Hangzhou, Shanghai, Xi'an (all in China), Shinagawa (Japan), Amman (Jordan), Gaza (Palestine), Hanoi, Ho Chi Minh-Ville (both in Vietnam), Conakry (Guinea), Dakar (Senegal), La Paz (Bolivia), Asunción (Paraguay), Paris (France), and Kiev (Ukraine). The report on the international activities of the city of Geneva (Ville de Genève 2007: 13, see below) mentions several additional partnership projects that are not based on a formal friendly contact basis but rather on an informal project-based cooperation scheme.

20   The city of Geneva signalled its intent to join the European coalition of cities against racism in 2005. As for the other city-regions under scrutiny, I did not include this network in my study (see page 41).

21   See pages 99ff.

The Global Digital Solidarity Fund (GDS) is an initiative to foster developing countries' access to the digitalisation of the world. The Global Cities Dialogue (GCD) network manages this fund. Geneva was among the three founding members of GCD (along with Lyon[22] and the region of Turin). The GDS was set up during an international conference on the information society in Geneva in 2003. The secretariat of the GDS is located in Geneva.

Geneva is the only Swiss member city of the International Association of Educating Cities (IAEC). The member cities cooperate on questions of education and organise a bi-annual conference in which the Director of the Department for Social Cohesion, Youth, and Sports participates regularly. Due to the engagement of the director, Geneva was among the founding members of the network in 1990. Additionally, the director was a long-standing member of the executive committee of the IAEC network.

Geneva is a member of two networks in the domain of sustainability and ecology, the International Council for Local Environmental Initiatives (ICLEI) and the Energie-Cités network. The city-region joined ICLEI in 1998, and policy-makers from the unit on the local agenda 21 participated irregularly in the network. Geneva is also a member of the Energie-Cités network, in which Geneva's delegate for energy issues has participated regularly in the exchange of best practices since Geneva joined the network in 2002.

The former mayor[23] of Geneva was significantly involved in the founding of the International Association of Peace Messenger Cities (IAPMC), the goal of which was to create a communal network for cities that commit themselves to peace. This network was inspired by the UN's decision to recognise sixty-two cities as peace messenger cities in 1987. Geneva initiated the creation of this network of those recognised cities and committed itself to a leadership role within the network, notably due to its close relations with UN authorities. The former mayor of Geneva served as president of the network for many years. The executive office of the network was located in Geneva for several years, and Geneva hosted the network's general conference in 1993.

The city of Geneva joined the Lighting Urban Community International (LUCI) network in 2003. The person responsible for economic development in Lyon invited the mayor of Geneva to join the network when he officially visited the festival de la lumière in Lyon in 2002.[24] This network brings together policymakers on all aspects of urban lighting. Several people from Geneva's urban planning department participated regularly in the LUCI meetings.

Geneva was a founding member of the United Cities against Poverty (UCP) network. This network of cities was established in 2002 by Geneva, Lyon,[25] and

---

22   See pages 99ff. for a discussion of Lyon's participation in this network.

23   The term mayor is a bit misleading in the case of Geneva. The special organisational form of Geneva's city government is explained on pages 54f.

24   The network was founded by Lyon; see pages 99ff.

25   See pages 99ff.

Bamako (Mali), and it endeavours to provide a platform for decentralised development aid through the exchange of knowledge with developing cities. Geneva has presided over the network since it began, and also hosts the secretariat. Several people from different departments of the Genevan city administration have participated in exchange programmes organised by the UCP network.

Geneva joined the Organisation of World Historical Cities (WHC)[26] in 2004 but participated only once in a conference that dealt with the preservation of historical towns.

Geneva joined the Association Internationale des Maires Francophones, i.e. International Association of French-Speaking Mayors (AIMF) in 1988. This important network of French-speaking cities is both a lobby organisation for the local scale towards upper-level governments and a multi-thematic policy cooperation network. However, the network focuses on the first aspect; hence, Geneva's membership was rather symbolic until 2002, when the city government decided to increase its engagement within the network. Geneva served as the AIMF's president of the working group on development aid in 2002, and the city-region has annually paid 50,000 Swiss Francs into that fund since 2004 (Ville de Genève 2007: 20).

Geneva was already a member of Eurocities in the late 1990s; for a long time, it remained the only Swiss member city of this highly influential lobby and multi-thematic policy cooperation network at the European scale. Eventually, political disputes over Geneva's role in a network that was closely attached to the EU led the city government to step down from its membership. The city government revised its decision in 2006, however, and Geneva again joined the Eurocities network as an associate member.

Geneva was one of the founding members of United Cities and Local Government (UCLG) in 2004. This was no surprise since Geneva was already a member of its two predecessor organisations, the United Towns Organisation (UTO) and the International Union of Local Authorities (IULA). Geneva even proactively sought to become the host city of UCLG, but the organisation eventually settled in Barcelona. Still, compared to the other Swiss cities under scrutiny, Geneva is relatively strongly engaged in the network. Geneva chaired the Information Society Commission and served as a member of UCLG's executive committee in its beginning phase but eventually stepped down from this position (Ville de Genève 2007: 22). Geneva is still a member of two commissions, urban diplomacy and decentralised cooperation.

Organisation of international contacts

The organisational structure of Geneva's international activities developed in two phases. In a first phase, which lasted until 2002, the activities were carried out by various different departments and were only marginally coordinated. The mayor

---

26 The OWC network should not be confused with the OWHC network. Although both networks cooperate in the same domain (the preservation of historical cities), the latter is attached to the UNESCO world heritage label, and the OWC is not. This competition of interurban networks is addressed on page 134.

of Geneva is only elected for one year (with a rotation principle among the members of the city government), which does not help to establish a coherent strategy on the international level. Hence, several engagements in networks are only followed irregularly (for example, the city's membership in Eurocities). In 2002, a new service for international activities was established; this service reports directly to the city government as a whole (not to the mayor, as in many other cities).

The duties of the service are twofold. On the one hand, it organises the international contacts for the city of Geneva, which includes overlooking the international networking activities that are carried out by different departments. On the other hand, the service manages several of the city's international contacts directly, primarily those that focus on the domain of peace and solidarity. The service for international activities published a report on its activities for the years 2004 through 2007 (Ville de Genève 2007), but the cooperation within the networks Les Rencontres and Energie-Cités is not mentioned. This underlines the problematic nature of the cooperation between the service for international activities and the different departments (see below).

Orientation of international contacts
The outline of the international contacts is very clear-cut; besides a few cooperation schemes that deal with specific policy domains (for example, education and public lighting), most international contacts address global peace and international solidarity. Geneva not only participates in many peace and solidarity networks but also has created its own networks in this domain and hosts several secretariats of these networks.

> In politics, there is a clear will of the city, which is governed by the left for several years, to demonstrate its international solidarity, to offer a place where representatives of conflicts zones can come and discuss.
>
> *(Head of the Service for External Relations)*

The city-region of Geneva does not participate in any international cooperation on economic matters. The city government decided, in 2001, to strengthen the international role of Geneva through an increased presence in international city networks, primarily those focusing on peace and solidarity. Thus, due to the city government's general agreement on the need for international visibility, Geneva has set a clear strategy for its international activities.

Overall, the level of international activity conducted by the city of Geneva is unrivalled in Switzerland. Geneva has participated in the newly emerging international activities of cities since the beginning of the 1980s, and it has intensified its engagement since the installation of a special service that deals with these contacts. Hence, Geneva is solidly Switzerland's leader in international urban networking, as one of the people responsible for the international activities mentions:

> It is true, if you look at international networks, Geneva is often quite alone.
>
> *(Employee of the Service for External Relations)*

Linking the economic situation with international activities

The links between a city-region's economic outline and its international activities are particularly clear in Geneva. Because the city-region is well known worldwide for hosting international organisations, policy-makers on the city level see a direct need to engage on the international level in order to maintain Geneva's reputation as an international city of peace and solidarity (see also *Neue Zürcher Zeitung* 2007, 6th February: 15):

> I think that Geneva profits from its trump card, its international image, its image as an international city. I think that it is quite sure that we will play this card to sell, to boost Geneva.
>
> *(Employee of the Service for External Relations)*

> The existence of this community, composed of international functionaries, of delegates that come to participate in conferences, the personnel of diplomatic missions, creates forcefully an international life in Geneva that is very important and that contributes enormously to the mission of the city.
>
> *(Head of the Service for External Relations)*

Geneva's engagement in peace and solidarity networks is directly linked to its role as a city in which international peace negotiations take place. Not only does Geneva focus on its collaboration in international networks that deal with these issues, it also steers its membership in multi-thematic networks (i.e. AIMF and UCLG) towards the same issues. Geneva strategically participates in workgroups that align with its interests in order to promote itself as an international peace city, as an employee of Geneva's Service for External Relations explains:

> What we now try to do is to go to places where Geneva can find a niche for peace, sustainable development, human rights [....]. We really try to find little niches which we can develop and finally play a role.
>
> *(Employee of the Service for External Relations)*

Geneva proactively tried to become the host city of the UCLG network when it was founded in 2004. Geneva viewed a central role in this worldwide organisation of communities and cities as an ideal complement for its role as an international city. The city-region's goal was to increase its international visibility through its participation in this major international network. If Geneva had successfully gained the privilege of hosting UCLG, then it would have hosted not only many international IGOs and NGOs but also the seat of the most important international organisation on the local scale. However, the organisation finally settled in Barcelona.

Policy-makers consider international visibility to be an essential goal for a city-region that is economically dependent on IGOs and NGOs. Geneva has therefore connected itself through international networks for many years. The decision to establish a new service for international contacts in 2002 was rooted in the need to develop a more coherent international presence for Geneva (Ville de Genève

2007: 3). The newly developed strategy strongly focuses on promoting Geneva as an international peace city. Therefore, the city's engagement on the international scale has predominantly emphasised involvement in networks from 2003 onwards, as one responsible for international contacts explains:

> There was a decision at the end of the 1990s and the beginning 2000s that Geneva has to become much more present on the international scale.
>
> *(Employee of the Service for External Relations)*

Thus, Geneva's clear orientation towards peace and solidarity is thus not as altruistic as it might immediately appear. Geneva develops an increasingly strategic vision of its international contacts in order to promote the economically important image of peace and solidarity. The international contacts that do not align with Geneva's general strategy are not abandoned, but cooperation is left to their respective departments, and the Service for International Contacts does not coordinate them. The city-region's strategy on the international level is clearly linked to its economic needs, and the involved policy-makers are fully aware of the need to remain clearly present on the international level, representing Geneva as a peace city, in order to retain the city's economic strength.

> We are fully aware that the international Geneva is strategic for Geneva; there are directly 35,000 jobs involved.
>
> *(Cantonal delegate for International Relations)*

Political actors fear the increasing competition for Geneva's role as a host city for IGOs and NGOs. Several other European cities, such as Bonn and Vienna, have started to challenge Geneva's lead in this area and to offer financial incentives that encourage IGOs and NGOs to relocate their headquarters. Genevan politicians are aware that the city's reputation as a host of international peace negotiations is not sacrosanct. Because this reputation is vital for Geneva's economy, Geneva's goal is to link its international networking activities to its image as an international peace city. The city-region's participation in interurban networks is part of its strategy to maintain its image as a city of peace and solidarity on the international level. The head of the Service for External Relations states:

> Effectively, the municipalities see that hosting international organisations on their territory obviously contributes to the economic development as well.
>
> *(Head of the Service for External Relations)*

Who governs?
The organisation of Geneva's city government is somewhat different from the organisation of other Swiss cities. The mayor is not directly elected by the people; rather, each year, one of the five city councillors takes the role of the mayor. Although some of the former mayors participated in the city's strategy for international networking by creating or joining certain networks, the mayor's overall influence remains limited. The fact that each mayor only holds the office for one

year complicates the continuity of the city's international activities. This also explains why the service for international relations is not directly attached to the mayor (as it is in other cities) but instead reports directly to the city government as a whole.

The administration deals autonomously with certain international contacts. The responsible city councillor is sometimes involved in international cooperation schemes, but the networking activities are clearly dominated by the administrations of their respective departments. Geneva's cooperation within the LUCI network is a good example of this practice; the city administration even used its international contacts to emphasise the significance of its work towards politics.[27] The city's membership of the LUCI network was used to highlight the importance of public lighting in urban marketing for other cities. The city's cooperation within the IAEC network is even more confined to the administrative level. Although Geneva's mayor is formally invited to the international meetings, the heads of the respective departments recommend to the city government whether the meetings are worth attending. Usually, the city government delegates the responsibility of attending the meetings to the head of the relevant department without any discussion of the topic.

The city government brought a political strategy into Geneva's international activities by setting up a special service for these activities in 2002. Although the service has a certain level of autonomy, the city government monitors its activities closely. The city government as a whole brought its diverse international contacts in line with Geneva's economic specificity. The city government linked its international activities with the importance of Geneva's international visibility. However, the communal administration resisted the centralisation of the city's international contacts, and the service for international activities had already experienced some difficulties in collecting the necessary information on international contacts from the various departments. The involved policy-makers from the different departments feared that the central service for international activities would take away their international contacts, as even an employee from this service states:

> It is true that [...] we have to search the information. It does not come to us, not just like that. [...]. It takes time to change the habits of the administration.
>
> *(Employee of the Service for External Relations)*

The policy-makers in charge of the departmental international contacts were also afraid that they would have to abandon certain international contacts that did not fit into the new focus on peace and solidarity. One example of this reluctance to cooperate on international matters is the cooperation within the ICLEI and Energie-Cités networks. Although they are closely linked thematically, two different services from two different departments manage contacts with the two networks, and each service is unaware of the other's international activities. In every

---

27   Although the original proposition to join the network originated from a city councillor (see above), the networking activities soon shifted to the administrative level.

other city under scrutiny, the networking activities in environmental networks are coordinated by the same service. There is thus a conflict between politics and the administration in Geneva. Moreover, the role of the relatively new service for international contacts is not yet clear to all involved policy-makers. The division of labour between the central service for international contacts and the different departments involved in international policy contacts is also not yet well-established.

Surprisingly, the political debate about international contacts is marginal in Geneva. The city parliament seems wholly uninterested in the city's international contacts. There have been no parliamentary requests regarding international activities since the establishment of the new service in 2002. Additionally, the public seems uninterested in Geneva's international connectedness. Absolutely no critical remarks have been offered by the public, and no concerns have been raised by anyone outside the city administration. Also surprising, NGOs are not directly involved in Geneva's international contacts. Although many international contacts are related to Geneva's role as headquarters for NGOs, the networking activities are restricted to politics and to the city administration.

Horizontal governance
Four of the eight agglomeration communities of Geneva are involved in international partnerships, but none of the communities are engaged in international networks (see Table 2.6).

Table 2.6: The international activities of the cities in the agglomeration of Geneva

Swiss city	Partner city/cities
Carouge	1st district of Budapest (Hungary)
Onex	Bandol (France)
Nyon	Nyons (France)
Thônex	Graveson (France)

However, there is no coordination between Geneva's numerous international activities and the international contacts of the agglomeration communities.[28] The city of Geneva is not aware of the international contacts of the agglomeration communities. It has never tried to involve the communities in its own international contacts. Although centrality burdens from the international contacts are the highest for Geneva due to the city's massive engagement on the international scale,

---

28   However, the communities in the agglomeration of Geneva, together with the canton, coordinate their budgets on development aid. Several of the agglomeration communities, as well as the city of Geneva, reserve a certain percentage of their budgets for international development projects. Because the amount provided by one community is usually too small to finance any significant project, these donations are coordinated under the umbrella of the canton.

there have been no attempts to use its international contacts against the agglomeration communities. Policy-makers have not reflected upon such a possibility, and it is undisputed that the international contacts are in the hands of the core city.

The same can be said about the international contacts of the agglomeration communities. Their proximity to the international city of Geneva seems irrelevant to their international contacts. The agglomeration communities carry out their city partnerships independently, and a possible involvement of the city of Geneva has not been considered. The international contacts of the agglomeration communities are not linked to Geneva's role as headquarters of IGOs and NGOs, and reflections on international contacts are not based on any economic pursuit of Geneva's international visibility. Although the internationality of Geneva fosters economic gains for the city-region as a whole, there is no common understanding of this economic necessity among the agglomeration communities. Although all the communities in the Geneva area are dependent on the economically important international visibility, they refrain from any cooperation regarding their international contacts. This lack of collaboration aligns with the generally competitive situation between the city of Geneva and its surrounding agglomeration communities, as mentioned by several policy-makers. As in many other Swiss city-regions, this competitive situation is caused by the fiscal competition between communities in general and the political divide between a left-oriented core city and right-oriented agglomeration communities.

Vertical governance

Relations with the canton
The canton of Geneva is quite active on the international scale. Through its delegate for international contacts, the canton of Geneva participates in several international cooperation schemes; some are close-border cooperation activities (Lezzi 2000: 36ff.), and others are more internationally oriented. The canton of Geneva is even a member of an international network on urban transport (POLIS), in which foremost cities participate.[29] The relationship between the canton and the city of Geneva is generally poor, as manifested in the canton's international contacts.[30]

Often, policy competences are not clearly separated between the canton and the city, and the competences for the communal scale are more limited in Geneva than in other Swiss cantons. Hence, international networking in these policy areas is difficult, since the city sometimes participates in international networks that deal with policy issues which are managed by the canton. According to policy-makers, collaboration on international contacts between the city scale and the cantonal scale is almost impossible. The cantonal delegate for international relations admits,

---

29   See the case of Stuttgart, on pages 114ff., for more information about the POLIS network.

30   This poor relationship is evidenced by the discussion of the seat of the WTO and its enlargement (see previous discussion). The negotiations took place between the WTO, the Swiss federal state, and the canton of Geneva, although the building was located in the city of Geneva. The canton did not want to involve the city of Geneva in these negotiations.

[…] that there is always a bit of competition, I do not want to say rivalry, this might be too harsh, but competition between the city and the canton.

(Cantonal delegate for international relations)

Although Geneva is the only case in which a formalised cooperation between the two levels exists, the contacts remain rather formal and minimal. The head of the city of Geneva's Service for International Contacts is a member of the steering committee for the international contacts of the canton of Geneva (Canton de Genève 2008). Through this committee, both sides exchange the knowledge they glean from their international contacts and cooperate on international contacts that require both the cantonal and city levels. However, both scales somehow perceive themselves as dominant regarding sub-national international contacts. Whereas the city tries to develop as many of its own independent international contacts as possible, the canton sees its own international contacts as much more important for the economic well-being of the Geneva area. Also, it is the canton and not the city of Geneva that publishes an annual report on the Geneva area's international competitiveness (Geneva Economic Development Office 2008c). Thus, there is no close collaboration on international matters between the canton and the city of Geneva. Rather, they compete for the lead in international contacts.

Relations with the federal state
Although the contacts between the city of Geneva and the national scale are important for the establishment of IGOs and NGOs, there is no collaboration between the two scales on Geneva's networking activities. The contacts between the two scales are established through channels other than an inclusion of the national scale in the city's international contacts. However, it is obvious to all policy-makers that no international contact of Geneva should contradict the Swiss federal foreign policy. Thus, there is no strategic consideration of using the city-region's international contacts against the national scale. On the contrary, Geneva's policy-makers are careful not to offend Swiss national politics by their international contacts.

The case of the GCD network and the GDS fund is somehow an outlier of the generally good understanding between the Swiss federal government and the city of Geneva. Originally planned as a network of nations, regions, cities, and private companies, GCD originated in two conferences. The first conference, which was for the cities, was held in Lyon in September 2003; the second, which was for national states, was held in Geneva in December 2003. Whereas several cities and regions joined the GCD network and began contributing to the GDS fund, the national states originally refused to do so. Several national states, including Switzerland, were displeased that the cities took the lead in the international cooperation on digital solidarity. Some of the national states eventually revised their positions and joined the previously city-dominated network. The GCD network is thus a rare exception as a multi-level international network that includes national, regional, and local authorities. The Swiss national state has not (yet) joined the network.

Thus, Geneva maintains a double strategy towards upper-level Swiss governments. The city competes with the canton for the lead in international contacts. The city uses its own international contacts to strengthen its role towards the canton, which is also quite active on the international scale. However, the city-region's relations with the federal state are characterised by an informal coordination and a good understanding.

Relations with the EU

Geneva's contacts with the EU are limited to cooperation within three networks: Les Rencontres, LUCI, and Eurocities. Within Les Rencontres, the member cities use their contacts to access the EU for funding for cultural politics. Geneva, although it is a member of Les Rencontres, cannot participate in these project demands. The involved policy-maker mentions that Geneva cannot become European capital of culture because only cities from EU member states can obtain that label, beginning in 2011.[31]

> When we signed up in this network, there was a rule which has changed now. It is now the rule that today, cities from countries not being formally members of the EU cannot postulate anymore, this is over.
>
> *(Co-director of the Department of Cultural Affairs)*

The involved policy-maker regrets this. As a result, the city of Geneva supported the candidacy of Lyon as a European capital of culture.[32] Through this support, Geneva is at least attached to this movement, which is viewed as important for the cultural sector. Geneva closely collaborates with Lyon on its candidacy, and the two cities would have developed common projects if Lyon had become European capital of culture.

The EU co-finances part of the LUCI network's activities through the Interreg III programme. This co-financing not only supports cities from the EU concerning the travel expenses of the involved policy-makers but also partially compensates them for their preparation activities. The city of Geneva cannot participate in this funding but instead must finance its networking activities within LUCI independently.

The city government decided to rejoin Eurocities in 2006 in order to express its commitment to Europe. Although the engagement within Eurocities is time-consuming and often related to the work of the European Commission, the city government nevertheless decided to invest in its membership in that highly influential city network. Geneva's membership in the Eurocities network also demonstrates a clear commitment to the EU. Although the network's lobbying activities are not at the forefront of Geneva's priorities, the city government still views its Eurocities membership as a sign towards the rest of Switzerland. The city government favours Switzerland joining the EU and sees membership in the Eurocities network as one way to emphasise its position on this topic, as the head of the Service for External Relations explains:

---

31 See the European parliament's decision 1622/2006/CE regarding the European capital of culture for the years 2007 through 2019.

32 See pages 99ff. on the candidacy of Lyon for the European capital of culture in 2013.

Geneva contributes to the Eurocities network although Switzerland is not a member of the EU, because it is an important place for exchange on the European level. Even if we are not part of the European community, we are still in Europe [...]. It is thus an indirect message that is given to the rest of Switzerland.

(Head of the Service for External Relations)

Other than the city's participation in Eurocities, Geneva's networking activities are oriented towards the global rather than the European scale. Because Geneva focuses on international peace and solidarity, collaboration schemes with cities from Africa or Asia are as common as collaboration schemes with European cities. Geneva's networking activities have no special relation with the EU.

Short summary
Geneva has established more international contacts than any other Swiss city. Although it has participated in the interurban networking movement since the 1980s, Geneva shows a clear recent increase in the intensity of its contacts. Geneva strategically reoriented its international contacts in 2002 through the establishment of a new service for managing international contacts. The city-region's strategy relies on promoting Geneva as an excellent location for IGOs and NGOs through engaging in international peace and solidarity networks. However, this strategy and economic focus remains limited to the core city's politics and administration. There is no political debate outside the city government, and there is no cooperation between the city and the agglomeration communities. The city's relation with the canton is competitive, not cooperative, concerning international contacts. Because the scalar orientations of Geneva's international contacts are global, Geneva has no special relation with the EU concerning its networking activities.

LAUSANNE: CITY OF INTERNATIONAL SPORT

International position and economic orientation
The city-region of Lausanne contains a total of 311,441 inhabitants who are spread over seventy communities. All of those inhabitants reside within the canton of Vaud. Lausanne, containing 124,914 inhabitants, is the core city of the agglomeration (Bundesamt für Statistik 2008a). Due to its small size, the city-region of Lausanne is not represented in any city or city-region rankings. The city-region of Lausanne is not specifically dependent on one sub-sector of the service economy. In addition to being the headquarters of a few international companies such as Philip Morris and Tetra-Laval (Schilt 2000: 30), the city-region of Lausanne is best known for its attachment to the Olympics and as an international city of sport.[33] Lausanne calls itself 'the capital city of modern Olympics' (SEGRE Lausanne 2008, author's translation).

---

33   Overall, twenty-four international sports federations and twenty international sports organisations have their headquarters in the canton of Vaud (Canton de Vaud 2008). Unfortunately, similar data are not available for the city-region of Lausanne; nevertheless, it can be assumed that most of the federations and organisations are within the boundaries of that city-region.

This city-region hosts the International Olympic Committee (IOC), the Court of Arbitration for Sport (CAS), and an Olympic museum. Several international sports federations locate their headquarters in Lausanne (IFSports Guide 2008). The Union of European Football Associations (UEFA) has established its seat in Nyon, which is between Geneva and Lausanne and which belongs to the agglomeration of Geneva but to the canton of Vaud. The UEFA moved its headquarters from Berne to Nyon in 1995 due to the canton of Vaud's more attractive fiscal conditions (Hödl 2004; *Neue Zürcher Zeitung* 2004, 15th June: 62).[34] The tax authorities of the canton of Vaud accepted the UEFA as a non-profit organisation; therefore, the UEFA is not required to pay taxes. The tax exemption highlights international sports associations' importance to Lausanne's economic well-being, according to the city-region's political actors (Canton de Vaud 2008). Clearly, Lausanne's international reputation is linked to sports, and this reputation is used as a promotional asset (Ville de Lausanne 2008a).

Apart from its strong reliance on sports for its international reputation, Lausanne also tries to foster its image as a city of culture. Lausanne is the Swiss city that invests the highest percentage of its budget to culture (Ville de Lausanne 2008c).

International activities

City partnerships and networks
The city of Lausanne is involved in seven international activities (see Table 2.7) and has no formal partnership with any city beyond the Swiss border. Although the city government has repeatedly received requests to establish formal partnerships with cities worldwide (*24 heures* 2006, 1st April), such offers have been declined with reference to Lausanne's special role as host city of the IOC.

Because several international sport organisations and particularly sport courts locate their domiciles in Lausanne, it would be problematic for Lausanne to prefer certain foreign cities (and their respective national states) through partnerships. Although these sport courts are formally independent from the city of Lausanne, Lausanne politicians believe that their neutral judgement on national matters (such as the sanctioning or non-sanctioning of an athlete's exclusion by the respective national sports court) could be endangered by the city's special relationship with any foreign city. An informal agreement between the city of Lausanne and the IOC provides the basis for this neutrality. Lausanne's non-engagement on the international scale is therefore much more explicit than in the case of Berne, where the reference to the city's role as the capital is not based on any formal command to avoid establishing preferred partnerships with non-Swiss cities. Lausanne's policy-makers consistently mention the city's close relations with the IOC as rationale for its non-engagement in city partnerships (see also *24 heures* 2006, 1st April).

---

34   Additionally, Nyon seemed to be more prestigious, and it is closer to an international airport (Hödl 2004).

Table 2.7: The international activities of the city of Lausanne[35]

International activity	Description	Categorisation
Les Rencontres	Cities cooperating on cultural policy	Thematic network
Energie-Cités	Cities for sustainable energy policy	Thematic network
IFGRA	Cities/Regions for sustainable development	Thematic network
DELICE	Cities with a relation to *haute cuisine*	Thematic network
UMVO	Cities with a relation to the Olympic games	Thematic network
AIMF	Multi-thematic network	Lobby network
UCLG	Multi-thematic network	Lobby network

The municipality has up to now always declined [partnerships] because we are the seat of the IOC, the Olympic movement. We never wanted to position ourselves, to prefer someone.

(Person responsible for external relations)

Lausanne has a peculiarity, as we are the Olympic capital city, [...] we do not have the right to make partnerships with other cities.

(Employee of the Department of Industrial Services)

Lausanne is one of the two Swiss cities that belong to the network Les Rencontres (along with Geneva[36]), which brings together European cities that want to share their best practices in the domain of cultural policy. The former city councillor, who was also the former head of the Department for Culture, Housing, and Heritage, was an executive member of Les Rencontres and participated regularly in the meetings. Today, the head of Cultural Services still attends the meetings, but irregularly.

Lausanne is also one of the three Swiss member cities of the Energie-Cités network.[37] Lausanne actively engages within the network on sustainable energy use in cities. Policy-makers from the department of industrial services (which manages energy policies) have participated in several projects on good practice exchanges in this European network.

Additionally, Lausanne has recently begun actively engaging in creating two new networks. First, the International Federation of Green Regions Association

---

35   The city of Lausanne signalled its intent to join the European coalition of cities against racism in 2005. As for the other city-regions under scrutiny, I did not include this network in my study (see page 41).

36   See pages 49ff.

37   Along with Martigny and Geneva. See also pages 49ff. on Geneva's engagement in this network.

(IFGRA) was set up during an international symposium on urban sustainability in Lausanne in October 2007 (SESEC 2007). So far, the network's founding has been its only activity led by the mayor of Lausanne, who is a member of the Green Party. The Association wants to share environmental best practices of green cities (IFGRA 2007).

The second network, the Union Mondiale des Villes Olympiques, i.e. the Union of Olympic Cities (UMVO), has not been formally established yet, but it has been announced in official documents as a strategic goal of the city of Lausanne for the near future (Lausanne Tourisme 2008; Ville de Lausanne 2008b). Lausanne's purpose is to create a network of cities that have close relations to the Olympic Games, either as host cities of past Olympic Games or as cities that are interested in hosting future games. The network will allow its members to share best practice rules for the execution of Olympic Games, and it will promote the spirit of the Olympic Games. The city of Athens originally established a similar network that relied on informal contacts between the host cities of the Olympic Games. The contacts among that network's members drifted, and Lausanne is now attempting to reanimate and formalise the international cooperation in this domain. The network's inaugural conference took place in Lausanne in October 2008 (Lausanne Tourisme 2008).

Lausanne recently joined the new network Délice (Réseau des Villes Gourmandes du Monde, i.e. Network of the Gourmet Cities of the World), which was established by the city of Lyon at the end of 2007,[38] as a founding member (*24 heures* 2008, 21st May; Lausanne Tourisme 2008).

Lausanne has been a member of AIMF since 1990. The city's engagement in this network is similar to its engagement in the UCLG network. The AIMF was primarily set up as a lobby network for French mayors, but its activities have been broadened over the years and now include some policy cooperation. The mayor of Lausanne irregularly participates in the AIMF meetings, and Lausanne supports the AIMF fund for French-speaking cities from developing countries. Lausanne's policy-makers would like to increase the city's engagement in this network. Hence, Lausanne recently assumed the presidency of the AIMF's commission on sustainability.

Lausanne is a direct member of the UCLG network. Although the UCLG is primarily an international umbrella organisation for national city-associations, its membership is also open to individual cities. Lausanne, along with Geneva and Zurich, has voted for such a direct membership, in addition to its indirect membership through the Swiss city association and the Swiss section of the Council of European municipalities and regions (CEMR). The latter organisation locates its seat in Lausanne, and the city has strongly committed to being a European city. Besides the mayor's participation at the inaugural conference in 2004,[39] Lausanne has not participated in any concrete policy cooperation programmes within the

---

38   See pages 99ff.

39   Two networks merged in 2004 to form the new UCLG network.

UCLG network. The city plans to do so in the near future but its policy-makers see the UCLG network as a bureaucratic organisation in which concrete policy cooperation is difficult to achieve.[40]

Organisation of international contacts
A division that is directly subordinated to the mayor partially coordinates the international activities of the city of Lausanne. The unit's name (Service des Études Générales et des Relations Extérieures, i.e. Service for General Studies and External Relations [SEGRE]) clarifies that the unit does deal not only with international relations but also with external relations in general. Accordingly, a subdivision of the unit deals with external relations. These external relations also include the city's relations with the canton of Vaud, with other Swiss cantons, and with the federal state. However, not all networking activities are coordinated by this service. The respective departments autonomously manage the city's engagements within Les Rencontres and Energie-Cités.

Still, the SEGRE knows about these networking activities and offers its assistance in organisational matters to the people who participate in networking activities that are not directly supervised by the mayor's office. The division of labour, whereby the departments carry out policy networking and the SEGRE manages organisational matters, guarantees the mayor's awareness of any ongoing international contacts. Nevertheless, because its resources are limited, the SEGRE focuses on newly established networks and on developing a strategy for Lausanne's international activities.

Orientation of international contacts
Lausanne's international strategy is based on the four pillars of its new urban marketing strategy: sustainability, sport, science, and culture. The city government has decided to focus on these four pillars because it views them as vital for the city's future economic development. This strategy responds to the city parliament's demand that the city government must focus more on interurban competition (Lausanne Tourisme 2008).[41]

These strategic considerations include international activities. Whereas Lausanne is already internationally connected in the domains of sustainability (through Energie-Cités) and culture (through Les Rencontres and Délice), it lacks any corresponding international cooperation in the domain of sports. Therefore, the city government, in response to the mayor's proposition, strategically decided to organise a network in the domain of sports and to increase its engagement in environmental politics through an additional network also set up by the city of Lausanne. All these decisions relate to the urban marketing strategy that provides the basis for these decisions.

---

40 Apart from these formal international cooperation schemes, Lausanne spends a fixed amount of two Swiss Francs per inhabitant every year on development aid projects (Ville de Lausanne 2008d).

41 Sustainability's link to economic development will be addressed on pages 128ff.

Lausanne is, besides Zurich, the Swiss city that is currently changing its international profile the most. Lausanne recently joined several networks, and its overall strategy in international cooperation is oriented towards sustainability rather than competitiveness. However, the two aspects are clearly interlinked in this case; Lausanne's international activities are managed by the same service that organises the city's promotional activities.

Linking the economic situation with international activities

Although the city-region of Lausanne is not heavily dependent on any economic branches, the city government still reflects strategically on the city-region's economic assets and urban marketing. Several of the city's international activities are linked to the four pillars that are defined in its urban marketing strategy (see previous section). Lausanne's networking activities within Les Rencontres support the marketing pillar of culture more coincidentally than strategically, and are not directly linked to the mayor's promotion of Lausanne abroad. However, the city's new engagement within the Délice network falls into this category since its intent is to attract high-quality tourism to Lausanne. *Haute cuisine* is part of Lausanne's cultural assets that can bring tourists to Lausanne. The city's linkages with sports, as another pillar of the marketing strategy, are also strong. Not only does the city of Lausanne refuse to engage in any formal city partnership due to its understanding with the IOC, it also is currently setting up an international network of Olympic cities in order to promote itself on the global scale as the 'capital city of the Olympics.' Because there was no well-established international city network in the domain of sports, Lausanne is taking the lead in re-establishing one. The city government sees an international cooperation in this domain as necessary for promoting Lausanne's role as a host city for sports organisations.

Lausanne also proactively tries to promote itself as a city that emphasises sustainability and ecology in general, which explains why the city is strongly engaged in international environmental networks and why it has invested in establishing a new network of sustainable city-regions (the IFGRA network). Lausanne tries to earn a label as a sustainable city, which is not surprising, considering that the mayor of Lausanne belongs to the Green Party. The label of a sustainable city is seen as an important locational factor because a green city is attractive for residents.

Lausanne's policy-makers increasingly view international networking as an important aspect of place promotion, and strategic reflections have lead the mayor to emphasise international environmental and sports networks. Correspondingly, the mayor of Lausanne has implemented a top-down, strategic approach to international networking whereas the international activities were previously rather uncoordinated. The starting point for the mayor's reflections was the need to develop a plan for urban marketing. The city's international activities have been integrated into the plan. Lausanne has developed a strategy for its international engagements that aligns with its economic specificities, especially its international visibility as a sports city. Therefore, Lausanne has recently increased its international activities, which are generally oriented towards promoting Lausanne on the global scale as a social-ecological city.

Who governs?
In the city of Lausanne, there have been two phases of network cooperation. Until 2005, the respective departments set up international contacts and there was hardly any coordination between the departments in doing so. That was the case for the engagement within the Energie-Cités and within the Les Rencontres network. Until 2005, the initiative to join international networks originated from the city administration, and the city government only participated in the decision to join these networks. No debate in the city parliament addressed these networks, nor was there any involvement of broader parts of the population. It was an era of uncoordinated technocratic international networking.

However, several changes have recently been instituted in the organisation of the city's international contacts and they have become politicised. After the city parliament committed the city government to developing a strategy for urban marketing, the city's international activities became a part of this strategy. The mayor thereafter developed a strategy that sought an increased coherence of the city's international contacts and economic profile. This has lead to an increased coordination of Lausanne's international contacts by a division that is directly subordinate to the mayor. The same division is now also responsible for setting up the two new networks in the domains of sustainability and sports. Lausanne also recently joined two networks (UCLG and Délice) where Lausanne's participation is now managed by the mayor's office. Clearly, the mayor is the driving force behind the city's increased international contacts and their underlying strategy. All recent networking activities are also in line with the political preferences of the Green-Party mayor.

The city parliament was not involved when Lausanne joined or formed any networks. It also never initiated a repeat of the discussion of international contacts. This is somewhat surprising, considering Zurich's harsh debates around its similar increase in international activities.[42] The involved policy-makers offer two reasons for the city parliament's lack of debate on the international activities. First, the parliament has already consented to the openness of the city of Lausanne.[43] The economic need to pursue international visibility seems to be accepted even among conservative politicians. Second, right-wing politicians accept the necessity of an international engagement in the city's place-specific economic assets of sports and sustainability. Lausanne has a well-reflected dependency on the international branch of sports, and right-wing parties do not question the city's corresponding engagement on the international scale.

Horizontal governance
Among the cities in the agglomeration of Lausanne (see Table 2.8), two of the five communities that contain more than 10,000 inhabitants each have at least one partner city, but none of the communities is engaged in networking activities.

---

42   See pages 84ff.

43   The inhabitants of Lausanne are sometimes called Europhiles because of the high percentage of Lausanne residents who favour joining the EU (Schilt 2000: 32).

However, a smaller community from the agglomeration of Lausanne, Lutry (containing approximately 8,700 inhabitants), is formally a member of the European Cities against Drugs (ECAD) network. Although the city is still listed as a member on the network's homepage, however, no one in Lutry was aware of the membership. Neither the communal councillor in charge of social policy nor the external drug delegate even knew about the network's existence. They asserted that Lutry has not paid any membership fees for the last several years.

The ECAD network was established as a response to the ECDP network, and it comprises cities that favour a more restrictive drug policy. In general, north-European cities dominate the ECAD network, which contains eighteen Swiss member cities. Most of the Swiss members are smaller communities from the French-speaking part of the country. The only other prominent member is Lugano, which is located in the Italian-speaking part of Switzerland. Within these networking activities, there is a gap between the German-speaking cities and the French- and Italian-speaking cities. The former favour a more liberal drug policy and therefore engage in the ECDP network, and the latter favour a more restrictive drug policy and therefore engage in the ECAD network. However, the larger cities from the French-speaking part joined neither ECDP nor ECAD. To the knowledge of the involved policy-makers, there has never been any cooperation between the core city and the agglomeration communities concerning an international engagement in drug policy.

There is absolutely no coordination between the two agglomeration communities engaged in city partnerships and the core city of Lausanne concerning their respective international engagements. No site is informed about the activities of the other, and no site has ever sought information on this topic. No agglomeration communities are included in any of the core city's networking activities, and they are completely disinterested in the international contacts of other communities. They have not reflected on the centrality burdens that the core city of Lausanne faces through its increased international engagement. The city's international contacts are not used in metropolitan governance, and the strategic use of them is a non-issue for the involved policy-makers.

Table 2.8: The international activities of the cities in the agglomeration of Lausanne

Swiss city	Partner city/cities
Morges	Rochefort (Belgium) / Vertou (France)
Pully	Obernai (France)
Lutry	ECAD

Vertical governance

Relations with the canton and the federal state

Questions of vertical governance are almost a non-issue for the international activities of the city-region of Lausanne. None of Lausanne's mentioned networking activities and none of the agglomeration community's city partnerships have any point of contact with upper-level governments. They are completely carried out on the communal level; upper-level governments are, if anything, only informally informed about these contacts. There are no established formal cooperation procedures between the communities and the canton of Vaud concerning international activities. In the case of Lausanne's international cooperation in the cultural and ecological sectors, policy-makers who are involved in communal international activities view the cantonal engagement in the respective sectors as unsatisfactory.

Regarding the city's cooperation within Les Rencontres, the responsible policy-maker notes that Lausanne uses its cooperation within the international network to connect with other similar-minded cities in cultural politics (i.e. cities that spend considerable amounts of money on culture). Clearly, the German-speaking cities are less engaged in this field:

> It is for us more interesting because we function in the same way, for example the opera, here we function like France and Italy or Belgium. We do not at all function as the German speaking part of Switzerland or Germany. [...] So, we are, I would say, culturally, we are evidentially much closer to France than to the German speaking part of Switzerland.
>
> *(Head of the Department of Culture)*

Accordingly, the city of Lausanne has searched for an opportunity to cooperate with similar-minded cities in order to share their knowledge and best practices, which the policy-makers see as impossible within the Swiss boundaries (Schilt 2000: 30). However, the city's international cooperation has not been used against the German-speaking cities; instead, the differences in spending on cultural politics have lead to Lausanne's international engagement in that policy field.

Lausanne uses its international cooperation within the environmental network Energie-Cités to strengthen its role as a leader in urban sustainable development in Switzerland. Lausanne emphasises the fact that Swiss cities and upper-level governments are not attentive enough to certain issues of environmental policy. In response, Lausanne's policy-makers have pointed to their international backup on this issue. This illustrates a strategic use of a city's international context in domestic relations, both towards other Swiss cities but also towards upper-level governments, particularly the federal state. Lausanne's position as an environment-friendly city clearly aligns with its general strategy of promoting its environmentalism. Lausanne uses this asset in intra-Swiss-city competition, and the city's policy-makers consider their position to be strengthened through their international cooperation on these matters. However, this conflicts with the canton of Vaud's relatively lax engagement in environmental politics, and Lausanne's policy-makers criticise the federal policy as insufficient in this respect.

The canton of Vaud maintains its own unit for external relations, primarily focusing on its relations with the federal state, other cantons, and close cross-border collaborations around Lake Geneva. There is no systematic inclusion of the communal level in the cantonal foreign policy, and the canton has no systematic overview of its communities' international contacts.

The canton's relations with the city of Lausanne are no different from its relations with any other cantonal community. The contacts remain limited to project-based cooperation schemes (for example, within an Interreg project) and informal activities. Contacts with the federal level are limited to Lausanne's international aid project. The city of Lausanne sometimes engages financially in programmes in which the DEZA is also involved. Lausanne's cooperation with the federal level remains restricted to technical and financial issues. The city does not maintain any political contacts or strategic use of communal international activities against the federal state.

Relations with the EU
Lausanne's points of contact with the EU are marginal. Only within the two networking activities regarding environmental and cultural policies have the respective policy-makers witnessed the EU financing some activities of the network's member cities. Occasionally, Lausanne has been able to profit from this funding through participating in EU-financed projects. However, the involved policy-makers have witnessed the general absence of Swiss cities from the increased co-financing of urban networking projects funded by the EU.

Short summary
The city-region of Lausanne is the Swiss city-region that has seen the most recent changes in its international activities (besides Zurich). There has also been a clear increase in the intensity of Lausanne's networking activities. Not only did the mayor recently decide to join two international networks, but he also decided, in line with the city's new economic strategy of urban marketing, to set up international urban networks in the domains in which it has been decided that Lausanne should become more internationally linked and visible. The new networking activities focus on Lausanne's label as an environmentally and socially sustainable location and as an international sports city. Therefore, these activities, which are managed in a top-down way, align with the city-region's economic outline. The mayor set up two new networking activities in the domains of sport and sustainability that align not only with the city's economic orientation but also with the mayor's own Green Party membership. However, the new engagement is limited to traditional political-spatial borders; only the city of Lausanne is involved in the international activities. Neither the agglomeration communities nor the upper-level governments are included in Lausanne's new international strategy. There has been no consideration of using these activities to strengthen Lausanne's domestic position. The city's relations with upper-level governments are not relevant to its communal international activities.

LUCERNE: PARTNERSHIPS FOR TOURISM

International position and economic orientation
The city-region of Lucerne contains a total of 196,550 inhabitants and is thus the smallest city-region under scrutiny. It spreads over three cantons and the city of Lucerne, which boasts 76,156 inhabitants[44], is the core city of the agglomeration (Bundesamt für Statistik 2008a). The city-region of Lucerne is not represented in any of the city or city-region rankings that were investigated. Even in the Swiss context, the city of Lucerne is rather small; it is ranked seventh according to number of inhabitants (Bundesamt für Statistik 2007). The city-region of Lucerne, although it is the economic centre of Central Switzerland, has become increasingly attached to the metropolitan area of Zurich. Its main economic cluster is the tourist sector (Hanser *et al.* 2003: 13ff.), due to its closeness to the mountains and its world-famous wooden chapel bridge. The hotel and gastronomy businesses comprise an extensive share of the city-region's economy (see below). Tourism has a long-standing tradition in Lucerne that dates back to the thirteenth century, when the path over the Gotthard was opened (Luzern Tourismus AG 2008b: 1). Lucerne became an important destination for people from all over northern Europe who travelled to and from Italy, and it was the last significant place to rest before the Gotthard pass. At the end of the nineteenth century, luxurious hotels were built along the lakeside, and they soon became the destination for wealthy tourists from all over Europe (Frefel 2005).

The city-region's accessibility by rail was another major factor for Lucerne's flourishing tourist industry in the late nineteenth and early twentieth centuries (Luzern Tourismus AG 2008b: 4). The very quick restoration of the wooden chapel bridge, which was accomplished in less than six months after it burnt down in 1993, was linked to the city's fear of losing one of its major tourist attractions and hence experiencing a decline in international visibility (Habegger 1998). The decision to construct a new culture and congress centre, which was finished in 2000, was also linked to the necessity of the city's international visibility. The city invested a great deal of money into that prestigious building (Bühlmann 1998; Hollenstein 2000).

In the year 2007, approximately 1,087,900 room nights were purchased in the hotels of Lucerne (Luzern Hotels 2008). Additionally, up to five million day tourists visit Lucerne every year (Luzern Tourismus AG undated: 4). The sales volume generated by the tourists equals approximately 1.5 billion Swiss Francs per year, and their added value is about 810 million Swiss Francs (Luzern Tourismus AG undated: 4). Lacking any other intensive value-adding sectors, Lucerne's economy is highly dependent on tourism (Hanser *et al.* 2003: 5).

---

44   After the amalgamation with the agglomeration community Littau in 2010.

International activities

City partnerships and networks

Lucerne currently has six city partnerships, which is more than any other Swiss city. The city is also engaged in one city network, and it used to be a member of another network (see Table 2.9).

Lucerne's partnership with France's Murbach/Guebwyler goes back to 1978 and, hence, is the city's oldest partnership.[45] The reason for this partnership dates back to the ninth century, when the cloister of Murbach owned the land of Lucerne. The partnership was formed at the 800 year jubilee of the city of Lucerne. Today, a private association manages Lucerne's side of the partnership, and contacts focus primarily on social exchanges.

Lucerne's partnership with the English city of Bournemouth was established in 1982. This partnership is also managed by a private association. Over the years, it has changed its focus from attracting tourists to pursuing social issues. Until 2005, the partnership also included the exchange of several school classes.

In 1994, Lucerne entered into two new partnerships with cities from Eastern Europe, Olomouc in the Czech Republic and Cieszyn in Poland. Both partnerships, which are clearly oriented towards development aid, endeavour to help those cities catch up with Western Europe. The city administration directly manages the partnership activities with these two cities.[46]

Table 2.9: The international activities of the city of Lucerne

International activity	Description	Categorisation
Bournemouth (England)		City partnership
Chicago (USA)		City partnership
Cieszyn (Czech Republic)		City partnership
Murbach/Guebwiler (France)		City partnership
Olomouc (Poland)		City partnership
Potsdam (Germany)		City partnership
ECDP	Cities for a liberal drug policy (until 2001)	Thematic network
Climate Alliance	Cities for a liberal environmental policy	Thematic network

45 The official charte d'amitié, however, was only signed in 1991.

46 In addition to the ongoing development projects for the two East European cities, the city government of Lucerne twice financially assisted the city of Olomouc for rebuilding programmes after severe floodings in 1997 and 2006 (*Neue Luzerner Zeitung* 7th April 2006: 24). These financial transactions were not included in the ordinary budget for the city partnerships (see below).

Another partnership, with the U.S. city of Chicago, was formalised in 1998. Again, a private association manages the partnership, which has a double orientation. On the one hand, it is used to promote Lucerne in the United States of America as a tourist city. On the other hand, cultural exchanges occur through the partnership.

Lucerne's last partnership, with Potsdam in Eastern Germany, was established in 2002, and it has an economic orientation. Although its concrete projects are still in the planning phases, its outline clearly states that the partnership is primarily used to promote Lucerne as a tourist city. In 1998, the city government of Lucerne decided to limit the number of its partner cities to six (Stadtrat Luzern 2001b: 11), due to increasing requests from the city parliament to reduce the money spent on the partnerships (see next section).

In addition to the city's predominant engagement in city partnerships, Lucerne is or was a member of two international policy networks. First, Lucerne was a very active member of the ECDP network. The city joined the network in 1992, shortly after Berne and Zurich, and cooperated within this network of cities that follow a liberal drug policy. Several people from different city departments participated in the network until the end of the 1990s, when the national states adapted their drug policies, as promoted by ECDP members. The network thereby accomplished its goal, and Lucerne's participation in it ended.

Second, the city government of Lucerne formally joined the Climate Alliance network in 2001. Informally, Lucerne had participated in the Climate Alliance network since 1993, but the city did not participate in any of its international conferences until 2006. Lucerne was also a founding member of the Swiss section of the Climate Alliance, the Swiss Climate Alliance Cities (Klimabündnisstädte Schweiz [KBSS]), and it hosted the secretariat of the KBSS for many years.

Organisation of international contacts
The organisation of Lucerne's international activities is twofold. The two networking activities are carried out by their respective departments, and there is no coordination on the city level. In 1998 (after the initiation of the partnership with Chicago), the city government decided to establish a special administrative unit under the direct control of the mayor (Stadtrat Luzern 2001b: 12). This unit prepared the two newest partnerships, since the need for coordination had increased. Endowed only with two part-time employees, the administrative unit for city partnerships does not coordinate existing international networking activities or establish new ones. The unit's duties are to organise the city's concrete partnership activities and to bring together the different actors from the private partnership committees and from politics, not to develop a strategically coherent international connectivity.

Orientation of international contacts
Looking at Lucerne's international activities reveals that their intensity has indeed increased over the last thirty-five years. This development is quite atypical, compared to other European city-regions, since Lucerne has emphasised partnerships rather than networking in an era in which most city-regions have shifted their engagement from partnerships to policy networks. The partnerships' direct subor-

dination under the mayor demonstrates their importance for Lucerne, whereas the city's networking activities are not coordinated.

The city-region's six partnerships and two networking activities only very rarely deal with economic questions directly. Only the two newest city partnerships purposefully foster tourism. The two partnerships with cities in Eastern Europe clearly focus on helping the developing cities in their transition processes, and Lucerne's two networks address social and ecological policies rather than addressing any economic activity. Only the city's partnership with Chicago has an economic orientation that goes beyond the attraction of tourists. Within this partnership, city officials hope to promote Lucerne as a place for financial investment in general.

Linking the economic situation with international activities

The city-region of Lucerne is highly dependent on tourism. Accordingly, its international activities are strategically oriented towards its international visibility as a tourist city. Several interview partners mention this fact, and even an official document of the city government on the international activities states that 'the city partnerships are part of our urban marketing with the goal to position Lucerne as a leading city of culture and congresses, as well as an attractive economic place with high quality of living' (Stadtrat Luzern 2001b: 10, author's translation).

The city's orientation towards international visibility is accomplished by a clear focus on city partnerships instead of networking. Within city partnerships, the idea is to promote Lucerne in other city-regions, preferably in attractive markets for potential tourists, which first meant France and England in the 1980s, and later meant Eastern Germany and the United States.[47] Hence, the two early partnerships were strategically selected from several possible candidates along the criteria of emerging tourist markets. However, this strategy failed in Lucerne's partnership with Bournemouth. The tourist promotion activities quickly ended when both cities realised that they were competing in the same market for tourists, which made cooperation in this domain almost impossible (Stadtrat Luzern 2003: 8). Accordingly, the partnership quickly moved on to non-economic aspects, such as the exchange of students.

Lucerne's outlook towards tourism has clearly affected the structure of its partnerships over the years. The last two partnerships (with Potsdam and Chicago), particularly, were established to increase Lucerne's visibility. The city government never intended to establish an equal partnership with the city of Chicago, which has 2.8 million inhabitants[48] and is fifty times larger than Lucerne. Rather, Lucerne desired to set its foot into the market of well-funded American tourists and to pro-

---

47 The two partnerships with cities from transformation countries in Eastern Europe do not follow this strategy; rather, they are oriented towards development aid. When they were established, the mayor wanted to do something on the local level that would help east-European cities transform from socialist to capitalist state structures.

48 This figure does not include the inhabitants of the agglomeration of Chicago, which comprise a total of more than 9.5 million (including the inhabitants of the core city; US Census Bureau 2006).

mote the city-region of Lucerne as an attractive place for investment in general, as a former city councillor confirms:

> […] primarily Chicago, but Potsdam as well, these partnerships were established out of touristy interests.
>
> *(Former Head of the Department for Social Affairs)*

The activities within Lucerne's partnerships do not always directly attempt to attract tourists; rather, they are part of a more general possibility of increasing the city's visibility within its partner cities. Therefore, the city indirectly uses its international contacts for economic benefit. It is no coincidence that three of the partner cities are located in countries whence most tourists who visit Lucerne originate: America, Germany, and Great Britain. People from these three countries compose 36 per cent of all room nights purchased in Lucerne (Luzern Tourismus AG undated: 4, figures for the year 2006).

The city-region's reluctance to engage in networking activities is explained and justified by its focus on tourism. Because no international city networks directly deal with tourism, Lucerne uses other channels to increase its visibility as a primary tourist destination. The city's scarce resources are invested in a relatively strong tourist promotion agency, and international networking is not seen as a primary option for improving the city's competitiveness.

Policy-makers perceive the use of city partnerships for the tourist sector ambiguously. Whereas the former director of tourism viewed them as 'nice to have, but not really useful', politicians in general consider them to be an important part of Lucerne's economic promotion strategy. That discussion has lead to several disputes over the necessity, importance, and orientation of Lucerne's city partnerships. Whereas the former tourist director would have favoured partnerships with new emerging tourist markets such as China or Japan, politicians note that the barriers to these cultures are too significant to allow formal partnerships and that the costs for partnerships with cities from Asia would be too high.

Although Lucerne strongly favours increased marketing activities in these emerging markets, the city government views city partnerships as a means of strengthening the city's visibility within certain cultural boundaries; moreover, the city's budget for partnerships has certain limits, and partnerships with cities from Asia would be cost-prohibitive. In addition, even the involved politicians agree that the search for promotional activities within city partnerships has not always succeeded and is difficult to achieve. The partnerships are usually one-sided, which means that Lucerne must increase its engagement in order to achieve their goals. The person responsible for international activities openly admitted the difficulties to increase the economic aspects of city partnerships.

Nevertheless, the city government devoted its efforts to promoting Lucerne as a cosmopolitan, tourist-based city-region. This explains the city government's higher involvement in international activities, compared to other city-regions. The city government, especially the mayor, view participating in receptions with international guests as a necessary duty:

If we present an overview, we have to see that the city of Lucerne is a tourist city. This clearly has the implication that many people come to Lucerne and some of them expect to meet people from the city, either with the tourist organisation which is normally the case, but sometimes, they ask for an official reception by the city government. This became daily business for us.

(Former Mayor)

The idea of an economically vulnerable, small city predominates the perceptions of the involved policy-makers. They know that Lucerne is reliant on tourists from all over the world. Thereby, the city is very dependent on global economic processes, although policy-makers do not perceive Lucerne as a highly globalised city. 'Tourism and the thereof resulting number of room nights react sensitively to economic crises and geopolitical events' (Luzern Tourismus AG undated, author's translation). The political actors are well aware that Lucerne, because of its niche in the tourist sector, is dependent on its visibility beyond national borders. Accordingly, the city government follows a policy of internationalism out of economic necessity:

We pursue the strategy of openness, think European and even cosmopolitan, also because of the tourism in Lucerne.

(Employee of the Department for City Partnerships)

Therefore, the international activities of the city of Lucerne are congruent with the city's specific economic situation; additionally, this congruence is well-reflected politically, and a corresponding strategy aims at promoting the city as a tourist destination on the international level.

Who Governs?

Lucerne's administrative organisation reflects the importance of international activities to the city's economic well-being. The unit that deals with partnerships, although it is relatively small, is directly subordinated to the mayor. Both the actual and the former mayor closely observe or have observed the city's international activities and are or were often involved in these contacts. Although other Swiss cities' international activities are dispersed among city councillors or delegated to the administration, this is not the case for Lucerne's partnerships. Clearly, the mayor is the key player in Lucerne's international activities:

This is why the mayor says [...], I am responsible for the city's foreign policy. The city partnerships are an instrument of our foreign policy.

(Employee of the Department for City Partnerships)

However, the city's networking activities are different. Because they are not directly linked to Lucerne's role as a tourist city, the mayor's office does not manage them. The two networking activities in which Lucerne has participated over the years are or were managed by different departments. The idea of joining the two networks originated from their respective administrative units. The city administration primarily controls the city's networking activities, although the respective members of the city government are or were included in both networks.

The distinction between the partnerships and networking can also be applied to the inclusion of the public. Within the two networking activities, the involvement of private actors is close to zero. Within the Climate Alliance network, neither the public nor the parliament has been involved at any time. The city government decided to join the respective networks (Stadtrat Luzern 2001a) and then never readdressed those decisions because the annual fees are very low and because no parliamentary or private request has ever addressed the city's membership within the network.

Once, both a private person and a right-wing city parliamentary politician requested that Lucerne abandon its membership in the ECDP network. These two persons argued for a more restrictive drug policy and viewed Lucerne's engagement within ECDP as an approval of an international network that lobbied for a more liberal drug policy. Because the annual fee for the ECDP network was so small, the city's decision to join the network was examined only briefly by the city government, and the city parliament's involvement was not mandatory (Stadtrat Luzern 1992). That argument was used to reject the request to abandon the ECDP membership. Although he was not obliged to do so, the person in charge of international networking within ECDP replied to the requests, arguing that the city of Lucerne had been at the forefront of promoting the four-pillar policy, which the national state later espoused, and that the city's membership within ECDP had proved to be valuable in promoting a more modest drug policy at the national scale.

Concerning the six partnerships, the involvement of the public is significant because several of the partnerships are managed by private associations (see above). These associations manage the partnership programmes but are supported by administrative aid from the unit for city partnerships. The partnership associations are managed by volunteers who feel somewhat connected to the respective partnerships. The partnership associations' close collaboration with Lucerne tourism concerning the organisation of events with partner cities is also a public-/semi-public-private partnership, since the tourist promotion organisation in Lucerne is privately managed. Although it is primarily financed by the city,[49] Lucerne's tourist promotion organisation is co-financed and controlled by twenty-three private actors (mostly businesses with specialisations in tourism; Luzern Tourismus AG 2008a). This has lead to some conflicts concerning the inclusion of city partnerships within Lucerne's broader tourist-marketing concept (see below).

Additionally, the engagement of Lucerne in the six partnerships has raised several questions from right-wing city parliamentarians, who have criticised both the relatively large amount of money that the city spends on partnerships (compared to other Swiss cities) and the partnerships' 'uselessness'. The latest critique occurred in July 2007, when the right-wing Schweizerische Volkspartei, i.e. the Swiss People's Party (SVP) criticised the annual credit of 25,000 Swiss Francs that is

---

49   The annual subvention of the city of Lucerne for the tourist promotion organisation will increase to 480,000 Swiss Francs per year in 2010. Currently (in 2008), the subvention equals 435,000 Swiss Francs (*Neue Luzerner Zeitung* 25th October 2005).

devoted to the atelier in Chicago, where artists from the canton of Lucerne can stay for up to six months. The SVP argued that absolutely no gains for Lucerne resulted from this cooperation and that the atelier only served as a place for artists to enjoy holidays paid for by public monies (*Neue Luzerner Zeitung* 2007, 17th July).

The mayor responded to these and former critiques by emphasising the importance of Lucerne's international visibility as a tourist city and by presenting detailed statements of expenses for all the involved actors (Stadtrat Luzern 2003, 2007). The city government also replied to the accusations by limiting its partnerships to six and thereby defining a temporary strategy of consolidation (Stadtrat Luzern 2001b: 11). In 2003, the city parliament responded by passing a four year global budget for the partnerships, imparting a democratic legitimisation to the city's strategy for international activities (Stadtrat Luzern 2003). The city parliament renewed its four year credit line in 2007 (Stadtrat Luzern 2007). The first credit line extended 720,000 Swiss Francs; the city government's proposal reduced it to 680,000 Swiss Francs for the period from 2007 to 2010.[50]

Additionally, in 2004, the city government published a report on all its foreign travel activities as well as those of the city administration members due to a request from a city parliamentarian. The right-wing politician asked for a list that delineated the purpose, destination, duration, and financial costs of each stay. The list described eighteen travels abroad, with total costs of around 90,000 Swiss Francs over the duration of eighteen months (Stadtrat Luzern 2004). Therefore, Lucerne is the Swiss city that is most encompassingly transparent about its international activities.

The city's engagement within partnerships is contested at several levels. The debate revolves around the existence of the above-mentioned causality between engagement in international city partnerships and increased economic gain from tourists. Even the former tourist director was not convinced of the benefits of political partnerships and would have preferred a focus on more direct marketing interventions in new emerging markets (Illi 2006: 7). In addition, members of the city parliament assumed that some of the partnerships were 'one-way relations'.

The mayor responded to these attacks by noting the impossibility of measuring the indirect impact of the improved international visibility accomplished through international engagement. Moreover, the partnerships with the two cities in Eastern Europe were explicitly formed as development aid projects and were not expected to benefit Lucerne directly. Later, there was a shift towards promotional activities, due to pressure from the city parliament (Stadtrat Luzern 2003). Overall, Lucerne's partnerships are most prominently controlled by the mayor, but they involve relatively significant parliamentarian control and private involvement.

Horizontal governance
An examination of the international activities of the cities in the agglomeration of

---

50 The labour costs of the two people working under the direction of the mayor are not included in this credit line.

Lucerne (see Table 2.10) reveals that only two of the six communities that contain more than 10,000 inhabitants each have at least one partner city and that none of the communities are engaged in networking activities.

Table 2.10: The international activities of the cities in the agglomeration of Lucerne

Swiss city	Partner city/cities
Kriens	San Damiano d'Asti (Italy)
Rothenburg	Five other Rot(h)enburgs (four in Germany, one in Poland)

Almost no coordination occurs among the different partnerships within the city-region of Lucerne. Only once, in the late 1990s, at a meeting of the communities of the canton of Lucerne, politicians debated the partnership engagements and their respective results. Apart from this and some informal contacts, no exchange of information or cooperation on international activities has ever occurred among the various communities within the city-region of Lucerne. This is astonishing because the economy of the whole city-region, not only the core city, is dependent on tourism (Hanser *et al.* 2003: 13). However, the policy-makers of the agglomeration communities do not perceive their engagement in city partnerships as supporting a strategy for promoting the city-region on the international scale. Perceptions of the city-region's international activities widely diverge between the core city, which has developed a strategic understanding of these activities as essential to economic promotion, and the agglomeration communities, in which policy-makers have not reflected on the correlation between the city-region's economic situation and its international contacts. The same general story can be told about Lucerne's networking activities. While cooperating in the ECDP and in the Climate Alliance network, the core city, which is solely responsible for the city-region's international connectivity, has never tried to involve the agglomeration communities. Additionally, none of the agglomeration communities have actively sought inclusion within international networking activities.

The involved policy-makers realised that increased drug use was a significant problem in core cities. Accordingly, the city of Lucerne joined the ECDP network. Although Lucerne found a mechanism for distributing the city's financial burdens that resulted from its central function as Central Switzerland's primary location for drug trafficking, this understanding involved only financial contributions from the agglomeration communities. It was taken for granted that the core city would continue to manage the international contacts.

In conclusion, the city of Lucerne has never tried to involve the agglomeration communities in its international activities. Although the policy-makers of Lucerne are fully aware that the core city bears centrality burdens by independently engaging in six partnerships and two policy networks, dispersing these burdens through increased cooperation on international matters is a complete non-issue. Only the core city realises that the city-region's international connectivity and consequential visibility are linked to its economic prosperity.

Vertical governance

Relations with the canton
The canton of Lucerne is the only direct upper-level government, among the seven city-regions under scrutiny that lacks a department for international activities. Most involved policy-makers ascribe this to the canton's centrality within Switzerland (i.e. its lack of a close border) and to its economy's relatively strong inward orientation. Since the canton pursues no international activities, the communities of the city-region of Lucerne are obviously not included in any such activities. The canton of Lucerne's only inclusion in a communal international activity is its co-financing of the atelier that Lucerne maintains in Chicago for short to midterm stays of Swiss artists.[51] The canton's involvement is clearly limited to a financial contribution[52] and concerns only that specific aspect of Lucerne's partnership with Chicago. Apart from that cooperation, the canton does not participate in any other international activity of the communities of Lucerne.

Neither the canton nor the involved communities have ever sought further cooperation in this area. This seems to be as much of a non-issue as the agglomeration communities' inclusion in the core city's international activities (see above). Because there is no direct contact person for international relations at Lucerne's cantonal level, policy-makers who manage the international activities of Lucerne's communities would not even know whom they should address if they were to seek cantonal support for their international activities. Also, with the exception of the ECDP network (see next section), the involved communities have never used their international engagement against the cantonal level to improve their position in the intergovernmental system.

Relations with the federal state
Lucerne continues this pattern in its relations with the national state; involvement here is minimal. The Federal council encouraged Swiss cities to conduct partnership projects with Eastern European cities, and the DEZA provided co-financing for early development projects within Lucerne's partnerships with Olomouc and Cieszyn. Despite that initial encouragement to engage in the two partnerships, national involvement was restrained to a purely financial contribution; and the state did not participate in planning, programming, or strategising for the respective partnerships. In addition, the DEZA has not offered any assistance in establishing the contacts or developing the partnerships, nor has it provided any guidelines. The national state only provided the original idea and some financial help for the two partnerships' initial phases.

As in the case of Berne, Lucerne's primary goal for its membership in ECDP

---

51 Consequently, artists from the whole canton of Lucerne, not only from the core city, can apply to stay in the atelier.

52 Additionally, the canton helps select the artists who are allowed to stay in the atelier in Chicago.

was to lobby at upper-scale governments for a more liberal drug policy.[53] Together with Zurich and Berne, Lucerne noted the centrality burdens of drug users in the early 1990s. At that point, Lucerne was the meeting point for almost all drug users in Central Switzerland. Lucerne's city government and the involved administrative units already favoured a more liberal drug policy when the city of Zurich demanded that Lucerne joins ECDP. The following cooperation, both with other Swiss cities and internationally, was used to promote a more liberal drug policy towards upper-level governments.

Relations with the EU
Lucerne's policy-makers have debated the city's relations with the EU more intensively than policy-makers in other Swiss city-regions, for several reasons. First, there seem to be increasing financial difficulties in communal international activities due to Switzerland's non-membership in the EU, which finances partnership activities among its member cities but which does not finance the partnerships of EU cities with non-EU-member cities. Accordingly, European partnership activities with Swiss cities have become more costly for any EU member cities. The person responsible for Lucerne's partnerships mentions that:

> Concretely, we do now have the problem with the youth camp in Bournemouth that the youth centre does not receive funding any more for the camp because Switzerland is not part of the EU. They only get money if someone from an EU-country participates.
>
> *(Employee of the Department for City Partnerships)*

Second, Switzerland's non-membership in the EU is problematic for Lucerne's local economy. Because its economy is highly dependent on international tourists, Switzerland's accessibility is a key aspect for Lucerne's local economies. Switzerland's non-participation in the common currency area poses a hurdle for tourists. More importantly, Switzerland has not participated in the Schengen treaties until late 2008. As a result, tourists had to acquire special visas for their journeys into Switzerland in addition to their general visas for the Schengen countries. In response, bigger tourist operators have increasingly organised European round trips for tourists that do not include stays in Switzerland. Because a stay in Switzerland usually meant visiting Lucerne, the difficulties with visas presented a major problem for the local economy.

As managers of an international tourist city, the city government and especially the mayor are committed to promoting a cosmopolitan view (Stadtrat Luzern 2003: 4). The person responsible for city partnerships considers this to be necessary for the city's economic well-being, and the city's openness is thus a combination of economic necessity and personal commitment.

Basically, I believe that Lucerne entered these partnerships with a clear focus

---

53   Because this argument is the same as in the case of Berne, I do not repeat its entirety here (see page 46).

on the tourism industry, which brings along cosmopolitanism. The combination of a political orientation with the slogans of Standortpolitik leads to the fact that Lucerne sees itself as a cosmopolitan city.

(Employee of the Department for City Partnerships)

Overall, the use of international activities by the city-region is very modest. Apart from its engagement within the ECDP network, there is no strategic use of these activities against upper-level governments. The country's absence from the EU, however, seems to be a more hotly-debated economic issue in the city-region of Lucerne than elsewhere.

Short summary
The city of Lucerne began to set up its international activities strategically in the 1980s. Since that time, there has been a clear increase in intensity of these activities. The orientation towards city partnerships instead of networking, although sometimes contested, was conducted in accordance with the city-region's economic outline on tourism. It is therefore not surprising that the partnerships are strategically coordinated by the mayor's office, whereas the networking activities are not coordinated at all. The mayor is the key player in Lucerne's international activities. A lively political debate surrounds Lucerne's international contacts, in contrast to most other city-regions under scrutiny.

The strategic orientation towards promoting the city-region's international visibility as a tourist city-region is limited to the core city itself. Despite the high economic interdependence between the core city and the agglomeration communities, there is hardly any cooperation on international activities. The policy-makers of the core city are fully aware of these centrality burdens. Still, there has not been any attempt to include the agglomeration communities or upper-level governments in the international activities of the city of Lucerne.

ZURICH: INTERNATIONAL BANKING AND INSURANCE

International position and economic orientation
The city-region of Zurich contains a total of 1,090,728 inhabitants. The 132 communities of the city-region of Zurich are spread over three cantons. The city of Zurich is the core city, and it contains 363,273 inhabitants (Bundesamt für Statistik 2008a). Throughout the early 1990s, Zurich consistently ranked as the sixth or seventh most business-friendly European city, according to the European Cities Monitor report's survey of 500 top businesspersons. In 2007, the city lost ground, dropping to the thirteenth position (Cushman&Wakefield/Healey&Baker 1990–2009: 5)[54], and was surpassed by Geneva for the first time since the ranking was conducted in 1990. Zurich is a 'beta world city,' according to Beaverstock

---

54   It remained in thirteenth position in the 2009 European Cities Monitor.

et al. (1999)[55] and Taylor (2004), and it consistently ranks as the city that has the highest living quality worldwide, according to Mercer's study (2009).[56] Zurich is not only Switzerland's largest city-region (approximately 13 per cent of the Swiss population resides in it) but also its economic powerhouse (Hitz *et al.* 1994: 172). One out of six jobs in Switzerland can be found in the city-region of Zurich (Frey 2004: 5), and the city's larger metropolitan area is responsible for about 30 per cent of Switzerland's added value (Credit Suisse 2004: 3). Zurich is thus solidly installed at the top of the national economic hierarchy.

The city's economic force is mainly due to the international banking and (re-) insurance sector, which dominates the city-region of Zurich's economic mix. Zurich has a long-standing tradition as a place for financial transactions, dating back to the nineteenth century (Straumann 2006). This economic specialisation increased after the Second World War, when the relatively strong industrial sector quickly vanished (Eisner 1997: 96ff.). Several leading international financial institutions, including UBS, Credit Suisse, Swiss Re, and Zurich Financial Services, locate their headquarters in Zurich. Roughly one fourth of worldwide cross-border private investment (3 trillion Swiss Francs) is managed by banks in Zurich (Schiffmann 2005).[57] Approximately 45,000 people work in Zurich's banking sector, not counting the large number of service provisions that are closely linked to this sector.[58] In total, the banking and insurance sectors compose about 25 per cent of the GDP of the city of Zurich (Blöchliger *et al.* 2004: 18). The canton of Zurich estimates that about 20 per cent of its workplaces (150,000) are dependent on the financial sector (Regierungsrat des Kantons Zürich 2006: 138). In addition, the Swiss stock exchange, domiciled in Zurich, is one of the leading stock markets in Europe (and worldwide), with a turnover of about 2.5 trillion Swiss Francs in 2007 (SWX 2008).

The research and development (R&D) sector has become increasingly important for Zurich's economy. Information technology companies have settled in the Zurich area, which is considered to prove the attractiveness of Zurich as a business location. IBM and Siemens maintain well-established research centres in the Zurich area. In 2006, Microsoft opened a development centre in the city of Zurich (Greater Zurich Area 2006: 3; *Neue Zürcher Zeitung* 2006, 31st May: 47). Zurich's biggest coup occurred in 2004, when Google decided to open a research centre there (Greater Zurich Area 2006: 4). By 2008, more than 500 people worked for

---

55   Beaverstock *et al.* (1999: 445) argue that 'Zurich is a world city but not a mega-city'. Zurich's importance on the international scale is much higher than its population size suggests.

56   Both international rankings are also used by policy-makers to emphasise Zurich's high living standard and its importance on a global scale (see for example Wehrli-Schindler 2006: 51 or *Neue Zürcher Zeitung* 2005, 8th July: 51, 2006, 5th October: 55).

57   For Switzerland as a whole, the figure is even more impressive. About one third (or 4.2 trillion Swiss Francs) of global cross-border private investment is deposited in Swiss banks (Standort-förderung Kanton Zürich 2004).

58   For the respective figures for the canton of Zurich, see Regierungsrat des Kantons Zürich (2006: 138).

Google in Zurich (*Neue Zürcher Zeitung* 2007, 18th January: 55). Despite the recent increase in R&D and information technology business, the banking and insurance sectors still dominate the economic mix of the Zurich area. In total, more than 90 per cent of all workplaces in the city-region of Zurich are in the service sector, which additionally highlights the economic importance of this sector. Accordingly, Zurich is considered to be 'not Switzerland's capital city, but its city of capital'.

Consequently, the Zurich economy depends heavily on international markets (Regierungsrat des Kantons Zürich 2006: 138). The volatility of international financial flows strikes the Zurich economy harder than other city-regions (Cox 1991b, quoted in Boudreau 2003: 182). The city's banking and insurance companies operate in highly globalised markets. At the same time, local politics is highly interlinked with (or rather, dependent on) the financial sector. The close linkages between city's local political system and its banking and insurance sectors are manifested in the fact that those sectors generate about 50 per cent of Zurich's tax revenues (Standortförderung Kanton Zürich 2004), thereby creating a political dependence on the well-being of the financial sector.

International activities

City partnerships and networks

The city of Zurich is currently involved in two city partnerships, five thematic networks, and two lobby networks (see Table 2.11). These various international activities (except for the two new networking activities; see below) are all carried out by different departments and are not coordinated, since there is no special entity within the city administration that manages foreign affairs.

A city partnership between Zurich and Kunming (China) began in 1982. In the beginning, the partnership primarily facilitated cultural exchange between the two cities, but it soon spilled over into issues that are more technical (*Neue Zürcher Zeitung* 2008, 24th September: 54). Experts from the city of Zurich shared their knowledge of water supply, public transport, spatial planning, and monumental protection policies. This cooperation was increasingly used to provide companies located in the city-region of Zurich with opportunities to contract business with Kunming (Präsidialdepartement der Stadt Zürich 2004: 4f.).

Zurich's relatively new partnership with the city of San Francisco was instigated by a private initiative by Swiss Re (a reinsurance company), the Swiss-American Chamber of Commerce, the Eidgenössische Technische Hochschule Zürich, i.e. Swiss Federal Institute of Technology Zurich (ETHZ), and the University of Zurich in summer 2003. Although the initiative was set up by the private sector and although most of the Zurich committee members were from the private sector (San Francisco – Zurich Initiative 2008), the city government decided to join and help pursue the initiative. The cooperation first focused on knowledge transfer for global companies and on cooperation among scientific institutions (*Neue Zürcher Zeitung* 2004, 3rd November: 49, 2005, 25th January: 49). In 2007, the two city mayors signed a declaration to increase the activities within the partnership. The

Table 2.11: The international activities of the city of Zurich[59]

International activity	Description	Categorisation
Kunming (China)		City partnership
San Francisco (USA)		City partnership
ECDP	Cities for a liberal drug policy (until 2001)	Thematic network
Climate Alliance	Cities for a liberal environmental policy	Thematic network
ICLEI	Cities for a liberal environmental policy	Thematic network
CVA	Cities with a relation to space industry	Thematic network
METREX	City-regions cooperating in spatial planning	Thematic network
Eurocities	Multi-thematic network	Lobby network
UCLG	Multi-thematic network	Lobby network

partnership's current goal is to establish an exchange of city employees, whereas previously the cooperation was restricted to the private sector (*Neue Zürcher Zeitung* 2007, 24th January: 57; Präsidialdepartement der Stadt Zürich 2007).[60]

Zurich's cooperation within ECDP dates back to the year 1990, when Zurich was one of four first-signature cities of the so-called Frankfurt Resolution (along with Amsterdam, Hamburg, and Frankfurt). In this document, the four cities expressed their view on drug policy, concluding that the 'present system of criminally prohibiting the use of certain drugs has failed' (ECDP 1990). Instead, the four cities argued for a more liberal drug policy. The engagement of the drug delegate of the city of Zurich in the network was intense, and Zurich hosted the second conference of the ECDP network in 1991.

Zurich joined the ICLEI and the Climate Alliance networks in 1993 by a vote of the city government in response to green politicians in the city parliament, who suggested increasing the city's international cooperation in environmental policy. This was seen as a response to the special need of urban areas to react to global

---

59   The city of Zurich joined the European coalition of cities against racism in 2007. As for the other city-regions under scrutiny,this network is not included in this study (see page 41). The city of Zurich also joined the new network Cities for Children (set up by Stuttgart; see pages 114ff.) in 2007. Because Zurich is not engaged within the network at the time of writing, however, it is excluded from this analysis of the city.

60   The declaration contains four elements regarding which the two cities want to increase their exchanges: a collaboration in economic and scientific questions (as before), the exchange of students (as before), research and technology exchanges between the two city bureaucracies (a new development), and a know-how transfer between several bureaucratic units (also new; Präsidialdepartement der Stadt Zürich 2007).

climate problems (Umweltschutzfachstelle der Stadt Zürich 1995: 22). The city government shared this view and did not oppose the parliamentarian request. The Head of the Department of Environmental Politics participated regularly in both network's meetings, and the city of Zurich hosted the 2007 general conference of the Climate Alliance. The city's environmental department managed the Swiss section of the Climate Alliance, presiding over the KBSS from 2004 until 2008. This coordinating role also involved a stronger engagement on the international scale. The city of Zurich now represents the other Swiss cities in international conferences since many of them refuse to participate regularly in international networking. A total of thirteen Swiss cities are members of the Climate Alliance, but Zurich is the only Swiss member city, aside from Geneva, that participates in the ICLEI network.

Zurich is the only Swiss member city of the Communauté des Villes Ariane network, i.e. Community of Ariane Cities (CVA), which brings cities together to address the space industry.

The city-region's involvement within the METREX network is somewhat complex. METREX does not cooperate directly with the city of Zurich but rather with the Regionalplanung Zürich und Umland, i.e. Greater Zurich Regional Planning Association (RZU), which includes the six spatial planning regions with and around the city of Zurich, containing a total of sixty-nine communities and the canton of Zurich. The RZU is the organisation responsible for regional planning. Because the METREX network covers the policy area of planning in metropolitan areas, the RZU is the logical networking participant for the Zurich area, although it is somewhat an outsider within the network since most other members are cities or city-regions.[61] Currently, the RZU is only an associate and not a full member of the METREX network. Although it regularly participates in the international meetings and has cooperated within a sub-project of METREX (the InterMETREX project, see RZU 2005: 12), the RZU has never paid the annual fee.

Recently, due to the mayor's new endeavours to strengthen the international visibility of Zurich (Ledergerber 2007: 19; see next section), the city joined two international city lobby networks: Eurocities and UCLG. The city-region's engagement within Eurocities is so far only technical, but Zurich has committed itself to strong engagement within several of Eurocities' policy sub-groups. Because networking activities within UCLG are mostly politically oriented (whereas Eurocities involves both a political component and concrete policy-making cooperation), Zurich's form of cooperation within the network has yet to be determined.

Organisation of international contacts
Zurich is the city-region under scrutiny that has undergone the most recent and most profound change in the strategy of its international activities. Additionally, it is still restructuring those activities. From 2003 to 2007, the department for city development, which was directly subordinated to the mayor, coordinated the two

---

61   See for example the membership of the Stuttgart region, which is addressed on pages 114ff.

partnerships (Präsidialdepartement der Stadt Zürich 2003: 14). The head of this department managed the city's international relations as one of her many duties. She did not manage the networking activities mentioned above, however, because they are carried out by their respective departments. The city does not maintain an encompassing overview of its dispersed international activities, and there is no coordination among the different activities:

> Primarily, it [the city of Zurich] did not have any strategy. It just had this city partnership with Kunming and nothing else.
>
> *(Head of City Development)*

This changed significantly at the end of 2006, however. The city government, upon a suggestion from the mayor, decided to make external relations one of its goals for the legislative period 2006–2010 (Stadtrat Zürich 2006: 8ff.). This decision included two main aspects: first, the city would join the two lobby networks Eurocities and UCLG (see above), and second, it would create a special sub-unit of the department for city development that would manage external relations. All coordination activities of the agglomeration communities, the canton of Zurich, other cantons, the federal level, and the international level would be managed by one unit. The mayor demanded that the city parliament accepts a credit line for employing three new people and creating the new sub-unit. However, the city parliament denied the credit in July 2008 (*Tagesanzeiger* 2008, 9th July: 12), so it remains unclear to what extent the city administration of Zurich will be able to accomplish the mayor's goal of deepening the city's networking activity.

Orientation of international contacts
Overall, among the seven city-regions under scrutiny, the city-region of Zurich has developed the most recent increase in the intensity of its international activities.[62] However, the organisation of its newly emerging international activities in international lobby networks has not yet been consolidated. Nevertheless, the international activities of the city-region of Zurich do not predominantly focus on economic questions, although there have been some changes towards this direction, especially within the city's two partnerships with Kunming and San Francisco.[63]

The partnership with Kunming started as a cooperation scheme oriented towards developmental aid and technical cooperation, and it did not cover any economic activities at first. This later changed due to political pressure from the right-wing party SVP (see below). Some people criticised the project for its lack of any specific gains for Zurich. In reaction to these attacks, the city government tried to change the focus of the partnership, instead emphasising the economic gains that flowed from it (*Neue Zürcher Zeitung* 2008, 24th September: 54). The mayor's office declared that the city partnership would work to provide a basis for

---

62   Besides Lausanne; see pages 63ff.

63   Additionally, the city government has set up a more informal network with economically strong city-regions close to the Swiss border (Munich, Frankfurt, Lyon, and Milan) in order to discuss possible cooperation schemes among these city-regions.

Zurich's business interests, and it stopped its financial contributions to the partnership in 2001 (*Neue Zürcher Zeitung* 2008, 25th September: 55). The partnership is now seen as an opportunity to set a foot in the Chinese market and to promote Zurich as a tourist location (*Neue Zürcher Zeitung* 2008, 24th September: 55; Präsidialdepartement der Stadt Zürich 2004: 5). It is doubtful whether this strategy change has been a success, since the Chinese partner city has not shown any substantial interest in these new economic cooperation schemes.

The San Francisco initiative was created in response to critics of Zurich's partnership with Kunming. This initiative was launched by the private sector. The city government decided not to provide any financial support for the initiative. Because of the problems with Kunming, the cooperation with San Francisco was explicitly named an 'initiative', not a partnership, although politicians were involved in the cooperation from the beginning.[64] Overall, the city acts very carefully within this initiative and focuses on economic aspects. However, the mayor of Zurich has mentioned several times (see *Neue Zürcher Zeitung* 2004, 29th and 30th May: 52, 2007, 24th January: 57) that the initiative with San Francisco helped convince Google to open its European research centre in Zurich (see above).

Because the city of Zurich has only recently and modestly engaged in international networking, the orientation of its networking activities is difficult to determine. Overall, Zurich's clear strategy on the international level is still missing. However, it has shifted towards a more economic orientation. Still, Zurich's international activities show no relation to finance.

Linking the economic situation with international activities

As discussed above, the economy of the city-region of Zurich is highly globalised (Sevcik 2007: 31). Its focus on the financial sector makes Zurich vulnerable to the development of the world market (Hitz *et al.* 1994: 172ff.). Therefore, local politics are expected to react to this situation by a respective internationalisation of its own domain. Although the importance of international contacts for the city-region of Zurich has increased, no comprehensive strategy to strengthen Zurich's role as a globally-connected city has been developed. The political globalisation of Zurich lags behind its economic globalisation (see also Klaus 2006). It is unclear why this is the case, although there are two possible explanations.

First, it seems very difficult to establish international political contacts in the areas on which the Zurich economy predominantly relies. No international city network specifically addresses the financial sector. Second, the financial industry is a sector in which the direct influence of the local political system is very limited. Although highly dependent on the financial sector, the connections between local banking and insurance companies and local politics are only loose. There is no close interlinkage between the local economy and the local political system, due to local politics' very limited role in regulating the business sectors (Regierungsrat des Kantons Zürich 2006: 140). Although Switzerland is a highly federalised

---

64   Additionally, an exchange of members of the cities' administrations is planned for the near future (*Neue Zürcher Zeitung* 2007, 24th January: 57).

country, the regulations that involve banking and insurance are predominantly managed at the national scale. The influence of local politics is mainly restricted to taxing local business. Contrary to many other sectors, the city's regulating influence on insurance and finance is therefore very limited. Certainly the most influential and most controversial regulation that influences the banking sector is the national bank secrecy[65]. This regulation is completely out of the control of local politicians, and there is no international cooperation on this aspect (Regierungsrat des Kantons Zürich 2006: 142f.). Surprisingly, the highly globalised banking sector is mostly dependent on the regulations of the traditional national scale and less on the local political-economic interplay.

The city's very modest relations to the local economic sector explain, at least partially, its relatively late engagement in international networking. Although Zurich's economy is highly international, it does not rely on political activities on the international scale. National political regulations play a much more important role (Regierungsrat des Kantons Zürich 2006: 134; 40; Straubhaar 2006: 13).

> The principal part of urban foreign policy is primarily a policy towards the national scale in Switzerland, [...] because the economically decisive general conditions for the development of a metropolitan area as Zurich [...] are primarily set by the national scale.
>
> *(Former Mayor)*

Hence, the new planned sub-unit within the service for city development was not set up as a unit for international relations but rather as a unit for external relations, and it primarily focuses on the city's relations with other communities in the city-region and with the cantonal and national levels (Stadtrat Zürich 2006: 8ff.). Unable to establish international activities in the domain of its economic strengths, Zurich focuses on the indirect possibilities offered by international activities. The city-region's goal is to increase its visibility on the global scale and to present Zurich as a city-region that has a high standard of living. This focus on softer locational factors illustrates the mayor's willingness to align the city's international contacts with its economic goals.

Who governs?

An analysis of the government structures of Zurich's involvement in its international activities shows considerable conflict between the mayor (and his department for city development) and the city parliament. Whereas the mayor has abandoned the reluctance of his predecessor towards the international level, he thereby faces considerable resistance from the local parliament. These different viewpoints first clashed under the reign of the former mayor. Several parties opposed the city's partnership with Kunming, which had begun in 1999, when the city parliament realised that the partnership lacked a legal basis and that the parliament had never approved a credit for it. The city government had split up the credit so that the city parliament could not vote on it (Gemeinderat Zürich 1997).

---

65   The bank secrecy is a legal principle that banks are not obliged to give information about their customers to the state.

The heavy opposition from the city parliament focused on three aspects of the partnership. First, the partnership represented Zurich's intervention in the domain of foreign policy, which was seen as a duty of the national state (Gemeinderat Zürich 2000a, c).[66] Second, Zurich was seen as spending too much money on an international aid project that did not offer any specific gains for the city (Gemeinderat Zürich 1998; Stadtrat Zürich 2000b).[67] Third, opponents suspected that the project merely provided opportunities for cheap travel for members of city government and their civil servants (Stadtrat Zürich 2000a).[68]

The climax of the debate was reached when the SVP successfully launched a referendum against the project credit for the years 2000 to 2002.[69] A clear 2:1 majority voted in favour of the partnership project in the public referendum.[70] Nevertheless, the political and public debates led to a major re-orientation and financial reduction of the project. In 2002, the city government decided that the technical cooperation between Zurich and Kunming should end in 2004, whereas the cooperation on cultural issues would continue. The city parliament agreed on a last credit of 915,000 Swiss Francs for the years 2003 and 2004 (*Neue Zürcher Zeitung* 2002, 21st November).

The interests of the mayor again conflicted with the interests of the parliament on the decision to reorganise the department for city development. The city government proposed to increase Zurich's presence, visibility, and international connectivity (Stadtrat Zürich 2006: 8ff.). The city parliament however denied the credit for the creation of a special sub-unit for external relations within the service for city development in July 2008 (*Tagesanzeiger* 2008, 9th July: 12). Hence, it remains unclear whether the restructuring of the service for city development and the international positioning of Zurich will effectively occur. A broad coalition of extreme left-wing, central, and right-wing parties opposes the mayor's statement that Zurich should increase its international contacts.

The debate about the city's partnership with San Francisco was much less controversial. After the problems in the city's partnership with Kunming, the city government decided not to provide any financial support to the initiative; consequently, there were fewer financial worries from the city parliament. Nevertheless, a right-wing city parliamentarian questioned the cooperation with San Francisco from the beginning (*Neue Zürcher Zeitung* 2004, 29th and 30th May: 52; Stadtrat Zürich 2004). In this case, however, there was no substantial debate and no exertion of influence from the city parliament. However, the inclusion of private actors

---

66　Additionally, opponents noted that a partnership with a city from a dictatorial regime is problematic (Gemeinderat Zürich 2000b).

67　For an overview of the arguments, see also *Neue Zürcher Zeitung* (1999, 9th December: 51).

68　See also Wagner (2000) for the responsible city councillor's reply to the accusations.

69　The credit line was 2.4 million Swiss Francs.

70　In 2007, the city population voted on a credit for the settlement of the Club of Rome in Zurich. The 1.8 million Swiss Francs credit line was rejected by a small majority. Thereafter, the Club of Rome decided to settle its new headquarters in the nearby city of Winterthur (see *Neue Zürcher Zeitung* 2008, 20th September: 55).

is relatively strong since companies from the Zurich area initiated the city's coop-eration with San Francisco. Accordingly, the Zurich-San Francisco initiative is a public-private partnership (*Neue Zürcher Zeitung* 2007, 24th January: 57); even the financing of its activities has so far been completely private.

The inclusion of the parliament and the public within the city-region's diverse networking activities is limited or even non-existent. The city government decided to join the ICLEI and the Climate Alliance after a request from Green Party city parliamentarians. Because the annual credit for those networks is very small, there has been no further discussion of the city's membership, either within the city government or within the city parliament. The city administration carries out the actual networking activities, although a city councillor occasionally participates in the international conferences.

The same is true for the METREX network; there was no formal decision to join the network since the RZU is formally only an associate member. The mem-bers of the RZU as a whole (see above), along with Zurich's city government, would decide whether or not to participate in METREX as an official member. Because the structure of the RZU and its membership in the METREX network are rather complex, neither any politician from a legislative body of the involved communities nor anyone from the public has ever noticed the membership.

The city's membership within the ECDP network has been highly politicised since the beginning, when the social department city councillor was at the fore-front of promoting the ECDP network to other Swiss cities. Because Zurich was a founding member of the network and because it was the city that had the most acute problems with drug users in the early 1990s, its political commitment to ECDP was strong at the beginning. However, the cooperation soon shifted to the administrative level, and the city's cooperation within the network became depo-liticised. In the beginning phase, attacks from the SVP on this international coop-eration were regular, but they never gained a majority within the city parliament or within the city government.

Interestingly, when Zurich recently joined the two lobby networks Eurocities and UCLG in 2007, there was no debate either in the public or in the city par-liament. The mayor did not promote the city's new memberships with a flashy ceremony but rather only submitted a short press release to the local newspapers. There was no reaction except for a few letters to the editors of the respective newspapers complaining that the city government should focus on local politics instead of international relations (*Neue Zürcher Zeitung* 2007, 30th November: 56). This lack of debate was surprising because the right-wing SVP had opposed all other international activities of the city of Zurich so far and because Eurocities is a strong lobbying network, primarily at the EU level, for promoting the concerns of large urban areas. However, when the city parliament wanted to assign the grant for the administrative unit that was necessary for cooperating within Eurocities and its diverse policy sub-groups, the parliament rejected its proposal (see above).

In conclusion, the parliament has limited the mayor's expansion plans on the international scale. Whenever the city parliament has been involved in the de-cision-making process, it has voted in favour of a more modest engagement in international activities, whereas the current mayor has continuously tried to push Zurich towards greater international visibility through networking activities. The public vote in favour of the city's partnership with Kunming in 2002 was a very rare occasion of the electorate's direct involvement in city-region's international activities.

Horizontal governance

Among the cities in the agglomeration of Zurich (see Table 2.12), only six of the twenty-three communities, that contain more than 10,000 inhabitants, have at least one partner city, and Dübendorf is a member of the international Climate Alliance. Dübendorf is the only agglomeration community in the five Swiss city-regions under scrutiny that is a member of an international network.

Table 2.12: The international activities of the cities in the agglomeration of Zurich

Swiss city	Partner city/cities
Uster	Prenzlau (Germany)
Dübendorf	Climate Alliance
Dietikon	Kolin (Czech Republic)
Adliswil	Vodnany (Czech Republic)
Illnau-Effretikon	Grossbottwar (Germany)
Meilen	Policka (Czech Republic) and Ebes (Hungary)
Affoltern a.A.	Litomysl (Czech Republic)

Almost all of the agglomeration communities' partnerships are with communities in the Czech Republic. This is no coincidence; the canton of Zurich initiated these contacts in the early 1990s (see below). The respective partnerships are therefore strongly interlinked. Although there are dozens of contacts from communities of the canton of Zurich with communities in the area of south-Bohemia, their development has been divergent. Many of them have been carried out as rather lose forms of cooperation and have never involved official partnerships.[71] For example, the partnerships of Affoltern a.A. and of Horgen have been inactive for several years, although they were intense at the beginning. Others, such as the partnerships of Meilen and of Dietikon, are still generally active. The number of active partnerships has diminished over the years, largely because the canton of Zurich stopped financially contributing to them (see below).

The city of Zurich never participated in the partnership programme of the canton (see below). There has been no contact between those managing Zurich's two

---

71   In Table 2.12 only the formal partnerships are listed, according to my definition of an international activity (see page 2).

partnerships and those managing the other agglomeration communities' partnerships. The city of Zurich administered its partnerships but did not involve any of the agglomeration communities in them. Several agglomeration communities participated in the cantonal partnership programme, but the city of Zurich refused to participate because of its generally poor relations with the canton. A closer cooperation between the core city and the agglomeration communities in their international activities seems to be a non-issue in the city-region of Zurich, as in many other Swiss city-regions.

Due to the personal engagement of the person responsible for the environmental politics of the city of Dübendorf, the city joined the international Climate Alliance in the late 1990s, although it never participated in any international conference. Due to internal restructuring, the position of responsibility for environmental politics was not renewed, and Dübendorf's participation in the Climate Alliance has been weak for quite some time. Although Dübendorf belongs to the agglomeration of Zurich, it never directly cooperated with the city of Zurich on its membership in the international Climate Alliance. The position of the Swiss cities is coordinated through the KBSS, but no further coordination addresses the cities' international cooperation. The fact that another city from the agglomeration of Zurich is a member of the same international network does not affect the cooperation schemes within either the agglomeration or the network.

Additionally, there is no cooperation between the international networking activities of the city of Zurich and those of its agglomeration communities except in the case of the METREX network. Cooperation within the ECDP, the Climate Alliance, and the ICLEI network is limited to the core city. No discussions have addressed the possible inclusion of any agglomeration communities or the city's strategic use of its international contacts towards the agglomeration communities. Again, there is also no strategic consideration to do so for Zurich's two new networking activities within Eurocities and UCLG. On the one hand, the policymakers of the city of Zurich, although they are fully aware of the city's centrality burdens, do not endeavour to include the agglomeration communities in the city's international activities or to use its contacts against them. On the other hand, the agglomeration communities show no interest in participating in Zurich's international contacts.

Within the METREX network, several communities are included. The RZU, as a spatial planning coordination organisation for several communities (and the canton, see below), is an associate member of the METREX network; the communities themselves are not official members. The dispersion of the knowledge gained from the networking activities within METREX to the communities is not at the forefront of the RZU. The involved communities seem to be only modestly interested. The cooperation is limited to the RZU itself; although the involved communities are very well aware of the RZU's membership within the METREX network, they do not seek to participate in any of its international contacts.

Vertical governance

Relations with the canton

There are a total of three points of contact between communal international activities and the canton of Zurich: the coordination of partnerships with Czech communities, the cantonal delegate for external relations, and the cooperation within the METREX network.

A cantonal councillor initiated contacts between the canton of Zurich and South Bohemia in the Czech Republic in 1991. Although the partnership focused on a regional international cooperation, it originally included an involvement of communities from both regions. Both regions initiated and financially assisted these communal partnerships. From the beginning, the cantonal councillor delegated the organisation of these cantonal and communal contacts to an external expert, who organised a first meeting for interested communities in 1992. The canton of Zurich continued to finance the partnerships with an annual credit that paid external experts to organise common activities. In close collaboration with a member of the cantonal department of justice, which monitors the partnership programme, the experts decided on a workshop theme and organised various get-togethers.

As mentioned before, several of the partnerships are currently inactive, but a relatively large number of communities are still involved.[72] From the city-region of Zurich, four communities are still officially involved in this partnership project, but only two partnerships (those of Meilen and Dietikon) are still more or less active. Although the person responsible for establishing and developing these partnerships tried to involve the city of Zurich in the programme as well, the city government refused to cooperate and instead focused on its already existing partnership with Kunming.[73] The canton of Zurich stopped its financial contribution for the communal partnerships after two years, and it now focuses on cantonal cooperation schemes.

The canton of Zurich has its own delegate for external relations. His activities focus on the external relations of the canton of Zurich within Switzerland and only very rarely address an international component. This is also the case in the tri-national cooperation around the Lake of Constance; the canton of Zurich, but not its communities, is involved. There is absolutely no involvement of the communities or the city within the canton's official external relations. Several involved policy-makers mention the rather disputed relationship between the city and the canton of Zurich. This conflict seems to manifest itself in international contacts; the involved policy-makers seldom communicate, although each is fully aware of the other's international activities.

Because the canton of Zurich is also a member of the RZU, the canton could the-

---

72 The cantonal coordinator of the programme assumes that ten to twelve of the original thirty-two communal partnerships are still active.

73 However, according to the project manager of the cantonal partnership programme, the city occasionally, upon request, delegated experts from the city administration to participate in the cantonal programme.

oretically participate in the cooperation within the METREX network. However, the canton has not shown any interest in cooperating within the METREX network because the concrete cooperation was carried out by the director of the RZU and included neither politicians nor people from the administration at the cantonal scale. Only once, within a specific project that was financed by the EU for the other cooperating city-regions (see below), the canton financed a part of the project costs, but it did not further participate in the actual project work.

Within the other networks, there has been no inclusion of any cantonal policy-maker, and neither the cantonal policy-makers nor the communal policy-makers have ever reflected upon such a possible inclusion. The involved policy-makers of the core city and the agglomeration communities have not considered a possible coordination or strategic use of their international activities against the cantonal level.

Relations with the federal state
There are two links between the city-region of Zurich's international activities and the national scale. The first link concerns the Kunming partnership, and the second link concerns the ECDP network.

The national development agency DEZA was involved in Zurich's partnership with Kunming, mostly through a co-financing of development aid projects.[74] Especially in the first phase of the project, the collaboration was rather close, although the role of the DEZA was primarily financial. The project leadership was always managed by the city of Zurich, although the city closely collaborated with the DEZA on several projects.

The ECDP network, as mentioned before, was established as a network of cities to lobby at upper-level governments for a more liberal drug policy. The policy-makers of the city of Zurich tried to broaden their already existing coalition of Swiss cities that favoured a more liberal policy beyond the national borders:

> The federal state was quite impressed [...] and a little bit irritated, because foreign policy is actually a domain of the federal state. We could use [the ECDP membership] there once or twice.
>
> *(Drug delegate of Zurich)*

Although the city government of Zurich could depend on relatively broad political support for its more liberal model of drug policy, the model opposed the position of the national parliament, which still favoured a repression-oriented drug policy in the early 1990s. Cities with liberal orientations in drug policy used the ECDP network to express their position against the regional and national governments that still followed restrictive drug policies. The international support from the ECDP network contacts was very welcome as the city of Zurich continuously lobbied for a more liberal drug policy on the national scale. This explains why the

---

74   For example, the DEZA spent 500,000 Swiss Francs on a project for disseminating the knowledge which had been extended to Kunming to other Chinese cities for the years 2000 and 2001 (Gemeinderat Zürich 2000c; see also Stadtrat Zürich 2001, 2002).

former city councillor and Head of the Social Department, along with the drug delegate of the city and with strong support from the former mayor, strongly favoured the international contacts developed within ECDP. Because the national scale later adapted to the more moderate drug policy favoured by ECDP members, the networking activity became obsolete. Currently, there is a broad national coalition in favour of the so-called 'four-pillar policy', which relies on prevention, therapy, harm reduction, and repression. The opposition between the city of Zurich and the upper-level governments thus gave way to a more cooperative collaboration between the different territorial levels regarding drug policies in the second half of the 1990s.

No international contacts other than the two mentioned above have been used to bypass the national scale. In the case of the Kunming partnership, the financial aid of the national DEZA even facilitated the cooperation. Thus, there is no conflict on international activities between the city of Zurich and the national scale. Because the regulations on the national scale are much more important for the economic well-being of the Zurich area than successful connectivity through international networking, this is no surprise. Zurich is increasingly pursuing its own international activities, but it never uses them against its good understanding with the national scale. The decision not to create a sub-unit for international relations within the service for city development but rather to create one for external relations in general, which includes the important relations with the national scale, aligns with the Zurich area's economic needs.

Relations with the EU
Zurich's relations with the EU seemed to be an issue of non-debate for a long time. Although several of the involved policy-makers mention the problem of the Swiss absence from the EU, they do not view it as a major issue. Only within the San Francisco initiative has the EU issue seemed to matter. In a press release, Zurich identified one of its reasons for setting up the initiative to be Switzerland's absence from the EU (Stadtrat Zürich 2003). Recently, Zurich increased its efforts to overcome possible shortcomings that result from its absence in the EU by joining the Eurocities network. The mayor, who initiated the membership, was well aware of Eurocities' purpose as a lobby organisation towards the EU. Thus, policy-makers in Zurich are increasingly aware of the EU scale's growing importance in urban policy-making.

The ECDP network tried several times to obtain co-financing from the EU, but it failed, largely due to the number of Swiss cities that participated in the network and the EU's resistance against co-financing a network in which many cities from a non-member country were involved.

Within the METREX network, the role of the EU is quite strong. From the beginning of the network's activities in 1996, the EU financially supported METREX. One of the goals of this network is to coordinate the needs of metropolitan areas in spatial planning towards the EU (Metrex 2000: 12). The RZU participated in the InterMETREX project that was partially funded by the Interreg III programme of the EU, but the RZU could not profit from these funds because they were open only to metropolitan areas of EU member states. Instead, the national State Secretariat for Economic Affairs and the canton of Zurich had to support the cooperation financially, compensating for the inaccessible financial contribution from the EU. The cooperation within the METREX network can therefore be described as truly multi-level; it is an international network of metropolitan areas, but the national level is also involved (by co-financing certain activities), as is the cantonal level (through the organisation of the RZU). However, the complex organisational form did not facilitate the cooperation, and it is partly responsible for the RZU's lack of full membership with the METREX network.

Within the international Climate Alliance and the ICLEI-network, several projects are co-financed by the EU, which hinders Zurich's participation. Zurich must either finance its share on its own (as in the eco-procurement programme; Clement and Erdmenger 2003) or reject participation in the programme. Zurich's inability to participate in several of the Climate Alliance's projects, due to the missing membership of Switzerland in the EU, is seen as an obstacle to deepened international cooperation:

> As long as Switzerland is not part of the EU, I mean, if the will of Switzerland is not there to participate in the EU, it is then very difficult for Swiss cities [...] to participate in these EU-wide projects. We witnessed that we would have to pay it on our own.
>
> *(Head of the Department for Environment)*

Short summary
Overall, Zurich is the city-region under scrutiny that has experienced the most recent changes and increased intensity of its international activities. The mayor promotes the strategy of achieving increased visibility on the international scale. This goal is linked to soft locational factors such as promoting Zurich as an attractive city-region in which to live. The city parliament blocked the credit for the restructuring of the department for city development and the creation of a special subunit for external relations. The city's anticipatory obedience to the national foreign policy aligns with its specific economic situation, which depends heavily on the financial sector and its respective national regulations. The city's new international activities are linked neither to the agglomeration communities nor to the canton.

LYON: GOING GLOBAL FOR THE TOP FIFTEEN

International position and economic orientation
The city-region of Lyon contains approximately 1.2 million inhabitants (Grand Lyon 2008b). The fifty-seven communities of the city-region of Lyon all lie within the département de Rhône. The core city Lyon contains 444,369 inhabitants. Lyon is the third largest city in France; it is half as big as Marseille, but it is far smaller than Paris, which has 2.15 million inhabitants (City Mayors 2008).[75] The city-region of Lyon has had a metropolitan government since 1969 (Mabrouk

---

75 The latter figure obviously only includes the city of Paris. Together with its agglomeration, the city-region of Paris is considerably larger and contains about ten million inhabitants (City Mayors 2008).

and Jouve 2002: 87).[76] Beaverstock *et al.* (1999: 456) rank Lyon as a city-region that shows 'strong evidence of world city formation'. Lyon is thus ranked lower than Zurich or Geneva, which are beta and gamma world cities, although they are much smaller. However, Lyon ranks higher than the other EU city in the sample, Stuttgart, in which there is only 'some evidence of world city formation'. Lyon is currently (2009) ranked number nineteen in the European Cities Monitor's study on business-friendly cities, conducted by Cushman & Wakefield and Healey & Baker (1990–2009). Lyon is also included in the quality of living index created by Mercer (2009); it is ranked thirty-seventh, slightly below Paris, the best-ranked French city, in the thirty-third position. However, Lyon is ranked considerably lower than the three Swiss cities of Geneva, Zurich, and Berne, which are ranked second, first, and ninth, respectively.

Lyon's international reputation is due to two facts. First, Lyon's light festival (festival de la lumière) in December attracts approximately four million visitors every year and generates a considerable boost for the tourist industry (Ville de Lyon 2008b). Second, the city of Lyon is known as an excellent place for gourmands because of its high-quality restaurants. Lyon describes itself as the 'world's undisputed capital of gastronomy' (Lyon Business 2008). Paul Bocuse, who is perhaps one of the most famous cooks worldwide, locates most of his restaurants in Lyon.

Economically, the city-region of Lyon is quite diversified. Its international reputation as a gourmet city and its festival of light are important for its tourist business. Nevertheless, Lyon's primary economic activity occurs in the sectors of banking, pharmacy, and several other domains. One of the largest French banking institutes, Credit Lyonnais, is seated in Lyon. Sanofi-aventis, the third biggest pharmacy company worldwide, maintains an important branch in Lyon. Originally, Rhone-Poulenc located its headquarters in Lyon, but this position was lost when the company merged with the German Hoechst AG in 1999. Another consolidation, with the French Sanofi in 2004, further decreased the importance of Sanofi-aventis' Lyon location (Sanofi-aventis 2005).

However, none of the mentioned economic sectors truly dominate the economy of Lyon. The region of Lyon lists fifteen economic clusters that include at least 10,000 jobs each (Grand Lyon 2007). Health and biotechnology, with about 67,000 jobs total, is the most important economic branch, but seven other branches involve more than 40,000 jobs each.[77] Because of its diversified economic structure, the city-region of Lyon is thus somewhat vulnerable to globalisation since the

---

76   In analogy to the other case studies, I use the English term 'city-region' to refer to the communauté urbaine de Lyon, which is the metropolitan governance structure for the Lyon region. For a historic overview of Lyon's metropolitan governance structure's evolution, see Mabrouk and Jouve (2002).

77   These seven branches are construction, public works, and materials (60,000), business services (58,000), industrial services (50,000), metallurgy, public works, and materials (48,000), finance and real estate (42,000), hotels, restaurants, and leisure (40,000), and logistics, and transport (40,000; Grand Lyon 2007).

mentioned clusters generally operate in internationally competitive markets. Still, the city-region of Lyon is not dependent on one specific economic sector, unlike many other city-regions under scrutiny. The city's strategy to diversify its economic profile is rooted in the city's history as an industrial city since the eighteenth century. Lyon faced modest deindustrialisation in the aftermath of the Second World War.

Politicians from Lyon have officially announced the city's goal of improving its economic position and becoming one of the fifteen economically strongest city-regions in Europe. This goal is termed 'Lyon – Top 15' (Grand Lyon 2005a: 5).

> The strategy of the city of Lyon is simple. The city of Lyon is today classified 23rd on the European level. The strategy of Lyon is to move up this ranking and to get into the top fifteen of the big European cities.
>
> *(Person responsible for international relations)*

Lyon is the only region under scrutiny that has such an explicit economic goal. Additionally, this goal is directly oriented against other city-regions since Lyon tries to improve its relative position in the European urban hierarchy. This goal also clearly demonstrates Lyon's orientation towards the European scale and away from the French scale. The top fifteen goal also refers to the European Cities Monitor (Cushman & Wakefield/Healey & Baker 1990–2009), in which Lyon wants to improve its ranking and become one of the fifteen most attractive city-regions for business location (Grand Lyon 2005a).

The international activities

City partnerships and networks
Because the services for the respective international contacts of the city and the region of Lyon merged in 2006 (see below), there is no distinction made between the two scales in the list of international contacts (see Table 2.13). In the following sections, there is a collective reference to the international activities of the region of Lyon.[78] The region of Lyon has seven partner cities and is engaged in fifteen international city networks.

Lyon's first partnerships were developed in the aftermath of the Second World War. The first partnership, with the English partner city of Birmingham, began in 1951. Then, Lyon took up partnerships with cities in states that were former wartime adversaries (Yokohama in 1959, Frankfurt on the Main in 1960, and Milan in 1966). Next followed a partnership with Saint-Louis in the United States in 1975 and one with Beer-Shiva in Israel in 1980. The last partnership, with the city of Canton in China, dates back to 1988. This was one of the earliest partnerships of aEuropean city with a Chinese city. The city-region of Lyon has established informal partnerships with numerous other cities worldwide.[79]

---

78 The description of the single activities will clarify which ones originated at the city scale and which ones began at the regional scale.

79 An overview can be found in Ville de Lyon (2008a).

Table 2.13: The international activities of the city of Lyon and of Grand Lyon[80]

International activity	Description	Categorisation
Birmingham (Great Britain)		City partnership
Beer-Sheva (Israel)		City partnership
Canton (China)		City partnership
Frankfurt (Germany)		City partnership
Milan (Italy)		City partnership
Saint-Louis (USA)		City partnership
Yokohama (Japan)		City partnership
Les Rencontres	Cities cooperating on cultural policy	Thematic network
Banlieues d'Europe	Cities cooperating on cultural policy	Thematic network
GCD/GDS	Cities for digital solidarity	Thematic network
IAEC	Cities cooperating on education policy	Thematic network
DÉLICE	Cities with a relation to *haute cuisine*	Thematic network
LUCI	Cities cooperating on lighting policy	Thematic network
IRE	Cities cooperating in location promotion	Thematic network
EURADA	Cities cooperating in location promotion	Thematic network
UCP	Cities fighting poverty	Thematic network
EMTA	Cities cooperating in transport policy	Thematic network
OWHC	Cities with a world heritage	Thematic network
AIMF	Multi-thematic network	Lobby network
Citynet/Proact	Asian-pacific cities (multi-thematic)	Lobby network
Eurocities	Multi-thematic network	Lobby network
UCLG	Multi-thematic network	Lobby network

---

80   The city of Lyon signalled its intent to join the European coalition of cities against racism in 2005. As for the other city-regions under scrutiny, this network is not included in this study (see page 41).

Lyon is a long-standing member of two networks in the domain of cultural policy. First, the delegate for cultural affairs of the city of Lyon regularly participates in the Les Rencontres network. Second, the committee for cultural affairs regularly attends the meetings of the network Banlieues d'Europe. The city's membership within the Les Rencontres network is closely linked to its candidacy for the European capital of culture (see below). Whereas Les Rencontres is attached to the EU and its funding of cultural activities on the city scale, Banlieues d'Europe is a rather informal network for alternative artwork in cities and for the use of art in disfavoured city areas.[81] Two different services within the city of Lyon carry out these two networking activities in the domain of cultural policy. However, involved policy-makers participate in both networks' meetings. The Banlieues d'Europe network has had its headquarters in Lyon since 2007.

The city-region of Lyon was among the founding members of the GCD[82] network, which endeavours to provide a fund (the GDS) to ease developing countries' access to new information technologies. Lyon is the seat of the World Digital Solidarity Agency, which manages (among other things) the technical cooperation for the GCD network, and the mayor of Lyon is the president of the World Digital Solidarity Agency. Lyon and Geneva share the leadership of this network, which addresses the digital divide between north and south on the local level.

The city of Lyon is also a long-standing member of the IAEC network on education policy. The head of the city's Department for Education regularly participates in the international meetings. Lyon also hosted the bi-annual general conference of the IAEC network in 2006 and has held a seat in the executive committee since that time. The IAEC is a two-level network since the French member cities have formed a sub-group of the network. They regularly exchange their knowledge on education policy in the French context. Lyon actively participates in this sub-network.

The city of Lyon independently created two new international city networks. First, the Délice network was established at the end of 2007. An inaugural conference in Lyon presented the network and endeavoured to attract member cities. The goal of the network is to bring together cities that focus on *haute cuisine*.

The second network initiated by Lyon is LUCI, which brings cities together to share their best practices in urban lighting. This network was set up in 2001. Its member cities join together at an annual urban light festival in Lyon in December every year. Lyon profited from the EU's co-financing of 667,000 Euros for setting up the network (Grand Lyon 2006a: 70).

Lyon is also a member of two international networks that deal with locational politics. However, neither the city nor the region of Lyon is directly a member; rather, the two organisations that deal with the Lyon region's locational politics participate in these networks. In the case of the Innovative Regions in Europe (IRE) network, the Chambre de Commerce et d'Industrie, i.e. Chamber of

---

81   However, the EU co-finances the network.

82   Together with Geneva; see pages 49ff. on the engagement of Geneva in this network.

Commerce and Industry (CCI) manages Lyon's membership. The CCI is the head organisation of the enterprises in the Lyon area. For the European Association of Development Agencies (EURADA) network, the Agence pour le Développement Economique de la Région Lyonnaise, i.e. Agency for the Economic Development of the Lyon Region (ADERLY) participates for the region of Lyon. Although formally separated, the ADERLY and the CCI work together closely. They are located in the same building, and the involved policy-makers frequently collaborate on their international contacts.

Lyon was also a founding member of the UCP network, together with Geneva[83] and Bamako. The goal of this network is to provide a platform for decentralised development aid through the exchange of knowledge with developing cities. The city of Lyon works in close collaboration with Geneva in this network and links its engagement within the UCP network to its other international activities that pursue international solidarity (see below).

As in the case of the IRE and EURADA networks, Lyon's cooperation within the European Metropolitan Transport Authorities (EMTA) network is not directly carried out by the city or the region but rather by the governing body for public transportation in the agglomeration of Lyon, the Syndicat mixte des Transports pour le Rhône et l'Agglomération Lyonnaise, i.e. Mixed Syndicate of Transport for the Rhone Region and the Agglomeration of Lyon (SYTRAL). The director of the SYTRAL participates irregularly in the meetings of the EMTA network that address best practices in urban public transport.

UNESCO recognised the old town of Lyon as a world heritage site in 1998. The city of Lyon decided, shortly afterwards (in 1999), to join the related OWHC network of cities that have UNESCO world heritages. The chief of the historic site of Lyon participates regularly in the international meetings of the OWHC network. The mayor of Lyon became one of the OWHC network's six vice-presidents for the period 2007–2009.

The city of Lyon is a long-standing member of the AIMF network, which brings together French-speaking cities. However, the city's cooperation within the network is not currently a priority. Membership in the UCLG network (see below) is seen as more important than the rather formal cooperation within the AIMF network. The city of Lyon does not even mention its membership in this network on its homepage,[84] and it only briefly mentions it in its annual report on international activities (Grand Lyon 2006a: 66).

The Lyon region joined Citynet in the early 1990s. This network of Asian-Pacific city-regions is the equivalent of the Eurocities network in the Asian-Pacific geographical area. The member city-regions cooperate in several policy domains to exchange knowledge and to lobby upper-level governments. For a long time, the region of Lyon was the only European member of this network. (It is now

---

83 See pages 49ff.

84 However, the mayor of Lyon presides over the commission on the European and international affairs of the association of mayors of large French cities, and Lyon is generally quite active in this national network.

joined by Ancona from Italy; see Citynet 2008). Lyon has a seat in Citynet's executive board, and, in 2005, Lyon hosted the network's annual meeting. The region of Lyon uses its membership in Citynet to establish business contacts in emerging Asian markets. The EU financed the Proact project, which was closely related to Citynet. The project was accomplished in close collaboration with the Eurocities network, and it brought together members of the two networks to discuss further European-Asian city-to-city collaboration possibilities (Grand Lyon 2006a: 39; Proact Asia Urbs 2005: 2).

Lyon was among the six founding members of the Eurocities network in 1996. In the beginning, the primary goal of this multi-thematic lobbying network of big metropolitan areas in Europe was to give secondary cities a voice in Europe. Because Lyon politicians perceived their own city to be in exactly that position, their commitment to the network was strong from the beginning. Lyon was a member of Eurocities' executive committee from 1986 to 1997, and it chaired several committees (Ville de Lyon 2002). Lyon then took a more passive role in Eurocities in 1997, when the goal of the network was broadened to include lobbying for cities' concerns at the EU. Within the past few years, however, after the election of a new mayor, Lyon has considerably increased its engagement in the network. From 2002 to 2005, the mayor of Lyon served as a member of Eurocities' executive board; in 2005 and 2006, he served as the network's vice-president; in 2006, he began serving as its president. Lyon also chaired one of Eurocities' six forums, a forum on economic development and urban regeneration, but stepped down from this position when the mayor was elected as president of Eurocities. Lyon also hosted the annual conference of Eurocities in 2005.

Lyon is also a very active direct member of the UCLG network. Because the city already belonged to the network's two predecessor organisations, Lyon became a member of UCLG at its inauguration in 2004. The city of Lyon is a member of the executive committee of UCLG. Since 2005, it has chaired the commission on the decentralised cooperation of UCLG, which is linked to the region of Lyon's engagement in development aid on the local scale in general (see below).

Although it does not fit into my formal definition of an international activity, Lyon's candidacy to become the European capital of culture is worth mentioning. Building on a huge marketing campaign, Lyon endeavoured to become the European capital of culture in 2013. The selection process is a national competition. The EU chose the national states for the 2013 cities (France and Slovakia). Four cities in France participated in the race for the title: Lyon, Bordeaux, Marseille, and Toulouse. The city's goal of becoming the European capital of culture is clearly linked to its general strategy of increased visibility on the European and global scales (see below; Ville de Lyon 2006: 12, 2007). Lyon also notes that its candidacy is part of its economic strategy to become one of the top fifteen European metropolitan areas (Ville de Lyon 2006: 3), and the city used its existing networking contacts (such as those formed through LUCI or Eurocities) to promote its candidacy (Ville de Lyon 2006: 6). Involved policy-makers believed that the international backup of Lyon's candidacy is an asset in the national competition and that Lyon outrivals the other competitors in this respect. However, Marseille finally won the battle to become European capital of culture 2013.

The organisation of the international contacts

Lyon's engagement in international contacts is also manifested in the city's organisational structure. The service for international contacts is directly subordinated to the mayor; additionally, a direct political actor (an adjunct, comparable to a city councillor in Switzerland[85]) is responsible for the international contacts. Together with the mayor, the adjunct is responsible for the political strategy of the city's international contacts. He also serves as the vice-president of the region of Lyon. This again underlines the importance of international contacts, both for the city and the region of Lyon. Lyon is also the city-region under scrutiny that first established a service for international contacts (in 1995).

Although the city's and the region's services for international contacts formally amalgamated in 2006, they still operate separately and are located in different offices. Bringing together two services with considerable overlap in their activities was more difficult than expected. Approximately twenty people work for the newly merged service, which makes it the largest staff that manages international relations among all the city-regions under scrutiny. The new service carries out many international activities on its own, and it dedicates relatively less time to coordinating the international contacts of other departments. In a rather top-down approach, the mayor decided which international contacts are of vital importance for the visibility of the region of Lyon, and the service for international contacts now carries out those networking activities. Contacts that are less in line with the city's orientation towards global visibility and increased economic performance are left to their respective departments. The city's service for international contacts has no systematic overview of all the different departments' international contacts.

Orientation of international contacts

In general, scholars see Lyon as a city that is at the forefront of a new inter-city competition (Gordon 1999: 1007). Already, in 1988, Lyon published a development strategy that highlighted the new territorial competition of metropolitan areas in Europe. Lyon adapted a growth-oriented strategy earlier than most other European city-regions.

> Heightened competition between the cities and regions of Europe for the location of firms, offices, factories and, ultimately, wealth and population. This heightened competition would give every chance to the most attractive cities, those who will know how to develop their geographical advantages and their growth assets, without compromising opportunities for cooperative ventures with other cities.
>
> *(SEPAL 1988: 23, cited in Gordon 1999: 1007)*

The region of Lyon follows a double strategy within its international activities. On the one hand, it promotes itself as an international solidarity city, and it is engaged in several development-oriented international cooperation projects (for example, in the GCD and UCP networks). The service for international contacts also

---

85   The French term is *adjoint au maire*.

coordinates these networking activities, which are an integral part of the region's strategy of international visibility. On the other hand, the region of Lyon follows a clear competitiveness-oriented strategy in several other international contacts. By delegating the international networking activities within the two networks that deal with locational politics to the CCI and the ADERLY, the city-region can maintain its image as an international solidarity city. The networking activities that clearly attempt to settle new enterprises in the Lyon area are officially not part of Lyon's international contacts; nevertheless, they are closely monitored by the region of Lyon (Grand Lyon 2006a: 2), and there is close cooperation on economic questions between the service for international contacts and the CCI and ADERLY.

The new mayor has clearly set a goal of using the city's international contacts to promote Lyon on the international scale in economic matters:

> What do the inhabitants want? They want prosperity, riches, and work. The international activities are a condition of prosperity, riches, and work. The world we are in is a world of competition. And the competition is international. To exist means to act, move, show yourself, emanate, have influence.
>
> *(Person responsible for international relations)*

This promotion is accomplished in two ways. First, the general goal is to increase the visibility of Lyon. Lyon therefore has increased its engagement in several important networks. Its engagement in the Eurocities network is the clearest example of this strategy. Although it does not provide direct economic benefits, the presidency of Lyon in this network is seen as an opportunity to emphasise Lyon on the European map. Second, Lyon directly enters or sets up international city networks that align with its economic orientation. Because the mayor of Lyon concluded that an international network was missing in the two domains in which Lyon's international visibility is best, *haute cuisine* and lighting, he decided to set up two respective networks on his own. These new networks' links to the city-region's economic development are specified in a promotional brochure, which states that 'the LUCI network is a major player in efforts to place light at the centre of [Lyon's] economic development' (LyonPhiladelphia 2006: 1).

The city's international contacts, as a whole, align with its general orientation towards becoming a competitive city-region. The city's collaboration with its economic actors on international contacts is close (Grand Lyon 2006b: 1), and these contacts primarily serve to increase the visibility of Lyon on the global scale and thereby to enhance the competitiveness of the region. This goal to create visibility represents both a strong commitment to the city's humanist tradition (Grand Lyon 2005b) and a reason for the city's engagement in development aid projects. As one employee of the service for foreign relations explains:

> The North-South cooperation, strategically yes, it is primarily solidarity but it is also valorisation of our image [...]. I do not want to be too negative, but it is also publicity for us, to have such a North-South cooperation.
>
> *(Employee of the Service for Foreign Relations)*

Because the policy-makers view the city's goal of increased visibility as more easily achievable through networking than through city partnerships, they have continually shifted their attention away from the city's long-standing established partnerships to its new international urban networks (Grand Lyon 2006b: 2). The traditional partnerships are strategically used to establish networking activities with those cities. Lyon promotes the networks it has formed through its city partnerships and searches for more project-based, economic-oriented cooperation within these partnerships. The city's partnerships with city-regions in Africa and Asia also align with the double strategy of development aid and economic gain, as the person responsible for these partnerships notes:

> The North-South cooperation has to bring economic exchanges in the long run.
> *(Employee of the Service for Foreign Relations)*

The clearest example of this trend is the city's partnership with Yokohama in Japan, which dates back to 1959. The partnership has recently undergone a considerable change of orientation. Originally, the partnership was used as a gate-opener for Citynet; nowadays, Lyon cooperates with several cities from Asia. This was accomplished, among other objectives, to establish economic links between the Lyon economy and emerging markets in Asia. Lyon has also hosted several international conferences of city networks (for example Eurocities and IAEC). This demonstrates the region's astonishing increase in international contacts over the last six to seven years (under the period of the current mayor). These international contacts are clearly linked to the more general goal of increasing the city-region of Lyon's competitiveness.

> To attract investors, the city has to be visible; this is evident, it has to be known. It is thus true that we have an extremely aggressive strategy in international events in Lyon within the networks.
> *(Employee of the Service for Foreign Relations)*

Linking the economic situation with international activities

Because the city-region of Lyon is economically diversified, there is no clear orientation in its international networking strategy apart from its two networks (regarding *haute cuisine* and lighting) in the domain of international visibility. Lyon seems to struggle with its diversified economic profile because it hinders a clear-cut international networking strategy that aligns with a specific economic profile. The region of Lyon consequently has increased its networking activities in multi-thematic networks (such as Citynet and Eurocities) rather than in single policy-issue networks. As in the two networks mentioned before, the region's goal in the multi-thematic networks is to increase its international visibility, which is seen as a precondition for the improvement of its economic situation (Grand Lyon 2005a: 5). The region's international contacts are therefore used indirectly to achieve its goal of becoming one of the top fifteen European metropolitan areas (Grand Lyon 2005a: 7, 2006b: 1).

Who governs?

The mayor of Lyon, who is also the president of the metropolitan government of Grand Lyon, has increased the international activities of the region of Lyon since shortly after his election in 2001. Although the service for international contacts already existed before the current mayor came into office, he increased the number of people who work for the service, and he turned its strategy towards increased international visibility. There seem to be broad political coalitions on both aspects. The need to improve the city's economic position in a European competition of metropolitan areas, which was originally promoted by a left-wing mayor, seems to be uncontested. The connectivity of the city's engagement in international contacts and its economic strategy also seems to be widely accepted. No parliamentarian requests concerning the international activities have arisen since the term of the new mayor and the consequent increase of the city's international activities.

However, the region of Lyon proactively publicises its international activities. The homepage of the city and the homepage of the region each display a section on international contacts on its front page; additionally, each scale disperses several printed brochures on its international activities. One of them, the 'carnet de retours de voyages' (i.e. booklet on return travel benefits; Grand Lyon undated), explicitly justifies Lyon's international contacts by emphasising the benefits they bring to the city-region. However, several policy-makers mention that the international contacts are known by political and administrative actors but not by the public.

The double strategy between international solidarity and competitiveness is also not a secret, as it is officially announced in documents and on the home page of the region's website (Grand Lyon 2006a: 1, 2006b: 2, undated: 3). The link between international solidarity and economic gains, which is accomplished by establishing contacts with emerging markets, is also mentioned in the brochure on Lyon's international contacts (Grand Lyon undated: 11) and in Lyon's annual report (Grand Lyon 2006a: 2).[86] The goal of this publication is to provide arguments to counter the possible criticism that the mayor of Lyon spends too much time abroad and not enough time in Lyon. Although this critique has not yet been brought forward, Lyon follows a proactive information strategy and demonstrates a certain anticipatory obedience to possible future critics.

Compared to other cities, Lyon uses a top-down approach to its international activities. The mayor strategically decides which international contacts align with the city's general economic orientation and its service for international contacts and then carries out these networking activities. The service for international contacts does not coordinate activities within other international networks that are judged to be less in line with the general strategy, such as Banlieues d'Europe.[87] The very

---

86 One of the goals of the city's engagement in international digital solidarity is to promote Lyon's strong local cluster of computer-industry businesses on the global scale.

87 Because the Banlieues d'Europe network was establishing its headquarters in Lyon at the time of the interview, the future collaboration between the committee for cultural affairs and the service for international contacts was somewhat unclear. The latter was informed about the network's move to Lyon, but it is not interested in a closer collaboration because the network does not fit within Lyon's general orientation of the international activities.

selective mentioning of the city's international contacts on its website's homepage underlines this point. Whereas the new networks established by Lyon (LUCI and Délice) and the networks in which the mayor of Lyon plays an important role (Eurocities, UCLG) are mentioned prominently, the other networks (such as AIMF, Les Rencontres, and Banlieues d'Europe) are not even mentioned.[88] The region's annual report on its service for international contacts (Grand Lyon 2006a) also fails to mention these networking activities. This has displeased certain policy-makers who are involved in international contacts, as they receive no support from the service for international activities. These policy-makers fear an increasingly centralised policy on international contacts that only pursues the goal of increasing Lyon's competitive position, rather than allowing for specific policy cooperation in fields that are not directly linked to the region's economic position.

Within the LUCI network, which was formed by Lyon, the inclusion of private enterprises is strong.[89] Firms like Philips and Bosch that operate in the lighting business sponsor LUCI's networking activities. In return, they are allowed to participate in the annual meetings and to present any new developments that might interest the member cities. These enterprises use the LUCI network as a platform for establishing contacts with city officials. Although this is the only example of a direct inclusion of private actors in Lyon's networking activities, the cooperation between the city-region's international activities and its private sector is closer than in any other city-region under scrutiny. The endeavour to become a top fifteen European metropolitan area is a joint understanding between the city-region of Lyon, the CCI, and the enterprises of the Lyon area (Grand Lyon 2006b: 1). The two networking activities closest to business interests (the activities in the IRE and the EURADA networks that deal with locational policies) are managed by the CCI and the ADERLY, not by the region of Lyon itself.

Horizontal governance

Lyon's horizontal governance concerns only the relation between the city government and the metropolitan government. The two services for international activities from the two scales merged in 2006. The two scales closely collaborate on their international activities.

Apart from that collaboration, there are no links between the core city of Lyon, which is very active on the international scale, and the agglomeration commu-

---

88   The city's cooperation within the AIMF network received some attention from the service for international contacts when the network held its bi-annual congress in Lyon in 2006. Because the organisation of international congresses is a key element of Lyon's strategy for better international visibility, the responsible policy-makers received considerable support for organising the congress from the service for international contacts. However, the support is clearly limited to the organisation of the congress, and there is no further cooperation between the policy-makers who are engaged in the AIMF network and those in the service for international contacts.

89   There is also a small occasional inclusion of private actors within the IAEC network. Because public and private actors often share responsibilities in education policy, Lyon has invited the latter to participate in the IAEC conferences.

nities, which are only engaged in traditional city partnerships.[90] Neither the city nor the region of Lyon is aware of the agglomeration communities' international contacts. There has been no direct inclusion of any other community in the common international contacts of the city and the region of Lyon, apart from one instance. In 2006, the city of Lyon, as the host city of the IAEC conference, invited the policy-makers responsible for education in the agglomeration communities to participate in the congress, and many of them did. This led several agglomeration communities to join the French sub-section of the IAEC, but none of them have engaged in the international IAEC.

However, the metropolitan government's strong engagement in international contacts results in an indirect inclusion of the agglomeration communities. This can be observed, for example, in Lyon's endeavour to become the European capital of culture in 2013. From the beginning, the city of Lyon, which took the lead for the proposal, included the region of Lyon in the candidacy procedure. This led to the discussion of the project in the assembly of the region of Lyon and to a reunion of the policy-makers responsible for culture of all fifty-seven communities of the region of Lyon. They discussed the project and the possible inclusion of their communities in the cultural activities that would have occurred in 2013 if Lyon had become the European capital of culture.

Because the city and the region of Lyon have merged their international activities, there is now an indirect inclusion of the agglomeration communities in the city's international activities. However, the co-financing of the city's international contacts by the region, and thereby indirectly by the agglomeration communities, is the only case of an integrated metropolitan governance approach to international contacts among the seven city-regions under scrutiny.

Vertical governance

Relations between the city and the region of Lyon
Because the two services on the international contacts of the city and the region of Lyon merged in 2006, the city of Lyon managed to evade the problem of centrality burdens caused by its international contacts, which are now co-financed by the metropolitan government and thereby indirectly by the agglomeration communities. This evasion was possible because of the strong position of both the city of Lyon as a whole and the mayor of Lyon in particular. The core city holds the majority of seats in the regional parliament, and the mayor of the city of Lyon is also the president of the region of Lyon. The close collaboration between the city and the region allowed the mayor of Lyon to amalgamate their respective services on international contacts in 2006. It also facilitates a common appearance on the international scale; for example, Lyon and the region of Lyon share their member-

---

90   As mentioned before, I was unable to investigate all international activities of the cities in the agglomeration of Lyon, for reasons of efficiency. A first glance, however, showed that, as in the other city-regions under scrutiny, none of the cities in the agglomeration of Lyon are engaged in international networking activities, although several of the agglomeration communities have one or more partner cities.

ship in the Eurocities network. They divide the annual membership fee and cooperate in numerous projects within Eurocities.

Relations with the département

There are two activities in which the city-region of Lyon and the département du Rhône cooperate.[91] First, the two scales cooperated for Lyon's candidacy to become the European capital of culture in 2013. Although the département formally supported the candidacy, however, it was not directly included in this project. Second, the development aid projects of the region of Lyon are sometimes loosely coordinated with the region of Rhône-Alps. Because the latter region is also engaged in decentralised cooperation schemes, both regions have pursued initiatives to coordinate their respective efforts. This has led to partnerships in the same geographical area.

There is thus a multi-level aspect of and some interscalar coordination among Lyon's international contacts. However, in the city-region of Lyon's networking activities, which are seen as very important considering the increasing competition among urban areas, there is no inclusion of the regional scale, with the exception of the département's small co-financing of the establishment of Banlieues d'Europe's headquarters. Still, the general understanding between the city-region of Lyon and the département concerning the international activities is described as good, and the responsible persons from both scales regularly meet to inform each other about their activities and to cooperate whenever possible.

Relations with the national state

Lyon's contact points with the national state are minimal. Only in the case of decentralised cooperation, where Lyon takes a leading position among French cities, does the national state recognise Lyon's role and financially support Lyon's endeavours (Grand Lyon 2006a: 38). Policy-makers of the region of Lyon do not reflect on national policies when considering their international activities. The international contacts of Lyon clearly do not support the respective national policy; rather, they are carried out independently. Lyon's increased international activities are a strategy against the national state, as one employee of the service for foreign relations explains:

> I think that we are in a competition between cities as well. [...] We in France, we have Paris that eats everything. We cooperate more easily, we also know better Birmingham than Paris [...]. In this domain, we are really in a competition with Paris.
>
> *(Employee of the Service for Foreign Relations)*

Because Lyon policy-makers perceive Paris as the uncontested economic and political powerhouse of France (Collomb 2005), they have redirected their attention from an intra-French competition towards a competition of similar-sized city-regions on the European scale. Another reason for this redirection was the city

---

91   There is another indirect inclusion of the département in the international activities of Lyon; because the département is one of the four constituting members of the ADERLY, it indirectly participates in the ADERLY's membership in the EURADA network. However, the cooperation within this network remains limited to the ADERLY and does not include the département directly.

of Lyon's discomfort within the highly centralised state system of France, which predominantly focuses on the development of Paris[92]. This perceived negligence by the national scale led Lyon policy-makers to change their scalar focus and to increase their international contacts. Lyon uses its international contacts to lobby for a better position in the French urban system and for greater national attention towards cities other than Paris. The president of the region of Lyon explicitly links the need to decentralise the French state to the function of urban areas as nodal points of an increasing interurban competition in Europe.

> Recent moves towards decentralization should have paid more attention to regional competition within Europe. France needs strong urban centres, integrated in productive regions. Only then can it assert itself as a driving force in building a strong Europe.
>
> *(Collomb 2005)*

The strategy against the national state and Paris is also reflected in Lyon's strong engagement in the lobby networks UCLG and Eurocities. The latter network promoted secondary cities, and Lyon was among its founding members because it shared the desire for an increased understanding across the borders of city-regions that feel uneasy within their national multi-level governance schemes. Because the Eurocities network is currently oriented towards the EU scale, Lyon uses its powerful position in the Eurocities network (attendant to the role of Lyon's mayor as the president of Eurocities) to bypass the national state of France in order to access the EU directly and to lobby at the EU scale for a stronger position of city-regions in Europe (Collomb 2005). Lyon is the only city that directly links its own international activities to the national state's loss of a monopoly on international contacts.

> In an evolving global context [...], the national state does not have the monopoly in international relations anymore. The exchanges and partnership programs between territorial collectives are intensifying and they clearly constitute an *urban diplomacy* today.
>
> *(Grand Lyon 2006b: 1, original emphasis)*

Relations with the EU
The region of Lyon concentrates its efforts concerning its relations with the EU to its engagement within the Eurocities network. Although Lyon has profited from the EU's co-financing of several of its international networking activities, Europe is not the primary scale of attendance for Lyon's international contacts. Rather, the logic of global competitiveness dictates the scale of the city-region's international political activities. Hence, the region of Lyon has established links to Asian city-regions, since contacts with emerging Asian markets are considered to be highly important for Lyon's future economic well-being. The scale of interurban competition dominates the scale of political networking, and the latter scale adapts to the first.

Lyon uses its strategic position within the Eurocities network in two ways. First, Lyon supports the lobbying of the Eurocities network at the EU. Second, the

---

92   The SYTRAL first refused to participate in the EMTA network that was set up by Paris in the late 1990s.

city-region's strategic position within Eurocities gives Lyon a head start on new EU legislation that concerns the local scale. Because the Eurocities network frequently operates as the EU's partner on the local scale, Lyon's engagement in this network allows the mayor to serve as a key addressee for the EU concerning issues of local governance. Policy-makers see the direct contacts through its leadership position within the Eurocities network as an asset for the city-region of Lyon, both politically and economically.

Lyon profits from a strong financial engagement of the EU in its contacts with Asian cities through Citynet. The programme Proact, which tried to increase the contacts between Asian and European city-regions and which was managed by the region of Lyon, profited from the EU's co-financing of more than 50 per cent of the project (Proact Asia Urbs 2005).[93]

Short summary
The city-region of Lyon has strategically increased the intensity of its international activities and is now aggressively engaged in several international urban networks. The content of these international contacts is clearly economically oriented. The city's international contacts serve its economic goal of becoming one of the top fifteen metropolitan areas in Europe. The mayor of Lyon is the leader of this new development, and he is personally involved in several international networks, most prominently as the president of Eurocities. This position places Lyon at the heart of the EU decision-making process. Lyon's mayor also instigated the merger of the separate services for international activities of the city and the city-region of Lyon, which now allows the city of Lyon to avoid the centrality burdens of its international contacts. The city-region's increased international activities are based on Lyon's position as a secondary city that cannot compete with the national leader, Paris. Accordingly, these activities compose a strategy against the national state. Lyon's links with the regional scale are minimal.

STUTTGART: GLOBAL MOBILITY

International position and economic orientation
The city-region of Stuttgart contains 2,666,849 inhabitants. The 179 communities of the city-region of Stuttgart lie within the Land of Baden-Württemberg. The city of Stuttgart, which contains 591,550 inhabitants, is the region's core city (Verband Region Stuttgart 2007: 2). Both the city and the city-region of Stuttgart are thus considerably larger than the Swiss cases in this study. The city-region of Stuttgart has had a metropolitan government since 1994 (Blatter 2006: 131).[94] Beaverstock *et al.* (1999: 456) rank Stuttgart as a city-region that shows 'some evidence of

---

93 The SYTRAL's membership in the EMTA network is closely linked to the EU's increasing influence in the domain of public transport. The SYTRAL uses its membership in the EMTA network to keep informed about new developments on the EU scale in its domain and to lobby at the EU scale for metropolitan public transport.

94 In analogy to the other case studies, the English term city-region is used to refer to the Verband Region of Stuttgart, which is the metropolitan governance structure for the Stuttgart region. For a historic overview of the Stuttgart metropolitan governance's structure and creation, see Blatter (2006).

world city formation'. Stuttgart is thus ranked lower than Zurich or Geneva, which are ranked as beta and gamma world cities even though they are much smaller. Stuttgart is not ranked by Mercer's quality of living index (2009). Although Stuttgart is the sixth biggest city in Germany, it is considerably smaller than the three largest German cities (Berlin, Hamburg, and Munich, which contain approximately 3.4 million, 1.8 million and 1.3 million inhabitants respectively; City Population 2007). The city-region of Stuttgart refers to a ranking of German city-regions' quality of living in which Stuttgart is ranked first (Wirtschaftsförderung Region Stuttgart GmbH 2001: 3).

Stuttgart's international reputation is clearly linked to the automobile industry. Gottlieb Daimler, who invented the automobile, was born in Stuttgart, and the Daimler company has located its seat in one of Stuttgart's agglomeration cities (Böblingen) since the early twentieth century. The city has a long tradition of automobile production and engineering, which are its most important economic sectors. Besides Daimler, Porsche is another major automobile producer that is located in the Stuttgart area. Daimler is the biggest German industrial company, and it provides work for approximately 362,000 employees in Germany (figures for the year 2003, Rüdiger 2005). Many smaller companies in the region are suppliers for the automobile industry. Stuttgart's dependence on the automobile sector and thereby on the manufacturing industry in general is quite high.

The city-region of Stuttgart is the German city-region that has the highest industrial density, which makes the city-region vulnerable to globalisation pressures. This economic mix of the Stuttgart area reflects this one-sided dependence on a single industrial branch. 40 per cent of the employees within the Stuttgart area hold blue-collar jobs (IHK Region Stuttgart 2008). Out of the 325,000 people who hold industrial jobs, 124,000 (or almost 40 per cent of all blue-collar jobs) work in the automobile sector, and many more work in its supplying branches (IHK Region Stuttgart 2008). Apart from the automobile industry, many other large industrial companies maintain their European headquarters in Stuttgart, including Bosch, Hewlett-Packard, IBM, and Alcatel (Verband Region Stuttgart 2008). Clearly, Stuttgart is economically dependent on the industrial sector. Because of its dependence on manufacturing, Stuttgart thus risks economic disaster if any of those few large industrial companies transfer their production bases out of the Stuttgart area to low-wage countries.

International activities

City partnerships and networks
The city of Stuttgart has nine city partnerships and is engaged in eight international city networks (see Table 2.14).

The city partnerships of Stuttgart can be divided into three categories according to the time of their inaugurations. The first four partnerships were set up to establish peaceful relations among the former opponents of the Second World War on the local level. The partnerships with the British cities of St. Helens and Cardiff were established in 1951 and 1955, respectively; a partnership with the U.S. city of St. Louis was formed in 1960; the French city of Strasbourg joined a partnership with Stuttgart in 1962.

Table 2.14: The international activities of the city of Stuttgart

International activity	Description	Categorisation
Cairo (Egypt)		City partnership
Cardiff (Great Britain)		City partnership
Lodz (Poland)		City partnership
Menzel Bourguiba (Tunisia)		City partnership
Mumbai (India)		City partnership
Samara (Russia)		City partnership
St. Helens (Great Britain)		City partnership
St. Louis (USA)		City partnership
Strasbourg (France)		City partnership
Climate Alliance	Cities for a liberal environmental policy	Thematic network
Energie-Cités	Cities for a liberal environmental policy	Thematic network
CLIP	Cities cooperating in integration policy	Thematic network
Cities for Children	Cities cooperating in youth policy	Thematic network
POLIS	Cities cooperating in transport policy	Thematic network
CIVITAS	Cities cooperating in transport policy	Thematic network
URB-AL Nr. 8	Cities cooperating in transport policy	Thematic network
Cities for Mobility	Cities cooperating in transport policy	Thematic network
UCLG	Multi-thematic network	Lobby network

The second group of partner cities includes cities from developing countries. Mumbai, in India, partnered with Stuttgart in 1968; Menzel Bourguiba, in Tunisia, formed a partnership in 1971; Cairo, in Egypt, began officially associating with Stuttgart in 1979. Stuttgart was among the first cities in Europe to establish links to these countries for social and economic reasons.

In the third phase, the city of Stuttgart established transnational linkages through partnerships with countries from Eastern Europe. Lodz, in Poland, partnered with Stuttgart in 1979; Brno in the Czech Republic, in 1987; and Samara, in Russia, in 1992. The goal was to help these cities adapt to the rapid transition process after the end of the Cold War. Stuttgart was one of the very few cities that established partnerships with cities from Eastern Europe before the end of the Cold War. Stuttgart has not entered any new formal partnership with a foreign city since 1992 because of the city's decision to focus on international networking rather than traditional international partnerships.

In 1995, Stuttgart joined the Climate Alliance network, which endeavours to reduce CO_2-emissions at the city scale, rather unwillingly; the city administration was forced, by a parliamentary motion of the Green Party, to join the network. Stuttgart's cooperation within the Climate Alliance network is minimal, and the city officials have debated resigning from the network. Stuttgart also joined the Energie-Cités network, which establishes first contacts among cities in order to share best practices for energy issues.

The city of Stuttgart initiated the new network Cities for Local Integration Policy of Migrants (CLIP) in 2006. The goal of this new network is to share best practices in integration policy. Stuttgart initiated this network due to its need of a workforce for its local economy. Because of its desire to attract migratory workers, Stuttgart was aware of the problems that attend a strong migration movement in city-regions. Stuttgart sought international cooperation in this policy area because the city's policy-makers felt unsatisfied about the overall cooperation within Germany regarding migratory workers. Many other German city-regions are in different situations because they face high percentages of unemployment. Because no international network in migration policy existed at that time, Stuttgart decided to form a new network to address this issue.

The arguments that endorse Stuttgart as a workplace led to the creation of the Cities for Children Network in 2006. The mayor of Stuttgart tries to promote the city as a family-friendly environment. This necessitates that the city remains attractive as a workplace. The goal of the new network is to bring cities together to cooperate in youth policy and to share best practices in this area. This new network closely cooperates with the UCLG network, and the mayor of Stuttgart uses his established contacts (see below) to promote the new initiative. The seat of the network's secretariat is consequently located in Stuttgart.[95]

In the domain of transportation policy, Stuttgart is a member of the existing networks POLIS and CIVITAS, which both deal with questions of urban mobility and which are both linked to the EU's engagement in this policy domain. Stuttgart was a leader in the URB-AL network, an EU-initiated cooperation between European and South American communities. Stuttgart managed the coordination of the programme nr. 8, which dealt with issues of mobility (Landeshauptstadt Stuttgart 2003c: 9). The URB-AL programme ended in 2002, but Stuttgart tried to continue the international cooperation in transport policy by creating an urban network out of URB-AL programme nr. 8. This led to the creation of the Cities for Mobility network, which coordinates actors from the private and public sectors to deal with broader issues of mobility. The network also cooperates closely with private enterprises from the Stuttgart area (see below).

Stuttgart is a very active member of UCLG. Stuttgart's engagement within this worldwide network of local authorities goes beyond the average member's partici-

---

95   Although it does not fit into my definition of an international activity, the One World initiative is an interesting project of Stuttgart (Landeshauptstadt Stuttgart 2006; *Stuttgarter Zeitung* 2005, 9th September). It has a twofold scalar perspective. First, in a now nearly completed phase, the city is building a coalition among different regional partners (mostly from the private sector) around the initiative and its goals (which are sustainability and developmental aid). Afterwards, Stuttgart plans to construct an international network of metropolitan areas, from both the developed world and the developing world, in order to establish a long-standing global partnership among cities on issues of sustainability and economic growth.

pation. Not only did Stuttgart join the network as an individual city, it also has developed two further specific engagements within the network. First, the mayor of Stuttgart is a world council member of UCLG. He is also the vice president of the European section of UCLG, the CEMR. Thereby, the mayor directly participates in the decision-making process within the UCLG network. Second, Stuttgart initiated a sub-group on mobility within the UCLG, and the mayor of Stuttgart is the head of this sub-group. The sub-group is closely linked to the Cities for Mobility network. Stuttgart uses the contacts it forms through its mayor's leadership position within UCLG to strengthen its position as a city-region that is an expert on mobility policy.

Organisation of international contacts
The city of Stuttgart has maintained two services for international contacts since the early 1990s: one for European and international contacts, which is attached to the Service of Economic Development, and one for international relations and city partnerships, which is under the control of the mayor. The two services merged in 2002, and the new Service for International Contacts[96] is under the direct control of the mayor. The head of the Service for International Contacts, in close collaboration with the mayor, is responsible for the strategy of Stuttgart's international activities.

The service follows a bottom-up approach to its international activities. Existing international contacts are managed by their respective departments but supported by the main service. Even in the newly established network CLIP, the service of integration – not the service for international activities – leads the network's development. The service for international activities directly carries out only the international contacts for city partnerships. The service monitors and supports all other international activities without interfering in the concrete networking contacts.

Orientation of international contacts
The new service takes a strategic approach to the city's international activities. It first evaluated Stuttgart's already existing international contacts that were managed by various departments. It thereby developed a strategy for its international activities that focuses on the city-region's economic strengths and that forms a more coherent approach to its diverse international contacts. The city's goal is to strengthen its economic links within its international contacts and to focus on its relations with the EU. The city also hopes to establish more project-based networking activities than traditional city partnerships.

Therefore, Stuttgart shifted the strategy for its city partnerships from traditional friendly exchange meetings between politicians towards economic and project-based cooperation schemes (Landeshauptstadt Stuttgart 2006d; *Stuttgarter Zeitung* 2005, 18th July). One of the strategy's goals is to use the city's existing partnerships to establish economic links with developing countries and to get a foothold in these emerging markets. Although the service for international activities closely observes the different international contacts maintained by the city departments, it focuses its coordination functions on networks that align with the new strategy. Networks that have fewer contact points with the EU or those that are not in line with the economic needs of the city-region are less closely monitored.

---

96   The official name of the new service is the 'staff section for European and international relations/ city partnerships' (author's translation).

Stuttgart's relations with the EU are a priority for the city's international contacts (Kreher 2006). Policy-makers view the EU as the most important scale for decisions in modern urban politics (Landeshauptstadt Stuttgart 2006c: 1; *Stuttgarter Zeitung* 2005, 4th August: 22). Consequently, Stuttgart's international strategy is oriented towards accessing the EU. Stuttgart thus engages strategically in EU-related policy networks and cooperation schemes.[97] Its goal is to become 'Europeable' as a city (Landeshauptstadt Stuttgart 2003a), which means that politicians in every department should reflect on EU legislation's possible impact on that respective domain. There is also a responsible person in every administrative unit who manages that unit's contacts with the EU. Stuttgart profited from seven million Euros provided by the EU for the years 1998 to 2005 to fund the city's participation in EU projects (Landeshauptstadt Stuttgart 2006c: 7).[98] Although Stuttgart is economically strong and therefore cannot easily access EU financing, it managed to obtain an additional fourteen million Euros from the EU social fund for the years 2000 through 2005 (Landeshauptstadt Stuttgart 2006c: 8).[99]

In conclusion, Stuttgart has enlarged its international contacts considerably over the last years, and its networking activities clearly evidence a transport-centred economic orientation.

Linking the economic situation with international activities
The link between the city-regions' economic situation and its international activities is very clear in the case of Stuttgart. Although the city-region is economically diversified, Stuttgart's dependence on the automobile industry and its corresponding supplier industry is still significant (Schuster 2006: 3). The automobile industry is under heavy pressure from globalisation, and its international competition is high; hence, the policy-makers who are involved in international activities greatly fear Stuttgart's loss of workplaces to low-cost countries:

> As an industrial location [...], we feel extremely challenged by India and China. [...]. Our region is today totally globalised, and this obviously challenges our work places.
>
> *(Director of the Stuttgart Region)*

---

97 A significant political debate has addressed Stuttgart's membership in the Eurocities network. The Christlich Demokratische Union, i.e. Christian Democratic Union (CDU) fraction of the city parliament repeatedly demanded that the government joins this network. The service for international relations originally rejected that proposal for three reasons. First, cooperating within Eurocities would require more resources, which would be difficult to obtain, especially because of the city's already strong engagement in UCLG. Second, Stuttgart preferred to engage in UCLG since that network is open to all communities, whereas policy-makers viewed the Eurocities network as a lobby organisation for large metropolitan areas. Third, the service for international contacts believed that the city administration was not yet ready to cooperate in Eurocities. Hence, the service endeavoured to strengthen the city administration's competences in EU matters first.

98 The four major policy areas that profited from the EU's co-financing were environment, transport/energy use, education/culture, and employment (Landeshauptstadt Stuttgart 2006c).

99 The funded projects sought the integration of unemployed people (Landeshauptstadt Stuttgart 2006c).

After the establishment of a new service for international activities, the mayor and the head of the service developed a strategy for the city's international contacts that sought to increase Stuttgart's international visibility. Although the city-region is economically very strong, not only in comparison with other German city-regions but also on the European scale, its financial success is seen as vulnerable since it depends on a few very international companies in a single industry. Policy-makers perceive that Stuttgart is participating in a global struggle to stay competitive as a relatively unknown global city-region. Globalisation is generally viewed as a possible threat to the popularity of the workplaces in the Stuttgart area. The city's international activities are clearly linked to the fear of a loss of economic strength due to globalisation pressures:

> The enterprises here are all international anyway; Stuttgart just has an enormous amount of global enterprises that are present all over the world. And I think that we, as a city, want to catch up there.
>
> *(Vice-director of the Department for European and International Affairs)*

The city of Stuttgart has therefore changed its goal for its city partnerships. These partnerships, which originated from the post-war ideas of understanding and development aid, were carried out in a traditional manner and were primarily based on contacts between the cities' political leaders and on an exchange of knowledge between the city administrations. The new strategy, enforced by the service for international contacts, now views the partnerships as opportunities for globally promoting Stuttgart as a workplace and for engaging in emerging markets (Landeshauptstadt Stuttgart 2003c: 9, 2006d). One of the city's goals is to use its contacts with its European partner cities to exchange knowledge about accessing the EU for the funding of urban projects. As a result of this clear change in the city's strategy, the city partnerships now must benefit Stuttgart.

A similar type of shift has transpired in Stuttgart's networking activities. The mayor has increased the city's engagement within the most important worldwide network of localities, UCLG, due to the city's need to stay visible on the international level. Additionally, Stuttgart has altered its policy networking activities and created new international city networks in the domain of its economic interests.

Although the city did not develop a specified strategy until 2002, the new service for international activities aligned Stuttgart's networking activities with the city's economic orientation towards the automobile industry. Stuttgart joined several networks that deal with urban transport policies and created several international contacts in that policy area. Stuttgart created a sub-group within UCLG that focuses on mobility (Landeshauptstadt Stuttgart 2006a). It also presided over a sub-group of the URB-AL network on urban transport issues, and it is currently establishing a follow-up network (the Cities for Mobility network; see Landeshauptstadt Stuttgart 2006b). One interview partner identifies the mayor's orientation towards the automobile in the city's international activities:

The mayor has the goal, not only for Germany, but worldwide, to become the Mecca for motorists and he does a lot on several scales at the moment, including the presidency in international networks.

(Employee of the Environmental Department)

The link between Stuttgart's international activities and its economic situation manifests itself most prominently in the new networks that the city has established. One of the persons responsible for these new networks explains:

Our mayor has a diversification strategy. He says that all important issues for the city have to be backed up by international networks. [...] There is a working paper [...] from the mayor, where he explains that he wants to promote the important issues of mobility, integration, and children both at the city scale as well as in international networks. He explicitly says that he has this double strategy within these issues: communal and global at the same time.

(Head of Coordination and Planning)

The Cities for Mobility network is probably the best example of the economic orientation of Stuttgart's networking activities towards the automobile industry. Focusing on every aspect of mobility, not only public transport, the network pursues the three goals of promoting socially just, economy-focused, and environmentally friendly mobility. Even the environmental aspect does not focus on public transport but rather on 'an intelligent mixture of the modes of transportation' (Landeshauptstadt Stuttgart 2006b: 3). The network's premium partners (i.e. sponsors) include the two automobile companies Daimler and Porsche (Cities for Mobility 2008). Thus, the network is not only a form of a public-private partnership in international networking but also a political contribution of Stuttgart to its automobile industry. The goal of the network is to promote Stuttgart as a city-region of automobile-oriented mobility, which aligns with the city's new profile 'as a competence centre for mobility in Europe' (Landeshauptstadt Stuttgart 2003b, author's translation).

It is thus unsurprising that the city of Stuttgart is only very reluctantly engaged in the Climate Alliance network. This network promotes a greener (i.e. more environmentally friendly) approach to urban politics, unlike the networks set up by Stuttgart. Stuttgart has even considered leaving the network because the responsible policy-maker does not think that this international cooperation provides sufficient benefits for the city. The Climate Alliance network does not align with Stuttgart's overall strategy for its international contacts[100].

The city's establishment of a network on immigration policy (the CLIP network) is also rooted in its economic strategy (Landeshauptstadt Stuttgart 2006e: 4f.). The economic powerhouse of Stuttgart has different needs than other German

---

100 To resign from the Climate Alliance would require the agreement of the city parliament, but the relevant policy-maker does not believe that the parliament would back such a decision. The environmental department has thus decided to stay in the network but to cooperate only when direct gains for Stuttgart are possible.

city-regions. Whereas the latter face problems of unemployment, Stuttgart requires immigration for its workplaces. Accordingly, Stuttgart decided to create an international city network that deals with immigration policy because its policy-makers viewed the cooperation possibilities within Germany's traditional multi-level system as unsatisfactory. The same logic applies to the new network on youth policy that Stuttgart created (Cities for Children). In response to the city's need to maintain an image as an attractive workplace for young females with children, the mayor increased his international efforts (*Neue Zürcher Zeitung* 2005, 21st July: 17). Because Stuttgart wanted to profit from best practice knowledge across the German border, it set up a new network in this policy domain.

Clearly, all the international contacts of the city of Stuttgart somehow reflect the region's economic situation. The annual report of the service for international activities contains a section describing 'the international contacts of the Stuttgart *company*' (Landeshauptstadt Stuttgart 2003c: 3; author's emphasis). This reference to the city as a company emphasises the outlook of Stuttgart's international contacts towards economic goals.

Who governs?

Among the city-regions under scrutiny, the mayor's leading role in international activities is most obvious in Stuttgart. Soon after the mayor's election in 1996, the city's international contacts became a key element of his programme. He decided that the city's international contacts should be bundled into one service directly under his supervision. He also decided to strengthen the city's international visibility and economic cooperation through international contacts.

The city's execution of these international contacts is twofold. First, the mayor participates in the UCLG network, serving as the president of its German section, as the vice-president of its European section, and as a member of its world council. This engagement is linked to the city's general goal of international visibility. Because UCLG is a political network, the mayor participates in its networking activities, although he relies on the service for international contacts for organisational matters. Second, the city administration, particularly the service for international relations, manages the major burden of international contacts. Together, the mayor and the service for international contacts are responsible for carrying out the city's economically oriented strategy and for executing its international contacts.

Although the service for international contacts reports on the mayor's activities annually, the service's inclusion of actors from outside city politics and administration is minimal. Other than forcing the city administration to join the Climate Alliance network, the city parliament has not intervened in Stuttgart's international activities. Although several criticisms have questioned the benefits of increasing the city's international orientation, the city parliament has never formally voted against any international contact. Additionally, the city's shift towards a competition-oriented policy for its international contacts has not raised any negative comments from members of the city parliament.

In fact, the parliament has raised questions about the economic gains provided by the city's international partnerships, viewing them as insufficiently oriented towards urban competitiveness. Despite the mayor's new emphasis on international contacts, Stuttgart's political parties do not seem to follow this strategy. The new movement towards a more economically coherent strategy in international relations is clearly due to the mayor's view of these contacts' importance. The parliament's inclusion in the strategy change has been minimal, and there is no clear division along the political parties either for or against the city's international activities.[101]

In general, private actors only rarely participate in Stuttgart's international activities. Within Cities for Mobility, however, the inclusion of private actors is common. Stuttgart uses its contacts in the automobile and industrial sectors to find local sponsors for this international network. In return, those companies can use the network's conferences as platforms to promote their products and to establish contacts worldwide, as the person responsible for this network explains:

> We are very well linked with enterprises like Daimler and Porsche. We allow these enterprises to become Premium Partners in the network Cities for Mobility and to engage as regards content as well as financially. This, of course, strengthens our image and allows us to globally merchandise Stuttgart as a centre of excellence in this respect.
>
> *(Employee of the Service for Coordination and Planning)*

Cities for Mobility is thus a rare example of an international city network that is sponsored by private industries.[102] By forming its own network, the city of Stuttgart clearly followed its double strategy of promoting itself as a leading international city in mobility matters and establishing links with local businesses in this policy area through sponsorship.

The city of Stuttgart has delegated the networking activities of the POLIS network to an external consultant. This consultant prepares Stuttgart's presentations for international meetings and then reports back to the city administration. Policymakers lack the time necessary to participate in the international network. Because participation in this network is of strategic importance for the city of Stuttgart (because of its general focus on mobility in international networks), it was decided that an external consultant should participate in the international networking. This is the only case among all seven city-regions under scrutiny in which the city administration does not carry out an international activity by itself.

---

101 The CDU fraction, for example, both argued for a more competition-oriented strategy for Stuttgart's international relations and encouraged the city to join Eurocities, which is a lobby network that demands considerable input from its member cities without giving them any direct economic benefit. Right-wing parties have not opposed these international activities, in contrast to some Swiss city-regions in which opposition against internationalisation originates from right-wing parties (see pages 78ff. and 91ff.).

102 The only other example is the LUCI network. See pages 109ff. for more information on LUCI's inclusion of private actors.

Horizontal governance

Stuttgart's multi-level governance setting is quite complex (see Figure 2.1). Even within the metropolitan government, there are three governmental levels. The communities are the first level, followed by the districts (Kreise); the metropolitan government is the third level, and comprises both five districts and the city of Stuttgart.

All five district towns (the Kreisstädte, i.e. the core cities of the five districts)[103] in the city-region of Stuttgart are engaged in several partnerships,[104] and three of these five cities are members of the Climate Alliance network (see Table 2.15).

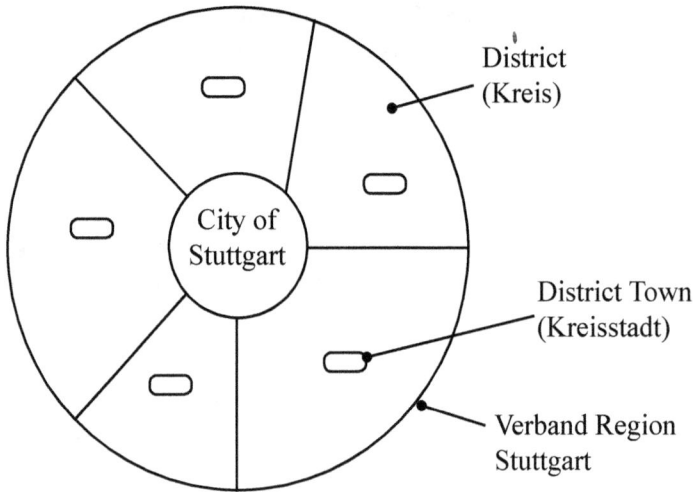

Figure 2.1: The multi-level governance system of the Stuttgart region

The Kreisstädte maintain an astonishing number of city partnerships, compared to the Swiss agglomeration communities. All of the Kreisstädte are involved in at least three partnerships; Esslingen is involved in ten. The partnerships were formed in two general waves. Many of them date back to the early 1950s and were formed in the aftermath of the Second World War; this formed the first phase of the Kreisstädte's partnerships. These contacts were established to bring together peo-

---

103 For efficiency reasons, it was not possible to investigate the international activities of the sixty communities within the city-region of Stuttgart that each contains more than 10,000 inhabitants. The study was limited to the cities that had significant political influence (as core cities of the sub-regions).

104 Some of the districts are also engaged in partnerships with foreign communities and/or regions. Thus, all layers of government in the city-region of Stuttgart are engaged on the international scale. However, the international contacts of the districts were not investigated any further, since these contacts do not seem to be connected to any international activities, neither those of the communities nor those of the Region Stuttgart.

ple of formerly enemy countries. The second phase transpired in the early 1990s, when German cities increasingly engaged in partnerships with cities from Eastern Europe in order to help them on the communal level and to promote Western European standards.

The Kreisstädte's international city partnerships are all independent from those of the city of Stuttgart. The cities carry them out independently, and neither side has pursued any inclusion of the other in its city partnerships or networking activities. However, the contacts are more closely involved in the Climate Alliance network. Although three of the five Kreisstädte are members of that network, none of them employ the large workforce necessary to participate regularly in the international meetings. The Kreisstädte's membership is mostly symbolic, and its contacts are only carried out through the Internet. The city of Stuttgart is the only actor within the region that is large enough to participate in the network's international meetings. The Kreisstädte often delegate members of Stuttgart's administration to participate in the international conference, informing them how to vote for the community. The Kreisstädte also maintain informal contacts through following up the international conferences, when the persons responsible for the cities' environments contact each other. Thus, there is a certain coherence of the position of the cities of the Stuttgart area in their cooperation within the Climate Alliance. This understanding is informal, and the city of Stuttgart has never used its predominant role within the network against the agglomeration communities, possibly due to its reluctance to cooperate within the Climate Alliance.

Table 2.15: The international activities of the district towns in the agglomeration of Stuttgart

German city	Partner city/cities
Esslingen	Vienne (France), Neath (Great Britain), Eger (Hungary), Udine (Italy), Schiedam (Netherlands), Piotrkow (Poland), Norrköping (Sweden), Velenja (Slovakia), Sheboygan (USA), Molodetschno (Belarus) Climate Alliance
Göppingen	Klosterneuburg (Austria), Foggia (Italy), Pessac (France)
Ludwigsburg	Montbéliard (France), Caerphilly (Great Britain), Jevpatorija (Ukraine), St. Charles (USA) Climate Alliance
Waiblingen	Jesi (Italy), Baja (Hungary), Devizes (Great Britain), Mayenne (France) Climate Alliance
Böblingen	Bergama (Turkey), Geleen (Netherlands), Alba (Italy), Glenrothes (Great Britain), Pontoise (France), Krans (Austria)

Some attempt has been made to include the agglomeration communities within Stuttgart's engagement in the URB-AL project on mobility. In the initiation phase, when Stuttgart hosted one of the network's first conferences, the city invited the agglomeration communities to participate. The response to the invitation was very modest, and the city later decided not to follow up on the possible inclusion of the agglomeration communities. This led to dissatisfaction from the one agglomeration community that was interested in further collaboration within the URB-AL project. Within the city's other international contacts (both partnerships and networking), the agglomeration communities are not included, and no effort to include them in the near future is planned.

Vertical governance

Relations between the city and the region of Stuttgart

The Stuttgart region with its own (relatively small) administration is also active in international networking. The Stuttgart region has some authority in the policy areas of economic promotion, public transportation, and spatial planning. Consequently, the region is active on the international scale within those policy areas. The region is a member of seven thematic networks, and it maintains an office in Brussels to lobby at the EU (see Table 2.16).

Table 2.16: The international activities of the Stuttgart region

International Activity	Description	Categorisation
IRE	Cities* cooperating in location promotion	Thematic network
EURADA	Cities cooperating in location promotion	Thematic network
METREX	City-regions cooperating in spatial planning	Thematic network
CIVITAS	Cities cooperating in transport policy	Thematic network
EMTA	Cities cooperating in transport policy	Thematic network
POLIS	Cities cooperating in transport policy	Thematic network
URB-AL Nr. 8	Cities cooperating in transport policy	Thematic network
EU-Delegate	Multi-thematic lobbying activity	Lobbying

*   Although the region cooperates in the international network, I use the term city because cities are the most common actors within international networks. The membership of a regional metropolitan governance structure is certainly an exception within most networks.

Although there is no formal coordination office for international activities within the Stuttgart region, the director himself coordinates these diverse activities, and presides over one of the transnational city networks (see below).[105] The decision to enter international cooperation schemes was made in 2000, when an evaluation of the region's activities concluded that the region's international presence was underdeveloped (Verband Region Stuttgart 2000). Before that decision, efforts had been dedicated to establishing the metropolitan government, and the region's international contacts had been neglected. Thereafter, the director of the region proposed the region's participation within certain networking activities (see next section). The regional parliament accepted his proposal, with some budgetary shortcuts (Verband Region Stuttgart 2001).

The Stuttgart region is engaged in two international networks that deal with the locational politics of city-regions. It joined the EURADA network in 2001. In this network, business development agencies cooperate on benchmarking and best practices. In the mid-1990s, the European Commission set up the Innovative Regions Europe (IRE) network, which endeavoured to establish regional innovation policies throughout European regions, in close collaboration with EU institutions.

The Stuttgart region joined the METREX network in 2001. This network of large metropolitan areas deals with spatial planning issues, and its cooperation within this network helped the region determine its new role in spatial planning. The head of the region's administration was also the director of the METREX network for several years.

The Stuttgart region is a member of four networks that address transport issues. The region participated in the URB-AL network nr. 8 on urban mobility, which the city of Stuttgart coordinated. Currently, the region of Stuttgart is not participating in the follow-up network Cities for Mobility, which the city of Stuttgart established (see above). The region of Stuttgart is also a member of the POLIS, CIVITAS, and EMTA networks, which deal with problems of urban and metropolitan mobility. Whereas the Stuttgart region is an individual member of the EMTA network, which focuses on public transport, both the city and the region of Stuttgart are members of the POLIS and CIVITAS networks, which deal with mobility more generally.

The Stuttgart region decided, in 2001, to send its own delegate to the EU in Brussels. Policy-makers noted the EU's increasing influence on metropolitan regions and the possibility of gaining access to EU funding programmes and therefore decided that a Stuttgart lobbyist in Brussels would support the region's general strategy of increased competitiveness (Schreiber 2007: 7; Verband Region Stuttgart 2001).

The international engagement of the region of Stuttgart is due to its perceived need to legitimise its own existence. This task is difficult to achieve within the region since several communities and especially the city of Stuttgart do not favour the regional coordination structure. Thus, the region of Stuttgart sees its interna-

---

105   The director of the region of Stuttgart also used to be the head of the 'initiative of European
       metropolitan regions in Europe' (Initiativkreis Europäische Metropolregionen in Deutschland).

tional contacts as a justification for its existence. The region is internationally connected in all policy areas in which it has some competences, and it thereby tries to provide additional benefits for the Stuttgart area.

The international activities of the region of Stuttgart clearly focus on the city-region's competitive position. The region's primary goal is to promote Stuttgart's international visibility as an economic cluster that has a strong focus on the automobile industry. Unsurprisingly, as in the city of Stuttgart, the region's international contacts focus on networking in transport policy. Another core competence of the region is its international cooperation in locational politics. The head of the administration of the region of Stuttgart explicitly refers to the Lisbon competitiveness goals of the EU in order to legitimise the existence of an internationally oriented metropolitan government (Initiativkreis Europäische Metropolregionen in Deutschland 2006: 1; Steinacher 2006: 3). Because one of the two networks in locational politics, IRE, is more closely related to EU policy-making, and because of the perceived importance of the EU in urban locational politics, the Stuttgart region shifted its attention away from the EURADA network and towards the IRE network.

Policy-makers generally describe the relationship between the city and the regional level as conflictive, and this manifests itself in their respective international contacts. Although these international contacts focus on the same policy areas, there is hardly any cooperation between the two scales. The city of Stuttgart and the region of Stuttgart compete regarding international networking. This is quite astonishing, considering both scales' active participation in urban networking and both scales' goal of increasing the city-region's international competitiveness. The city does not want to share the revenues from its international contacts with the agglomeration communities, and the region of Stuttgart does not treat the core city preferentially through its own international contacts. This leads to a special situation; the city and the region of Stuttgart belong simultaneously to two international networks that address transport issues (POLIS and CIVITAS). Both scales have some policy competences in this field, and they both perceive international networking in the domain of transport as important for their competitive advantages. Table 2.17 provides an overview of their partially overlapping international contacts.

Interestingly, the two scales conflict less on the administrative level. Policy-makers who deal with public transport informally share the knowledge they gain from their international contacts, and there is even an informal division of labour between the two scales. Whereas the city is more active in the POLIS network, the region focuses on cooperating within the CIVITAS and EMTA networks. The city also dominates the city-region's cooperation within the URB-AL project nr.8, on urban mobility; the region is only included occasionally. It is thus not surprising that the region does not participate in or intend to become a member of the follow-up project Cities for Mobility, which is also clearly dominated by the city. The political conflict between the city and the region has fostered increased international networking on the regional scale.

Table 2.17: The (partially overlapping) international activities of the city and the Stuttgart region

Network	The City of Stuttgart	The Stuttgart Region
Cities for Children	x	
Cities for Mobility	x	
CIVITAS	x	x
Climate Alliance	x	
CLIP	x	
EMTA		x
Energie-Cités	x	
EURADA		x
IRE		x
METREX		x
POLIS	x	x
UCLG	x	
URB-AL	x	x
Total	9	7

In conclusion, the existence of a metropolitan government has led to an increase in the city-region's international contacts. However, the Stuttgart region directly carries out these contacts, and the agglomeration communities are hardly involved. The contacts of the city-region of Stuttgart are in competition with those of the city of Stuttgart. Thus, there is an internal conflict between the city and the region regarding the lead in international contacts.

Relations with the Land
Apart from the conflictive relations between the city and the region of Stuttgart, the city-region's relation with the upper-level German government is not particularly relevant to its international contacts. Although there is some cooperation in the two scales' contacts with the EU, since the Land Baden-Württemberg has its own office in Brussels,[106] there is no inclusion in other networking activities or in city partnerships. Stuttgart tries to overcome the traditional multi-level governance scheme through its international contacts. The vice-director of Stuttgart's department for European and international affairs explains the city-region's changed scalar orientation:

---

106 However, Blatter (2006: 136) mentions that the region's creation of a separate office in Brussels was not appreciated by the Land, at first.

If one has a scalar strategy, you do not have to look at the close-by cities Karlsruhe or Mannheim, this leads to nothing. And also not to the national scale, this is not the scale to look at anymore if you want to progress, you have to be international [...]. We have to look at Barcelona or at Lyon.

(Vice-director of the Department for European and International Affairs)

The contacts between the city of Stuttgart and the Land Baden-Württemberg are somewhat different from those between the Stuttgart region and the Land. The policy-makers of the city do not see any conflict with the Land regarding the city's international activities. The region, however, maintains its own office in Brussels and uses its direct contact with the EU against the Land. This is part of a general strategy against a rurally oriented Land that, according to involved policy-makers, neglects urban areas, especially the metropolitan area of Stuttgart.

Relations with the federal state
The city-region of Stuttgart's connections with the national state concerning its international activities are scarce. Within development aid, cooperation between the two scales became more prominent in 2006. Within the project One World (see above), the city of Stuttgart cooperates closely with the Deutsche Gesellschaft für Technische Zusammenarbeit, i.e. German Organisation for Technical Cooperation (GTZ), which is a branch of the national state that deals with development aid (Landeshauptstadt Stuttgart 2007). One staff member of the GTZ has worked in Stuttgart's town hall since 2006, coordinating between the city and the national state regarding their respective development aid projects. No other international cooperation schemes of Stuttgart include the national scale.

In several aspects, the city of Stuttgart is somewhat isolated within Germany, since most other city-regions are different regarding economic orientation and success. Stuttgart, as an industrial city in need of qualified immigration, is in a unique situation that differs from most other German cities' situations, especially East German cities that face economic decline and high unemployment rates (Oswalt and Rienits 2006). This has lead the city of Stuttgart to initiate the two networks CLIP and Cities for Children, through which Stuttgart wanted to profit from best practices in the policy areas of urban immigration and family politics. Stuttgart saw an international cooperation on this topic as more fruitful than one within Germany's traditional multi-level governance system. However, the city-region's dissatisfaction with the traditional multi-level governance scheme has led neither the city nor the region of Stuttgart to use its international contacts against the national scale. Stuttgart's increased engagement in international cooperation schemes does not correspond to its changed relationship towards upper-level governments, since the city-region's international contacts are not used against the national state.

Relations with the EU
The EU's involvement in the Stuttgart region's international activities is significant. On the one hand, the EU finances many of the city-region's international contacts. On the other hand, the EU is the addressee of many of these activities. Both

Stuttgart's city partnerships and its interurban networks benefit from the EU's co-financing. Even the smaller agglomeration communities have maximised this opportunity to gain partial EU funding for their partnership activities, as has the city of Stuttgart. The URB-AL project nr. 8 on urban mobility, which the city of Stuttgart directed, was completely financed by the EU, and the two international networks on mobility (POLIS and CIVITAS) are partially financed by the EU as well. Thus, the EU directly impacts the local level's international contacts. Although all policy-makers think that the application process for acquiring funding for international activities at the city-region scale is relatively complex, most of them have successfully obtained funding at one time or another. The city of Stuttgart strategically assesses all possibilities for acquiring EU co-financing, not only through its international contacts but also through urban policy-making in general.

Stuttgart uses its international contacts to access the EU, mainly through interurban networks; therefore, the city and the region of Stuttgart are more involved than the smaller agglomeration communities. The region of Stuttgart even decided to set up its own office in Brussels in order to influence the heart of the EU's decision-making processes. Although the city does not rely on such direct contacts but rather prefers making regular policy-specific visits to Brussels, it closely monitors the decisions on the EU scale that are relevant for Stuttgart. The city also tries to participate proactively in the EU's decision-making process when its interests could be affected by a possible new EU regulation. The CIVITAS, POLIS, and EMTA networks lobby at the EU scale for projects on urban mobility. Participating in these networks grants Stuttgart easier access to the EU's decision-making process in this policy area, and the EU often co-finances the city networks' common projects. The same change of a network's orientation happened within the Climate Alliance, where the network itself applied for EU funding for a project of its member cities. Stuttgart participated in this EU-funded cooperation. City networks therefore link the EU and the city-region scales in two directions, both from the EU to the city-region of Stuttgart and from the city-region of Stuttgart to the EU.

Short summary
The city of Stuttgart has increased the intensity of its international activities since 2002. This increase is based on the city-region's economic need to connect its workplace, which is dependent on the automobile industry, to the global scale. This has led Stuttgart not only to orient itself towards existing interurban networks on mobility but also to create additional ones in its areas of economic need (mobility, immigration, and youth policy). The city's mayor initiated the change towards competition-oriented international activities and towards accessing the EU scale.

The metropolitan government of the Stuttgart region has also increased its international contacts since 2001. Although the region's international networking is also oriented towards competitiveness and access to the EU, the region and the city of Stuttgart compete for predominance on the international scale. There is hardly any cooperation between the district towns and the city of Stuttgart regarding international contacts. The involvement of the Land and of the national state in the international activities of both the city and the region are also minimal.

A FIRST OVERVIEW: THE NETWORK'S SIDE

Although the international strategies of the city-regions are at the core of this analysis, the partnerships and the networks will be examined first. Table 2.18 presents an overview of the first element of urban foreign policy: city partnerships. The partnerships of the seven core cities[107] under scrutiny are divided along the provenances of their partner cities.

Only one of the seven core cities, Stuttgart, has established partnerships with African cities. Most partnerships are with other European city-regions. Four of the seven city-regions under scrutiny have American partner cities, and three of them have at least one Asian partner city each. The rows also show each city-region's number of partner cities. The two city-regions from EU member states, Lyon and Stuttgart, are very active in this respect, maintaining seven and nine partnerships respectively. Among the Swiss cities, only Lucerne maintains a large number of partnerships (six), and Berne, Geneva, and Lausanne have no partner cities at all.

Interurban networks are the second element of urban foreign policy. Table 2.19, which presents an overview of all the international networking activities of the seven city-regions under scrutiny, reveals two important conclusions. First, the rows illustrate how many city-regions are members of the listed international urban networks. There is considerable variety among the networks' membership structures. This aspect will be further analysed later in this section. Second, the columns note the number of international networks in which each city-region participates. Again, there is a considerable variety among the city-regions' engagement in international networks. This aspect will be discussed further in the first section of the next chapter.

Table 2.19 shows that many of the thirty-three analysed networks have only one or two members from the chosen seven city-regions. This is partly because of Swiss city-regions' generally greater reluctance to engage in international networks and partly because the two city-regions of Lyon and Stuttgart are generally not members of the same interurban networks. Thus, few international city networks have broad membership bases among the seven city-regions. Additionally, most city-regions pursue international engagement in networks that are specific to their individual economic and policy interests, and since each city-region specialises in a different area, it also participates in different networks. The only international city network that has five member cities out of the current sample is UCLG. This is somewhat surprising since all cities in Europe are already indirectly members of the UCLG network through their respective national city organisations. However, because the network is also open for individual membership and because it is viewed as an important lobby for cities on the global scale, five of the seven cities under scrutiny have joined the network as individual members. The city of Stuttgart shows the highest engagement in this lobby network since its mayor leads the network's European section and serves on the international executive board.

---

107 Here, the comparative analysis has been limited to the partnerships of the core cities because the seven city-regions under scrutiny differ too widely concerning their numbers of agglomeration communities. Considering all the partnership activities of every community in the seven city-regions under scrutiny would skew the comparison.

Table 2.18: An overview of the city partnerships of the seven core cities under scrutiny

Provenance of Partner City \ Core city	Berne	Geneva	Lausanne	Lucerne	Zurich	Lyon	Stuttgart	Total
Africa	–	–	–	–	–	–	2	2
America	–	–	–	1	1	1	1	4
Asia	–	–	–	–	1	3	2	6
Europe	–	–	–	5	–	3	4	12
Total	0	0	0	6	2	7	9	

The network that boasts the second-most members from the sample is the Climate Alliance. This network also provides the clearest example of another astonishing conclusion; there is a clear language gap in international urban networking. The four member cities of the Climate Alliance network from the sample are all German-speaking cities, whereas the three French-speaking cities from the sample are absent from the network. In fact, this closely aligns with the general orientation of the Climate Alliance network, which has a large membership base in German-speaking countries. The network has only few member cities from countries other than Germany, Switzerland, and Austria.

The French-speaking cities are much more actively engaged in the Energie-Cités network. The language gap is less clear in this network, however, since the city of Stuttgart joined this network recently and since the network's membership structure, in general, is quite diversified concerning the national provenances of its member cities. Nevertheless, two networks operate in the same general policy domain; although the activities within these two networks overlap considerably, their membership is mostly divided along language borders. Stuttgart is the only city under scrutiny that is a member of both networks.

The same is true for the membership structure of the Les Rencontres network. Within this network, which is dominated by French-speaking cities, the two French-speaking cities Lausanne and Lyon are members, but none of the German-speaking cities participate. The involved policy-makers explain this discrepancy by noting the parties' different approaches to state cultural politics. Whereas culture in English-or German-speaking countries is considered to be controlled by private actors, the public state primarily coordinates and finances cultural activities in the French state system. Since this understanding of the state's influence in cultural policy strongly affects a city's international networking, Les Rencontres focuses on French-speaking cities that share an understanding of the state's role in cultural politics.

The same language barrier is evident in IAEC. Barcelona established this network, which has an incredible number of member cities in Spain, France, Portugal, and Italy. However, only one is in Germany and none are in Great Britain, and the member cities from France have formed their own national sub-section of the network. Again, the only Swiss member city, Geneva, is from the French-speaking part of Switzerland.

Clearly, the interurban networks compete with each other, as suggested by Leitner and Sheppard (1999). A few networks operate in the same policy domain, resulting in a competition for member cities. A broader membership base not only creates more revenue but also gives the network greater legitimacy to represent the interests of its member cities in its particular policy field. Networks therefore have a clear incentive to compete for members. The most striking example of this phenomenon is the competition between the OWHC network, which deals with the preservation of sites recognised by UNESCO as having world heritage, and the OWC network, in which cities cooperate to preserve their historical sites that are not recognised as world heritage by UNESCO.[108] Whereas Berne and Lyon are members of the OWHC network, Geneva is a member of the OWC network since its old town has not been termed a historical site by UNESCO. Clearly, the OWC network provides a platform for the city-regions that want to cooperate in the OWHC network's domain. Since entrance to the latter network is closed for cities that lack a UNESCO world heritage, such cities created another method of interurban networking for the preservation of historical sites by setting up their own network.

The networks also compete in the domain of environmental politics (see also Keiner and Kim 2007; Schmid *et al.* 2007), although these networks are not as closely related as the previously mentioned networks for historic preservation. Among the three international interurban networks on environmental politics, the global city network ICLEI has the broadest scope, whereas the Climate Alliance network focuses more on urban areas' reduction of CO_2 emissions. The Energie-Cités network is even further specialised in urban energy policy. Although the scopes of the three networks differ, their activities overlap. The ICLEI network's activities include addressing the more specific goals of the other two networks. The involved policy-makers, however, perceive the ICLEI network as too global in its orientation, which makes policy learning among the member cities more difficult than in a more regionally restricted network such as the Climate Alliance or Energie-Cités.

The membership structures of the seven city-regions in environmental networks are quite heterogeneous. Whereas all four German-speaking cities are members of the Climate Alliance network, only Zurich and Geneva are members of the more international network ICLEI. The French-dominated Energie-Cités

---

108 Another example of this phenomenon was the competition between the ECDP network of cities that followed a more liberal drug policy and the ECAD network of cities that proposed a more abstinence-oriented drug policy. Three of the cities under scrutiny were among the members of the ECDP network. None of the seven cities under scrutiny has ever belonged to the ECAD network.

Table 2.19: An overview of the networking activities of the seven city-regions under scrutiny

Network \ City-region	Berne	Geneva	Lausanne	Lucerne	Zurich	Lyon*	Stuttgart**	Total
AIMF		x	x			x		3
Banlieues d'Europe						x		1
Cities for Children	x				x		x	3
Cities for Mobility							x	1
Citynet/Proact						x		1
CIVITAS							x	1
Climate Alliance	x			x	x		x	4
CLIP							x	1
CVA					x			1
DELICE			x			x		2
ECDP	x			x	x			3
EMTA						x	x	2
Energie-Cités		x	x				x	3
EURADA						x	x	2
Eurocities		x			x	x		3
GCD/GDS		x				x		2
IAEC		x				x		2
IAPMC		x						1
ICLEI		x			x			2
IFGRA			x					1
IRE						x	x	2
Les Rencontres		x	x			x		3
LUCI		x				x		2
METREX					x		x	2
OWHC	x					x		2
POLIS							x	1
UCLG		x	x		x	x	x	5
UCP		x				x		2
URB-AL							x	1
UMVO			x					1
WHC		x						1
Total	4	12	7	2	8	15	13	

* Along with Grand Lyon (see pages 99ff.).

** Along with the region of Stuttgart (see pages 114ff.). Although it is somewhat problematic, since the city and the region of Stuttgart do not share their memberships in international networks, their activities are merged here in order to enhance comparability among the seven city-regions. See Table 2.17 to view the city's and region's memberships in international networks.

network boasts Lausanne, Geneva, and very recently Stuttgart among its members. Lyon is the only city-region that is completely absent from environmental international interurban networks.

Two additional networks that operate in the same policy field of locational politics are IRE and EURADA. Although there are small differences in their scalar orientations (e.g. the IRE network is more oriented towards the EU), the two networks clearly compete for members. Stuttgart and Lyon are members of both networks, but policy-makers in both city-regions perceive their activities in the two networks as duplications, and they are considering withdrawing from one of the two networks. Interestingly, none of the Swiss city-regions under scrutiny is a member of any of these international networks that deal with urban locational politics.

This focus on non-competitiveness-oriented networks is the current study's most important finding from the networking side of urban foreign policy. The Swiss city-regions are absent from the above mentioned networks on urban locational politics, and only a very few networks deal with the competitive position of urban areas. Neither the policy networks nor the more general lobby networks are primarily oriented towards locational politics. Rather, the networks cooperate in almost all policy domains of urban politics, without a clear focus on either competitiveness, social issues, or ecological matters.

So far, this analysis aligns with the scholars who have linked the trend towards increased interurban cooperation with a general hope for a more sociopolitical, rather than economic, orientation of urban politics in rescaled statehoods (see Heeg *et al.* 2003). However, as will be shown in the following chapter, this preliminary conclusion is misleading. The perspective of the involved city-regions will be addressed next. This will facilitate a better understanding of the motives for interurban networking, which are much more closely related to competitiveness goals than the analysis from the network's perspective might predict.

chapter three | why do city-regions go global?

After presenting the case study results, I will now conduct a comparative analysis along the theoretical model presented in Chapter One. This chapter will begin by addressing the determinants of a city-region's foreign policy. An elaboration of the intrascalar and interscalar changes in city-regions' international activities will follow in Chapter Four. This chapter will first discuss the macro theoretical analysis of the rescaling approach, then the varieties of capitalism approach on the meso level. These two approaches will be coordinated at the end of this chapter.

GLOBALISATION AND THE RESCALING OF THE STATE

The analysis along the macro theoretical rescaling approach will start with an investigation of the intensity of city-regions' international activities. The general proposition from the rescaling theory was an increase in the intensity of city-region's international activities in the age of globalisation. Thereafter, the content of urban foreign policy will be examined. My first hypothesis predicted an increased economic orientation of such international activities. I will then further investigate the discrepant conclusions regarding competitiveness orientation from the network's side and from the city-region's side.

Increasing global connectivity

In an examination of the intensity of the seven city-regions' urban foreign policies, a variety of engagement strategies are apparent (see Table 3.1 and again Table 2.19). Berne is only a member of four international activities, whereas the other Swiss cities pursue between seven and twelve international activities. However, all the examined Swiss cities lag considerably behind the two EU city-regions, which manage twenty-two international activities each.

Table 3.2 offers a first overview of the findings along the rescaling approach. The rescaling approach proposed that city-regions would increase their international activities. To clarify this further, the period of the increase was specified because the time dimension is closely linked to the intensity of international activities. City-regions that have long-standing traditions of international contacts will most likely engage in more international activities. Indeed, six out of the seven city-regions under scrutiny have increased their international activities. However, the analysis did not confirm the rescaling approach's hypothesis that the international activities of city-regions have economic orientations.

For analytical purposes, the two forms of urban foreign policy (networking and city partnerships) will be treated independently here, and the two aspects will be merged in a second step.

Table 3.1: Summary of the networking activities of the seven city-regions under scrutiny

Int. act. \ City-region	Berne	Geneva	Lausanne	Lucerne	Zurich	Lyon	Stuttgart
Thematic networks*	4	9	5	2	6	11	12
Lobby networks	-	3	2	-	2	4	1
City partnerships	-	-	-	6	2	7	9
Total	4	12	7	8	10	22	22

* I did count all the memberships here, even though the case study sections did not include the networks in which the observed cities established memberships after the period of my investigation. I only include the partnerships of the core cities here.

Table 3.2: Increase of economically-oriented international activities

City-region	Increase of international activities	Time period of increase	Direct economic orientation of international activities
Berne	–	–	–
Geneva	✓	Since late 1980s	–
Lausanne	✓	Very recently	–
Lucerne	✓	1978002	–
Zurich	✓	Very recently	–
Lyon	✓	Since late 1990s	(Partly)
Stuttgart	✓	Since 2002	(Partly)

Looking first at the city-regions' engagement in interurban networking, the seven city-regions can be divided into three categories according to the intensity of their international activities. First, the two city-regions of Lucerne and Berne only incidentally became members of an international network. Currently, they are only very reluctantly engaged in interurban networking, as demonstrated by their two and four memberships respectively. Lucerne predominantly focuses its international engagement on partnerships, not networking. Berne has only two networking activities and no partnership engagement and is therefore the only city-region under scrutiny that does not act in accordance with the general tendency of an increase in city-regions' international activities.

Second, some city-regions have only recently discovered interurban networking as an element of urban policy-making. This is the case for Lausanne and Zurich. Both city-regions are currently developing strategies for their international activities, and they both became members of several international networks only very recently. The city of Lausanne has even established two new interurban networks in the domains of its economic interests. Lausanne is currently a member of seven and Zurich of eight international urban networks.

Third, in some city-regions, international activities are already well-established and are integral parts of urban policy-making. This is the case for Geneva, Lyon, and Stuttgart. Geneva started its international engagement back in the 1980s and, for a long time, was the only Swiss city-region that pursued considerable international engagement. Geneva is currently a member of twelve international city networks. Lyon also has a long-standing tradition of international engagement, and this tendency has increased recently through the amalgamation of the separate services for the international contacts of the city and the region of Lyon. Taking both scales together, the city-region of Lyon is a member of no less than fifteen international networks, which is the highest number for any of the seven city-regions under scrutiny. Stuttgart has also increased its international engagement within the last decade. The city and the region of Stuttgart are together members of a total of thirteen international city networks.[1]

The second form of urban foreign policy is partnerships, and the general picture of the two EU city-regions' greater engagement in international activities than their Swiss counterparts remains intact (see again Table 3.1). The French city of Lyon, with seven partnerships, and the German city of Stuttgart, with nine city partnerships, are only challenged by Lucerne, which has six partnerships. In general, the Swiss cities' reluctance to engage in city partnerships is astonishing. Berne, Lausanne, and Geneva all actively refuse to enter city partnerships. Geneva and Lausanne refuse because of their commitments to international organisations to engage in city partnerships. Berne's refusal is related to its role as Switzerland's capital city. Considering city partnerships thus widen the gap between the EU city-regions, which have long-standing traditions of urban foreign policy, and the Swiss city-regions, which are generally still reluctant to engage in international activities (with the exception of Geneva).[2]

Thus, one conclusion of this analysis is that Swiss city-regions still lag considerably behind their EU counterparts regarding international connectivity. The rescaling theory's prediction that city-regions have increased their international engagements must be viewed in its proper context, and it cannot be generalised for all city-regions. A city-region's international activities are not necessarily part of an increased steering capacity at the city-region's scale, due to the process of 'glocalisation'.

---

1   As already mentioned, taking the international activities of the city and the region of Stuttgart together is somewhat misleading since the two scales compete rather than cooperate on their international contacts. This aspect is addressed in more detail on pages 167ff.

2   And partially with the exception of Lucerne, but only concerning partnerships.

This argument is true for the two EU city-regions under scrutiny, Lyon and Stuttgart, and for the Swiss city-region of Geneva. It is partially true for Lausanne and Zurich, although these city-regions have only very recently discovered the possibilities of urban foreign policy. It is still uncertain whether these two city-regions will catch up with the general trend of interurban networking or whether their recent attempts will remain their only activities. The city-region of Berne is completely absent from this trend and therefore does not follow the rescaling theory's proposition. Lucerne, with its focus on city partnerships rather than on networking, follows a comparatively exotic strategy. What Lefèvre and d'Albergo (2007: 318) called the convergence theory is only partially supported by this analysis. Although most of the city-regions under scrutiny have increased their international activities, there is still considerable variety among their methods of increase and involvement, and one city-region (Berne) totally avoids this convergence path.

The analysis of the rescaling theory's proposition thus produces a mixed and rather unclear picture. Although the rescaling theory is generally correct to assume an increase of city-regions' international activities, the various strategies regarding the content of these developments is still somewhat puzzling. As will be shown subsequently, this can be tackled theoretically only by incorporating the varieties of capitalism approach into the argument. First, however, the first hypothesis will be analysed, which was deduced from the rescaling approach.

Social cohesion at a first glance

The first hypothesis, deducted from the rescaling theory, predicted a direct economic orientation of the city-regions' international activities. It was noted that it was theoretically unclear whether the increased steering capacity at the city-region scale is used as part of a counter-strategy against neo-liberal policies or whether city-regions use their new competences to engage in increased interurban competition. A distinction is made between social and economic orientations of city-regions' international activities.

According to neo-Marxist scholars (such as Harvey 1989; Keil 2003; Swyngedouw 1997), it would be ideal for city-regions to increase their networking in social domains due to their increased steering capacity in the age of globalisation. However, the hypothesis was extracted from the more pessimistic strand of the rescaling approach, stating that the international activities are part of the turn towards urban entrepreneurialism and that they directly focus on economic questions. The empirical analysis does not support this conclusion (see Table 3.2).

As mentioned in the previous section on the analysis from the networks' angle, many networks do not deal with economic questions. Consequently, the same is true for the city-regions engaged in those networks. Their engagement is much more diversified than was expected. The city-regions under scrutiny cooperate in several policy domains, many of which are entirely unrelated to economic questions or locational politics. The international activities of city-regions are therefore not *per se* devoted to questions of economic competitiveness. As will be argued later, however, the involved policy-makers intend to pursue economic benefits even though the content of the city-regions' international activities is not specifically oriented towards competitiveness.

The clearest example that disproves the rescaling theory's hypothesis is the case of Geneva. The only Swiss city that has a long-established tradition of international cooperation does not focus on economic questions in its networking activities. On the contrary, Geneva predominantly focuses on issues of international peace and solidarity, and it has even created new networks in these domains. Lausanne, through its recent founding of international interurban networks, has also positioned itself in its particular fields (sport and sustainability), not in urban competitiveness or locational politics. The other Swiss city-regions also maintain many city partnerships and networking activities that never or rarely address questions of competitiveness directly.

Only the two EU city-regions (partially) focus directly on economic issues in their international contacts. Both city-regions are members of the two international networks that deal with locational politics (IRE and EURADA), and they both have shifted the outline of their established partnerships from traditional exchanges on the political level to cooperation schemes that emphasise economic exchanges and the establishment of business relations. Stuttgart has strongly shifted the orientation of its international contacts towards a strategy of increased competitiveness. The old established city partnerships were reoriented and are now partially used to establish economic contacts with emerging markets. The policy-makers in charge of Stuttgart's international contacts based their decision to form new networks on an analysis of the area's economic needs. This led to the creation of three networks; one in the domain of mobility, one dealing with youth policy and one dealing with immigration policy. The later aspects are seen as domains in which Stuttgart should profit from best practices in other urban areas due to the city's economic need to become friendly both to children and to immigrants.

The city-region of Lyon has followed a somewhat similar path in reorienting its long-established international contacts. Here too, city partnerships are increasingly seen as a gate-opener for economic contacts. The prominent and dominant discourse on becoming one of the top fifteen European metropolitan areas has affected most of the city's networking activities. In new activities, such as the city's candidacy to become the European capital of culture in 2013, and in already established networking activities, such as within the Les Rencontres network on cultural politics or within the lobby network Eurocities, the city's international strategy is oriented towards competitiveness. However, even Lyon and Stuttgart are active in numerous city networks that never address questions of competitiveness or economic matters.

Therefore, the empirical analysis does not confirm the first hypothesis, derived from the rescaling approach, which assumed a primary orientation towards economic issues in interurban networking. According to a first glance, the rescaling theory is therefore wrong to assume a general and coherent path towards neo-liberal policy-making on the urban level, at least in the content of the city-regions' international activities.

However, it would be too early to assume that interurban networking is a means of strengthening the political steering capacity of city-regions in social cohesion through policy cooperation on these matters. As will be argued later, the international activities closely align with the turn towards urban entrepreneurialism, but in an indirect way. This argument will become clearer after the analysis that uses the varieties of capitalism approach. Meanwhile, the question remains; why do city-regions only very reluctantly engage in interurban networking on matters of competitiveness and locational politics?

The illogicality of cooperation in competition

It is inherently logical that city-regions do not cooperate on economic matters. Through interurban networking, a single city-region not only learns from the other city-regions participating in the network but also necessarily provides information to the other city-regions about its own activities in that policy area. Policy learning, which has been mentioned repeatedly as one of the main goals of interurban networking (see Keiner and Kim 2007; Kübler and Piliutyte 2007: 367; Ward and Williams 1997: 461), is only possible if best practice examples exist within the respective network. Bluntly, there must be someone to learn from, or else there is nothing to learn.

The lead city-regions within such networks strategically reflect upon their willingness to provide the information basis that will allow other city-regions to catch up with them. Policy learning will necessarily lead to an equalisation in the respective policy fields, with a tendency to copy best practices from lead city-regions. Whereas this does not pose any problems to lead city-regions in policy fields in which there is no or only little competition among city-regions (e.g. public transport),[3] it becomes problematic when city-regions are expected to provide information on their best practices in policy areas in which they directly compete with other city-regions in the network. Sharing knowledge on best practices would necessarily lead to a diminution of the competitive advantage of the lead city-regions in these policy areas. The motivation to cooperate is thus weaker in proportion to the strength of the concerned policy area's relation to the competitive advantages of the involved city-regions (see also Keating 2001: 386).

Therefore, too many authors have assumed too easily that policy learning is automatically an achievable and desirable goal of interurban networking. Results from the seven city-regions under scrutiny prove that policy learning in city networks is not automatic. Perhaps an analysis of city-regions' international activities should instead start from Betsill and Bulkeley's (2004: 471) pessimistic conclusion 'that those local governments most effectively engaged with the network are mobilised more by the financial and political resources it offers'.

---

3   This is of course an oversimplification, since connectivity through public transport is increasingly seen as an element of the competitiveness of urban areas (see Kübler *et al.* 2007). However, policy-makers dealing with public transport only very rarely perceive that policy area as linked to questions of competitiveness. Therefore, knowledge sharing on these matters is still relatively easy.

It is thus no surprise that the involved policy-makers view interurban networking as most difficult in the policy field of locational politics. Here, the involved city-regions are very reluctant to provide information on their strategies for attracting enterprises to their area. They view the other city-regions that participate in these networks as competitors, not partners. The policy-makers engaged in interurban networking on locational politics from Lyon and from Stuttgart mention that both city-regions joined networks to learn from others about their operations within locational politics. However, they also both admitted to avoiding the provision of full information about their own strategies and organisations to these international interurban networks. This rational type of strategy leads necessarily to a strategic unwillingness of all participating city-regions to share information on these matters.

In many other policy areas, the policy-makers involved in international networking are much less reluctant to share their experiences because they do not perceive losing their competitive advantage through sharing best practices. One of the main reasons why city-regions do not cooperate on questions of urban locational politics, as predicted by the rescaling approach, is thus the inherent logic that cooperation is most difficult where competition is highest (see also Parkinson and Harding 1995: 55). The partnership of Lucerne with Bournemouth is a clear example of this logic. Soon after its initiation, Lucerne tried to promote itself as a region attractive for tourists from the Bournemouth area. Because Bournemouth itself was trying to establish itself as a tourist region, cooperation between the two cities became inherently problematic and nearly stopped. Only when the city partnership was shifted away from tourism towards non-competitive issues was cooperation again possible.

Therefore, the conclusion of Ramasamy and Cremer (1998) that sister city relations are a first step towards the establishment of economic relations between two city-regions may also be doubted. Although several city-regions have tried to use their well-established partnerships as gate openers into emerging markets, it is still unclear how economic activities and political engagement in sister cities' relations can be linked. According to the examples from the seven city-regions under scrutiny here and according to the logic presented above, this shift is highly conflictive and illogical within the development of a city partnership. The case of the partnership between Zurich and Kunming is a clear example of a failed move towards an economic orientation in a city partnership, since Zurich's desire to establish more economic links was not shared by the Chinese sister city. This caused severe problems and led to a major re-dimensioning of the partnership.

The strategies of city-regions are thus not responsible for their strong focus on questions of social cohesion and ecology in interurban networking. In fact, according to the logic just presented, city-regions would be very willing to learn from others in the policy area of locational politics as long as they are not required to provide any information about their own activities. However, the inherent logic of competition makes cooperation very unlikely in this domain. This would therefore suggest that there are grounds to strongly disagree with Friedmann's (2001: 120) notion that 'city-regions have much to gain (and nothing to lose) by associating with other regions in networks'. On the contrary, they risk losing their competitive advantages by sharing their best practices in policy areas in which they compete. Therefore, the argument on the content of interurban networking can be summarised as 'competition or cooperation' rather than 'competition through cooperation'. Interurban networking is most likely to occur in policy areas in which the competitiveness of the involved city-regions is less directly affected (see also Leitner and Sheppard 1999: 240).

This does not necessarily mean that interurban networking is *per se* a zero-sum game. This depends on the scalar viewpoint. Theoretically, if all city-regions in Europe would cooperate in policy areas relevant to their competitiveness, then the competitiveness of the whole European area would be increased. However, since most policy-makers see their city-regions as engaged in an inter-urban intra-Europe competition, this logic does not apply. Hall and Hubbart (1996: 167) are only partly right to state that 'with all cities competing in the same global market, there are bound to be winners and losers'. If inter-urban competition was truly global, then inter-urban networking would not be likely, according to the logic of competition presented above. If, however, forms of cooperation within certain geographical boundaries are possible (as through interurban networking in Europe), they could — like a merger of two private companies — lead to a mutually strengthened position towards other contestants (such as North-American and Asian city-regions). As far as this investigation revealed, however, the scalar orientation of policy-makers at the urban level in Europe is still mostly limited to the intra-European competition. Lyon is the only city-region of the seven under scrutiny that has started to orient itself strategically towards Asia in order to gain a competitive advantage over other European city-regions by maintaining a foothold in emerging Asian markets.

Castell's (1994: 29) notion that the competitiveness of city-regions is increasingly determined by their connectivity to other major metropolitan centres might be true for the economic exchanges. Here, the connectivity to global (mega-) city-regions might be of vital importance for the economic well-being of city-regions. However, this logic does not automatically apply to the political connectivity of city-regions as well. The link between increasing networking activities and increasing the competitiveness of the respective city-region is not as clear as many policy-makers believe. Therefore there can only be partial agreement with Church and Reid's (1996: 1302, with reference to Cappellin 1992) statement that 'joint initiatives [...] are thus primarily economic in intent and are designed to generate network economies, lower transaction costs and economies of scale through resource sharing and controls on competition'. Although this might be true for the intent of the involved policy-makers, it is not true for the content of interurban networking. This analysis of city-regions' international activities casts doubt on the idea that 'controlled competition' can be achieved through interurban networking.

The analysis of city-regions' international activities along the rescaling approach leaves several questions unanswered. The different paths of the seven city-regions' international activities could not be explained. According to the rescaling approach to urban foreign policy, these activities have no clear economic outline but are extremely diversified and very often directed towards social or ecological goals. To determine whether this argument is valid, an analysis will now be conducted along the varieties of capitalism approach, before merging the two approaches. Only with the combination of these two approaches, as will be argued, can it be fully understood why city-regions engage in international networking.

VARIETIES OF CAPITALISM AND THE INTERNATIONAL ACTIVITIES OF CITY-REGIONS

The previously presented conclusion (which was based on the rescaling approach), regarding urban networking's missing competitiveness orientation, is misleading. Considering the specific economic situation of the city-regions under scrutiny reveals that their policy-makers often follow an economic logic in their international engagements. However, the city-region's international activities and the economic orientation of their urban policies are only indirectly linked. The city-regions adapt their strategies for international activities according to their economic needs. Therefore, the city-regions do not primarily focus on international city networks that deal with locational politics. Still, their engagement in interurban networking often intends to promote the economic strengths of the respective city-regions on an international scale.

To develop this argument, the congruence between the city-regions' economic outlines and the orientation of their international activities will first be analysed. An explanation of what policy-makers at the city-region scale must consider when deciding to join existing networks or to establish new ones will follow. This decision is also linked to the city-region's economic outline.

Congruence of economic outline and international activities

Table 3.3 shows the results of the analysis along the varieties of capitalism approach. Clearly, the empirical analysis confirms the second hypothesis. The international activities of four of the seven city-regions directly align with their respective economic outlines. In the three other cases, there is an indirect or at least intended congruence between the city-region's international activities and its economic specificity. This close relationship between economic orientation and international political connections can be observed in exactly the four cities that have developed clear strategies for their international contacts. In each of those cases, strategic reflections on the region's economic needs lead to a clear strategy for the region's international contacts.

In the following sections, each of the seven city-regions will be examined to determine whether their international activities align with their specific economic outlines. The examination will start with the cases in which the connection is most clear before turning to the city-regions in which the relation is more subtle.[4]

---

4   In this section, the focus will be on the international activities that align with the relevant city-region's economic specification. This decision is based on a somewhat deterministic logic since all city-regions have some international activities that do not align with their specific economic settings.

Table 3.3: Varieties of capitalism: international activities in line with economic specificity

City-region	Economic specificity	Orientation of international activities	In line
Berne	National administration	–	(Indirectly)
Geneva	NGOs/IGOs	Peace and solidarity	✓
Lausanne	Sports administration	Sports and sustainability	✓
Lucerne	Tourism	City partnerships	✓
Zurich	Banking and insurance	–	(Indirectly)
Lyon	Diversified	Diversified	(Partly)
Stuttgart	Automobile industry	Mobility	✓

Geneva owes its international reputation to its role as an international city of peace negotiations. The city-region's international activities are clearly oriented towards international peace and solidarity, and the goal of this engagement is to promote Geneva in international interurban networks as a host city for IGOs and NGOs. This strategy is clearly effective; many IGOs and NGOs have settled in the Geneva area, and they comprise an important economic sector of the Genevan economy. The city-region's international activities are part of a larger strategy for remaining attractive to these organisations.

Geneva's engagement in peace and solidarity networks is thus not as altruistic as it might first appear. Instead, Geneva's international engagement is clearly linked to the economic needs of the city-region. Additionally, Geneva's decision not to enter any formal city partnership is also based on its role as a city for international peace negotiations. Although many cities have asked for a formal partnership, the city consistently refuses these demands, with reference to its neutrality. According to the involved policy-makers, this neutrality is crucial for the acceptance of Geneva as a host city for IGOs and NGOs. Geneva clearly devotes its international engagements to the city-region's economic needs.

The same is true for the city-region of Lausanne, which increased its international contacts in response to a parliamentarian demand to promote the city-region's economic space more effectively. The mayor responded to this demand through the intensification of existing international activities and the establishment of new ones. Both types of activities are pursued within the two domains of sport and sustainability, in which the mayor identifies the economic assets of the city-region. Alongside its long-standing tradition as a host city for international sports organisations, Lausanne is proactively reanimating the network of Olympic cities (UMVO). The city's decision not to enter any formal partnerships with foreign cities is also directly linked to its economic need to stay independent in order to facilitate impartial decisions within the domiciled sports organisations.

Lausanne's neutrality is thus clearly rooted in an economic goal. Additionally, the Green Party mayor sees Lausanne as a precursor of Europe's overall development towards better sustainability in urban areas. Again, this view is linked to the city-region's perceived economic needs, specifically its goal of becoming a more desirable city in which to live and thereby attracting new residents.[5]

The city of Lucerne orients itself towards city partnerships and is therefore only very modestly engaged in interurban networking. This is quite contrary to the international development in the other city-regions. However, this strategy is clearly linked to the city-region's main economic sector, tourism. Although opinions of the partnerships' usefulness for the city-region's economic well-being are divided among the involved policy-makers, several of these partnerships at least intend to promote the city-region of Lucerne in important tourist destinations.

In Stuttgart, the city-region's international activities and its economic outline are clearly connected. Because they depend on the automobile sector and its subcontractors, both the city and the region of Stuttgart are predominantly engaged in interurban networks that deal with mobility. The new network, Cities for Mobility, which was set up by Stuttgart, focuses on mobility in general, whereas other interurban networks in this domain often focus on public transport. The network is partly sponsored by Daimler and Porsche, the two largest automobile manufacturers in the area. Thus, in the case of Stuttgart, the economic outline indirectly influences the international activities, and the important economic actors are directly included in the new networks.

In these next two city-regions, the argument is a bit more complex but no less convincing. Berne has displayed an astonishing absence of international activities. This inconsistency can be plausibly explained by noting the economic orientation of the city-region. As the capital city, Berne's economic outlook is predominantly inward-oriented. Because of its high economic dependency on the national administration, an international engagement of the city-region would quite clearly contradict its economic orientation. The city's focus on good relations within Switzerland and its emphasis on the traditional multi-level governance system are thus unsurprising.

The city government of Berne refuses to enter any formal partnerships with foreign cities because of its special role as the capital city of Switzerland. Although the argument that capital cities generally do not enter partnerships is clearly wrong (see, for example, the cases of Rome or Paris, presented in Jouve 2007), this case still shows the predominant importance of good relations with the national state over possible gains from international contacts for the city-region of Berne. In this area of study, the international activities of city-regions and their relations to the cities' economic orientations must be analysed, but so must the possible absence of such activities. The case of Berne strongly supports the varieties of capitalism approach in the analysis of city-regions' international activities since the city-region's absence of international contacts clearly aligns with its economic needs.

---

5   As discussed later (on pages 153ff.), the ecological orientation of international networks is linked not only to the economic needs of the city-region of Lausanne but also to the personal engagement of the Green Party mayor.

The case of Zurich is somewhat similar. Although the scalar orientation of the Zurich economy is clearly global, and although the dependence on global incidents for the banking and insurance sectors is nowhere higher than in the case of Zurich, the respective political scale of importance is the national scale. The scalar orientation of the city-region's economy and the respective political regulations do not necessarily coincide. Most important decisions for the well-being of the Zurich economy are made at the Swiss national scale because most regulations of the banking and insurance sectors are determined by the national state. The most prominent example is bank secrecy, a national policy that entices a global inflow of money into Switzerland (and especially into the Zurich area).

Zurich struggles to form a useful strategy on the international level because international activities that align with the city-region's economic mix of banking and insurance are almost impossible since no international interurban networks address this topic. The city's primary orientation towards a good understanding with the national scale clearly complements the area's economic needs. Additionally, the highly globalised economy in the Zurich area does not need the state to connect it to the world market, since it is already connected (van der Heiden and Terhorst 2007).

Although there is a similarity between Berne's and Zurich's reluctance to engage in international activities, i.e. the importance of the national scale for both regional economies, there is also an important dissimilarity. The orientation of the local economy is inward for Berne but global for Zurich. However, the conclusion is the same for both city-regions; the political need to go global is quite low because the important scale for the city-regions' economic well-being is the national one. The distinction between an export- and an import-oriented economic system is thus not useful in analysing the need to pursue international political activities at the city-region scale. The local economy's perceived vulnerability to globalisation pressures better explains the intensity of city-regions' international activities.

Lyon faces the same problem of an impossible congruence between its economic orientation and its international activities. Because the Lyon economy is not clearly dependent on one branch, the city-region's international political contacts are also quite diverse. They focus on two primary aspects. First, Lyon attempts to increase it visibility on the global scale and thereby to contribute to the area's economic prosperity indirectly. Second, Lyon focuses on international engagement in multi-thematic lobby networks such as Eurocities, UCLG, and the Asian Citynet. This more general outlook aligns with the region's diverse economic profile.

For the case of Lyon, policy-makers indeed consider the city-region's economic profile, but its diversity makes an adjustment of the international contacts towards this profile difficult. The city-region's orientation towards lobby networks and networks that labour in the domains in which the international visibility of Lyon is highest thus indirectly serves the area's economic needs. Accordingly, the city-region of Lyon set up two networks (LUCI and Délice) in domains where its international visibility is high (lighting and *haute cuisine*), although this visibility is not directly linked to the region's economic outline. The theoretical approach of the varieties of capitalism reaches its limits when a clear definition of an economic profile cannot be obtained. Lyon might be the only case in which the rescaling approach's more general thesis on the economic orientation of international activities is more adequate than the more specific approach of the varieties of capitalism.

The argumentation from the varieties of capitalism approach is thus very convincing for the seven city-regions under scrutiny. Six of the seven city-regions affirm the prediction of an orientation of international activities along the respective city-regions' economic outlines. In four of the city-regions, the link is straightforward. In two cases, the link is more indirect because the economic orientations explain the reluctance towards an international engagement. Lastly, the diversified economic profile of Lyon hinders policy-makers' adaptation of their strategy for international activities along this economic profile, despite their active efforts.

Choosing between joining and creating networks
Another interesting aspect of interurban networking is the formation of new networks. Although the number of networks increases, the relevant city-regions' motives for initiating them are less clear; luckily, they can be analysed with the varieties of capitalism approach. The city-regions, and very often the mayors themselves,[6] strategically create networks in the domains of their respective city-region's economic necessities. In at least three of the city-regions under scrutiny, policy-makers have strategically considered forming new networks.

The network-creation procedure is usually quite straightforward. First, the decision makers analyse the economic needs of their city-region. Second, they analyse the existing interurban networks in these domains. If relevant networks already exist, then the city-region usually joins these networks and tries to play a key role within them. Third, if there are no or only unsatisfactory interurban networks in this domain, then the city-region often initiates a new network.

The city-region within Switzerland that has followed this strategy most clearly is Lausanne. The city parliament forced the mayor to develop a marketing plan for the city. He responded by creating new networks that reflect not only the Lausanne area's economic dependence on sports (through the UMVO network) but also the city-region's new strategy for promoting the area as a precursory sustainable city-region (through the IFGRA network). Similarly, Geneva set up one international network of cities that is committed to peace (the IAPMC network), and it was a co-founder of an urban network that deals with international digital solidarity (the GCD network). Here too, Geneva's new networks completely align with its economic dependence on its reputation as an international city-region of peace and solidarity.

Lyon, which has a diversified economic profile, also formed new international interurban networks. The mayor of Lyon decided to create two networks in the domains of Lyon's international visibility, although this was not necessarily congruent with the city-region's economic interests.[7] The two networks LUCI (in the

---

6   This aspect is addressed on pages 153ff.

7   However, as was argued in the relevant case study, the international activities indirectly pursue increased competitiveness through enhancing international visibility.

domain of urban lighting) and Délice (in the domain of *haute cuisine*) were the result of this strategy.

Stuttgart joined several international interurban networks that deal with mobility, which is the city-region's most important economic cluster because of its high dependence on the automobile industry. However, since these networks primarily focus on public transport, the city of Stuttgart was discontent with the existing interurban networks on mobility and hence set up its own network, Cities for Mobility. This network clearly has a more encompassing approach on mobility and does not predominantly focus on public transport.

Establishing new international interurban networks is a costly strategy. The founding city-regions must commit considerable resources to financing the project, provide the secretary for the initial phase of the network, and invest heavily in convincing other city-regions to join it. Because of the fierce competition for members among interurban networks in almost any policy field, this is a challenging task.

The experiences of past efforts to set up networks demonstrate that this strategy does not automatically succeed. Many of these international urban networks disappear as quickly as they emerged. It is therefore too early to predict the possible success of the newly established networks mentioned above. Nevertheless, one thing is clear; the city-regions that initiate new networks clearly aim for increased international visibility. The advantage of setting up an international city network is increased visibility as a lead city in the relevant policy domain. All investigated new networks are closely linked to their initiating city-regions' respective economic specificities. In conclusion, a city-region's decision to take a leadership position in setting up an international interurban network is only explainable by analysing the city-region's economic specification through the varieties of capitalism approach.

COMBINING RESCALING AND VARIETIES OF CAPITALISM

In this last step, the rescaling and the varieties of capitalism approaches are combined. Only when the varieties of capitalism approach is considered can the rescaling approach reach its true potential in analysing city-regions' international activities. As shown previously, the international activities are very often oriented towards social or ecological goals. The specificity of the city-regions' economic outlines, however, reveals that most of these engagements in social or ecological networking are linked to the respective city-regions' place-specific economic assets. Lefèvre and d'Albergo's (2007: 312) statement that 'even some apparently socially oriented international activities might actually be interpreted as motivated by economic aims' is thus absolutely correct.

This analysis even discovered that most of the socially oriented international contacts are truly motivated by the economic goal of increased competitiveness. Interurban networking is thus a significant part of the neo-liberal trend at the urban scale, although this does not automatically lead to a competitiveness orientation in the networking activities. An examination of the motives and strategies of the city-regions involved in interurban networking reveals that the city-regions choose international activities that align with their specific economic outlooks.

Using the varieties of capitalism approach was essential to unveiling this causality. Interurban networking *per se* is thus not necessarily economically oriented, but the underlying motivations of the city-regions are indeed focused on economic gain. Examining the strategies of the involved city-regions is thus necessary when analysing the phenomenon of interurban networking.

Consequently, the rescaling approach's pessimistic argument about city-regions' international activities, as presented by Brenner (2004: 286ff.), is correct that these international contacts are part of the shift towards urban entrepreneurialism. The hope that these international activities will provide opportunities to form monopolies of the economically important city-regions (as presented by Heeg *et al*. 2003) and will thereby eliminate the negative effects of increased interurban competition was thus not fulfilled. International activities of city-regions are not part of a counter-trend against the neo-liberal turn of statehood, but they are connected to the neo-liberal developments of a post-Fordist multi-scalar state. The increased importance of the city-region scale has not been used by that scale's actors to regain their redistributive power of the Fordist era. The international connections through networks are seen as place-specific assets within interurban competition, not against it.

Brenner (2004: 26) is thus accurate in concluding that interurban networking 'deepened rather than alleviated the political-economic dislocations, regulatory failures, and territorial inequalities that were generated through previous rounds of urban locational policy.' City-regions' newly emerging international activities are an instrument for place marketing, locational politics, and positioning the city-region in the international marketplace. The 'wasteful competition between cities' (Begg 1999: 805) is thus not stopped or hindered but rather is accentuated by interurban networking.

Leitner and Sheppard's (2002: 166) conclusion that 'neo-liberalism has successfully appropriated network discourses for its own purposes' must be redefined because networking *per se* is not infiltrated by neo-liberalism; rather, city-regions involved in interurban networking have altered their strategies towards increased competitiveness. The city-regions brought neo-liberalism into the interurban networks through their strategies for international activities. Interurban networks themselves are often wholly unconnected to neo-liberal policy goals.

The shift towards neo-liberal strategies in city-regions' international activities can also be witnessed in the transformation of city partnerships (see also Cremer *et al*. 2001: 383; O'Toole 2001). At least three of the seven city-regions under scrutiny (Zurich, Lyon, and Stuttgart) have tried to shift the content of their long-standing partnerships towards economic orientations. Many of these partnerships were formed as means for providing developmental aid, financial aid, and technical help for transitioning city-regions. Nowadays, however, these partnerships must offer specific gains to both city-regions. They are increasingly viewed as opportunities for reaching emerging markets and fostering business contacts that benefit the local economy. Although not all city-regions under scrutiny have followed this trend so far, there is still considerable evidence for such a shift in the content of city-partnerships. Within the seven city-regions under scrutiny, no new city partnerships that target developmental aid have been formed since the year 2000.

The intensity and the content of the international activities are thus clearly interlinked. The varieties of capitalism approach has correctly emphasised the importance of regional economic outlines for strategic decisions concerning city-regions' engagements in international contacts. The intensity of city-regions' international activities can therefore be explained by the needs of their respective local economies. The more decision makers perceive their city-region as vulnerable to global economic pressures, the more they will engage in interurban networking. Only the detour via the varieties of capitalism approach allowed for a full understanding of the neo-liberal turn in city-regions' international activities. The content of networking itself is hardly oriented towards competitiveness, but the strategy behind the networking is clearly linked to competitiveness goals. In this area, this analysis of city-regions and their strategies has offered new insights to existing analyses of interurban networking.

The detour via the varieties of capitalism approach has proved that the basic concept of the rescaling approach is correct. The international activities of city-regions are indeed part of the shift towards urban entrepreneurialism. However, the rescaling approach was unable to explain the different paths of the city-regions towards this goal. Only their economic specifications, as predicted by the varieties of capitalism approach, plausibly explained their different trajectories. Although 'all roads lead to Rome' (i.e. urban entrepreneurialism), it was still important to investigate these different roads (i.e. economic specificities). Gaining this insight was only possible through examining the city-regions' side of interurban networking.

chapter four | intrascalar and interscalar changes

After presenting an explanation of city-regions' international activities, the changes that have followed from the new urban setting's international activities will now be examined. This section will treat city-regions' international activities as the independent variable. Three different scales or interscalar relations will be investigated: first, the policy-making process within the city-region will be addressed; second, the interplay between the core city and the agglomeration communities will be investigated and third, the relations with upper-level governments are inspected. In the last section, the findings concerning the scalar changes will be combined with the conclusions from the examination of urban foreign policy factors.

THE MAYOR AND THE BUREAUCRACY GOVERN

The goal of this section is to analyse the decision-making procedures followed in city-regions' international activities and possibly to detect power shifts towards an executive and output-oriented way of policy-making. This was the third hypothesis, which was derived from the pessimistic strand of the rescaling approach (Keil 2003; Smith 2002; Swyngedouw 1997). These scholars propose a top-down method of policy-making regarding international activities due to the activities' link to the city-regions' increased competitiveness orientation. As the preceding chapter showed, city-regions' international activities are indeed part of the shift towards urban entrepreneurialism.

The purpose however is to also identify any resistance against this policy change, as hoped for by certain scholars of the rescaling approach (see Bulkeley 2005; Castells 1994; Leitner and Sheppard 1999). To comprehend the shifts in urban policy-making, the involvement of four actor groups will first be separately analysed before combining the findings in a second step. The analysis will start with the role of the mayor, then the role of the bureaucracy, next the inclusion of the parliament, and lastly the involvement of the public in city-regions' international activities. In a final step, the role of PPPs will be studied in this policy field before offering some concluding remarks.

Mayoral leadership

In five of the seven city-regions under scrutiny (see Table 4.1), the mayor is the key player in the international activities since he[1] is directly responsible for the city-region's strategy on the international scale. The service for international contacts, where one exists, is directly attached to the mayor (with the exception of Geneva, where the service reports to the city government as a whole). This organisational structure allows the mayor to monitor the international contacts closely.

---

1   There is no female mayor in any of the seven city-regions under scrutiny.

Table 4.1: Who governs? Strong role of the mayor and the bureaucracy

City-region	Strong role of the mayor	Strong role of the bureaucracy
Berne	–	–
Geneva	–	✓
Lausanne	✓	✓
Lucerne	(✓)	(✓) Democratic control
Zurich	(✓)	(✓) Democratic control
Stuttgart	✓	✓
Lyon	✓	✓

In Lausanne, the mayor has developed a particular response to the city parliament's demand to develop a strategy of locational politics. International activities are part of the mayor's response, which is not surprising. However, the Green Party mayor created new international networks in the domains of sport and sustainability. Within the sustainability network, he clearly linked the international strategy of the city-region to his personal political values. The mayor's position is thus quite strong, since he can reply to a demand for increased locational politics by forming an international network of sustainable city-regions. The networks' mutual purpose is to promote Lausanne as a precursor in sustainable urban areas and thereby to gain an indirect economic benefit. Among the seven city-regions under scrutiny, Lausanne is the example that best supports Martins and Rodriguez Alvarez' (2007: 393) conclusion that 'the institutional strengths and above all the personal traits of the local leaders are crucial to understanding mainly why cities have developed a strategy and, to a certain extent, the way they do it'.

In Stuttgart, the mayor is not only the initiator of several new international interurban networks (e.g. Cities for Mobility and Cities for Children); he is also personally engaged in the city's international contacts. The city's strong emphasis on the EU as the important scale for modern urban policy-making is based on the mayor's personal commitment to the EU. He has repeatedly been called a 'Europhile', and his Europhile nature is clearly visible in Stuttgart's international activities.[2] No other city-region under scrutiny has devoted as much effort to relations with the EU. The mayor also participates actively in the UCLG network. As the president of its German section, vice-president of its European section, and member of its world council, he spends considerable time in this network and therefore abroad.

---

2   The mayor of Stuttgart was recently elected to the EU's 'Council of Wise Men to Rethink Europe'. He is the only representative of the local scale on this board, which discusses important steps for the EU's future development (see Landeshauptstadt Stuttgart 2008; *Stuttgarter Zeitung* 2008, 16th October).

The mayor of Lyon shows a similarly strong commitment to the international scale. As the current president of the Eurocities network, which is probably the most important interurban network on the European scale, he holds a strong position beyond the city-region scale. He also appointed a city councillor to be responsible solely for the city's international contacts.

Besides these three city-regions in which the mayors have a strong and direct influence on international strategy, there are two more city-regions in which the mayors clearly control the international contacts, although their predominance in this policy area is not as clear as in the three city-regions discussed above.

The mayor of Lucerne has managed the city's international contacts for a much longer period than in the other city-regions. As early as the late 1970s and early 1980s, when the first city partnerships were established, the mayor during that period devoted his city's international contacts to promoting Lucerne as a tourist destination. However, the discussions in the parliament and among the public partially restricted the mayoral lead in this policy domain (see below). The mayor of Lucerne is much more constrained than his colleagues in the other city-regions regarding operating on the international scale.

The same is generally true for Zurich. The current mayor proactively tried to develop a strategy for the city's international activities and to increase them in strategically important networks. However, the city parliament severely restricted his propositions, repeatedly refusing to permit a credit line that would finance an increase of the city's international activities. Zurich is the only examined city in which a mayor has been severely restricted in his attempt to strengthen the city's position through international contacts.

Besides these five city-regions in which mayoral leadership plays an important role in international activities, there are also two city-regions in which mayors do not maintain strong positions in the cities' international contacts. In Berne, neither the former nor the current mayor have shown any interest in international activities. The city government as a whole has decided to focus on intra-Swiss relations instead of cross-border contacts. The current mayor has never shown any interest in reversing this reluctance towards international activities.

In Geneva, the mayoral position rotates every year among the members of the city government. This structural constraint hinders coherent leadership in international contacts. Within the one-year term, it is almost impossible for a mayor to develop a strategy for the city's international contacts or to establish new networks. Although this has been accomplished in the past, the current organisation of international contacts, through a service that reports to the city government as a whole, clearly demonstrates Geneva's different organisational approach to international activities. Nevertheless, this has not prevented the city government from developing a coherent strategy for its international contacts. Still, the role of the mayor is considerably less important in this area than it is in other city-regions.

These observations therefore lead to disagreement with Martins and Rodriguez Alvarez' (2007: 406) conclusion that 'only cities with strong mayors can strategically play the international game'. The case of Geneva is a clear counter-example against this notion of a necessary link between a strong mayor and a strategically coherent international strategy. Among the Swiss cities under scrutiny, Geneva has both the weakest mayoral position and the most clear-cut strategy for international activities.

However, not only interurban networks but also city partnerships are relevant to an analysis of the role of the mayor. In this more traditional form of urban foreign policy, the role of the mayor as the city's chief ambassador is crucial. Although some of these partnerships have been reoriented towards a more competitiveness-oriented logic, their political contacts are still important. The role of the mayor as the chief ambassador is unquestioned since he must receive delegations from partner cities. However, the role of the mayor within city partnerships is usually less devoted to the strategic orientation of the city-region as a whole and more towards formal duties.

Because the city partnerships are the most important (and almost the only) international activity of the city-region of Lucerne, the role of Lucerne's mayor in the city's international activities is clearly that of a leader. The mayor not only participates in the operational aspects of the partnerships but also serves as the key decision maker. He chooses Lucerne's partner cities strategically, since they are crucial for Lucerne's orientation towards competitiveness in the tourist sector.

In the cases of Stuttgart and Lyon, the current mayors, together with the heads of the Service for International Contacts, are responsible for the strategic shift of partnerships towards an economic orientation. In the two EU case studies, the mayors not only have used their influence in interurban networking but also have aligned their long-standing city partnerships with their general strategy in international activities. Therefore, a clear urban foreign policy is most apparent in these two cases since the mayors have developed coherent strategies that encompass both partnerships and networks.

Mayors strongly influence the content and the orientation of the international activities of city-regions. Two aspects demonstrate mayors' ability to manoeuvre independently. First, the mayor's party affiliation influences his city-region's international strategy. The clearest example is the Green Party mayor of Lausanne, who used his power to increase Lausanne's global visibility as a sustainable city-region. Second, the election of a new mayor often leads to a boost in the respective city-region's international activities. Newly elected mayors in Lyon and Stuttgart have strategically increased the presence of their city-regions on the international scale.

Still, the logic of the varieties of capitalism approach remains valid in explaining city-regions' international activities since the mayors always consider their respective city-region's economic specificities when deciding to enter certain international contacts or not. There is thus a structuralist logic of the general intensity and orientation of city-regions' international activities. Within these structuralist boundaries of the economic specificity of the city-region, a mayor has some freedom in choosing actual international activities. The international activities of city-regions cannot be fully understood without an analysis of the mayors' motives (see also Martins and Rodriguez Alvarez 2007).

Bureaucracy's influence

The administration is clearly the key player in the international activities of city-regions. A distinction can be made between the politically steered international activities that the mayor initiates and those that the service for international activities (if one exists) conducts and the more policy-oriented cooperation schemes that the city administration manages. The first contacts are usually highly important lobby networks (such as Eurocities and UCLG). The latter are not only carried out but often also initiated by the city administration.

There seems to be an ideal development path for such international contacts on the departmental level. The initiative to join an international interurban policy network originates from the relevant department. One employee of the department proposes to the department chief that the city should join the network. Thereafter, the city government decides, usually without any discussion, to join the network. Because the annual credit line (i.e. membership fee) is usually very low, the city government seldom readdresses its decision, except when a city councillor or someone from the city parliament demands it, which happens only very rarely (see below).

The departments therefore have almost a *carte blanche* in carrying out their international contacts. In cities in which the departments have considerable freedom to engage in international contacts on their own, this opportunity is often maximised. Even the head of the department (i.e. the relevant city councillor) is only very rarely informed about the international contacts of the policy-makers in his or her department. Because the majority of existing interurban networks are clearly policy-specific, the city bureaucracy deals with most international networking activities behind closed doors. Only when the mayor strategically decides to join a more lobby-oriented network is politics involved.

The role of the city administration is also strong in city partnerships, although the city government is much more involved than in the interurban networks, because the partnerships inherit more formal contacts in which the involvement of elected politicians is desired. Because policy learning between city administrations is often a goal of the partnerships, it is not surprising that the bureaucracy plays an important role in city partnerships.

Among the various services for international activities (in those city-regions where they exist), there is considerable diversity in their responsibilities. The city-region of Lyon has the most encompassing respective structure; it maintains a service for the city and the region.[3] The current mayor has increased the duties of this service, which now deals directly with the majority of the networking activities and with all city partnerships.

Only very few international activities are completely left to the departments, mostly the ones that do not align with the general strategy of achieving increased visibility through international activities (for example, the cooperation within Les Rencontres). However, most of the city-regions that maintain services for inter-

---

3   As mentioned before, the two services have only formally merged.

national activities have adapted a more dualistic approach. The service directly attached to the mayor deals with city partnerships and with the most important international activities, and it often creates new networking activities; meanwhile, the less important international policy networking activities are left to the departments. However, the service usually observes these departmental contacts closely.

The cases of Geneva, Lausanne, Lyon, and Stuttgart reveal that the contacts between the policy-makers responsible for international contacts in the various departments and the policy-makers in the centralised service for international activities are not always in harmony. Quite often, the policy-makers in the departments fear a possible centralisation of their own international contacts. They are therefore reluctant to cooperate with the service for international activities, and sometimes they actively refuse to do so. These internal conflicts even increase the tendency towards policy-making behind closed doors. International activities that become public risk being centralised, which is what bureaucrats often fear.

The information policies of the services for international activities also reveal interesting differences. Whereas Lucerne, Stuttgart, and Lyon proactively inform about their international contacts through public brochures, informative Internet sites, and internal reports for interested policy-makers, the other city-regions follow a more restrictive information policy. This is unsurprising in the case of Berne, for which there is not much to communicate in this area. It is more surprising in the case of Geneva, which has a long-standing tradition of international interurban contacts. Geneva's service for international activities, although it was established in 2002, first published a report on its activities in 2007 (Ville de Genève 2007). In Lausanne and Zurich, there are no systematic reports on their international contacts; this is certainly connected to their recent increase in international activity and their organisational structures, which are not yet well-established. Therefore, the administration, together with the mayor, is the most important player in city-regions' international activities. There is a certain tendency towards a top down policy-making process that occurs behind closed doors, obscuring the international activities.

Parliamentary inclusion or exclusion

Two important points must be noted concerning the role of city parliaments in international activities. First, in general, the city parliaments are only marginally included in the policy-making process for international activities. Second, in the rare cases where the parliament has been involved, it has had a moderating effect on the international activities.

The two city-regions, in which there is a considerable inclusion of the parliament in the decision-making process for international activities, will be examined first. In the case of Zurich, the parliament became aware of the financial dimensions of the Kunming partnership in 1999. In response, a right-wing parliamentarian from the SVP requested that the city government inform the parliament about this aspect. The SVP criticised the partnership's absence of gains for Zurich and the city bureaucrats' long stays in Kunming. The city government finally decided to stop contributing financially to the partnership, in response to the continuing criticisms from the parliament.

The debate about the Kunming partnership then influenced all the upcoming decisions concerning Zurich's international activities. For example, the city's partnership with San Francisco was set up privately, and the city did not engage financially in the partnership for a long time. This reluctance is clearly due to the controlling function of the parliament, which closely monitors the new city partnership. The parliament very recently blocked the mayor's credit proposal to establish a service for external activities within the service for city development (*Tagesanzeiger,* 9th July 2008: 12). Once again, the parliament hindered the mayor's plans to increase the city's international activities. The mayor pushed for a more proactive strategy on the international scale, especially through the two new memberships in Eurocities and UCLG. The parliament could not vote on the decision to join these two networks because the credit lines were too small. However, the parliament refused the credit line for the human resources that were necessary to manage the new networking activities. Thus, there is clearly a conflict in Zurich between the mayor, who seeks a more active international strategy, and the much more reluctant parliament.

In the case of Lucerne, the function of the parliament is the same as in Zurich; it controls the partnership activities. However, there is no conflict between the parliament and the mayor in Lucerne. The parliament has always voted in favour of the credit lines for the city partnerships, and critical remarks from right-wing parliamentarians are rare. Still, the city parliament repeatedly discusses the intensity and orientation of Lucerne's city partnerships. The city government has reacted to these critics by providing a detailed report on its international activities.

In the other five city-regions, there is very limited inclusion of the city parliament in the decision-making processes concerning international activities. In Lyon and Stuttgart, the services for international contacts produce annual reports; based on this report, the city parliaments decide on the annual credits for the services. According to the involved policy-makers, this has never led to long discussions in the city parliament, and the credit lines have always been passed with comfortable majorities. Additionally, there are no lines of conflict along classical cleavages in these two EU city-regions. Parties from the left and right sides of the political spectrum acknowledge the need to engage in international activities.

In the two city-regions in which the parliament has debated the cities' international activities, there is a clear divide between the populist-right parties that oppose the international contacts and the moderate-right and left parties that favour such activities. The openness of Switzerland has been an even more hotly debated issue on the national scale since the early 1990s. This debate divides the political spectrum into right-wing isolationistic parties and more open left-wing parties (Lachat 2008).[4] As the analysis of urban foreign policy shows, this debate has even trickled down to the urban scale. Clearly, political cleavage concerning foreign policy is the same on the local as on the national scale.

---

4   Of course, this is a clear over-simplification of actual cleavages concerning the openness of Switzerland. For a more elaborate analysis, see Lachat (2008).

Public inclusion or exclusion

As mentioned above, the inclusion of the city parliament is already minimal. The direct inclusion of the public is even less significant. Only in the two cases in which the parliament is included is there also a limited inclusion of the public. The only public vote on an international activity among the seven city-regions occurred in Zurich, and the vote favoured the partnership that the politicians had hotly debated. Still, the existence of a referendum against a city partnership is a sign of some considerable public discontent. Accordingly, the city government and especially the mayor have promised to reform the dimensions of the part-nership and to reorient it towards more bilateral cooperation. Hence, although the vote favoured the partnership, the direct democratic procedure still indirectly changed the intensity and the orientation of the partnership.

A different form of inclusion of the public is present in some of Lucerne's city partnerships. Private associations manage several of these partnerships, in close cooperation with the service for partnerships. Citizens with special relations to one of the partner cities organise the meetings and cultivate the friendships along with the more formal political contacts. Several former city councillors are engaged in one or several of these partnership committees. However, the membership ba-sis of these partnership committees is rather small, and the knowledge about the partnerships beyond these committees is rather low, according to the involved policy-makers.

In the other five city-regions, there is no inclusion of the public in the decision-making process concerning international activities. Although several city-regions organise some events related to their international activities (mostly the partner-ships) in which the broad public can participate, there is nowhere a significant influence of the public on the intensity or content of the city-regions' international activities. This is surprising, at least for the Swiss city-regions, which have long-standing traditions of direct democratic instruments and which are open in the local political system for bottom-up initiatives (Linder 2003). It is less surprising, how-ever, if the small number of these city-regions' international activities is considered.

Lefèvre and d'Albergo's (2007: 322) statement that the international activities of city-regions grant 'a very important role [...] to civil society groups and asso-ciations' cannot be supported by the analysis of the seven city-regions under scru-tiny here. Lefèvre and d'Albergo's (2007) statement addressed city-regions that have social orientations in their international activities. According to this idea, the biggest inclusion of civil society groups should be evident in the case of Geneva, the city-region that has the most social orientation in its international activities. However, even in Geneva, with its focus on peace and international solidarity, the inclusion of NGOs in these activities is close to non-existent.

The international activities of city-regions, at least for the seven cases under scrutiny here, are clearly in the hands of the mayor and the city administration. There is no inclusion of any organised civil society in the seven city-regions' internation-al activities. The inclusion of NGOs in interurban networking is sporadic, and their influence is far from important in the decision-making processes. City-regions' international activities are therefore not an issue in which the public is involved.

Public-private partnerships

The critical strand of the rescaling approach proposed an increasing influence of PPPs in city-regions' international activities. However, the direct influence of private actors on the decision-making procedure in the foreign policies of city-regions is very limited. As already noted the strong indirect influence of the city-region's economic structure on its international activities. Still, there are only three examples of PPPs participation in city-regions' international activities. First, in the Cities for Mobility network, established by Stuttgart; the automobile industry not only sponsors this network's activities but also participates in them directly. Second, the LUCI network, set up by Lyon, promotes a similar inclusion of companies from the lighting industry. Third, in the Zurich-San Francisco initiative, the city government delegated the development of this new partnership to the private sector after the city's negative experience in its partnership with Kunming (see above); nevertheless, it is increasingly involved in that cooperation scheme.

Reconsidering the number of networking activities analysed (see again Table 2.19), PPPs are only rare examples in this domain; the decision-making process is still highly concentrated in the hands of politicians. Insofar, there has been no shift from government to governance in city-regions' international activities, as proposed by Blatter (1997: 167f.) for transborder contacts in general. The significant roles of the mayor and the bureaucracy demonstrate that the international activities of city-regions might comprise a political response to the economic trend of globalisation and therefore an attempt to (re)gain political steering capacity. It is thus no surprise that the economy's direct influence in these activities is very limited.

These findings do not directly contradict Keiner and Kim's (2007: 1382f., with reference to Reinicke and Deng 2000) argument that 'a growing number of transnational challenges require a form of tri-sectoral collaboration: public sector (i.e. states and international public organisations), civil society (i.e. NGOs), and the for-profit private sector (i.e. corporations, other businesses, and their associations)'. Nevertheless, it must be concluded that this form of tri-sectoral cooperation does not (yet) exist in city-region's international activities.

Top-down policy-making

In summary, the mayor and the city bureaucracy clearly control the city-region's international activities. The mayor controls the city-region's membership in strategically important (usually lobbying) networks, which are often managed by a special service for international activities. The city administration carries out the more policy-oriented networking activities, often independently. The mayor and the city bureaucracy work together closely in this respect, especially in city-regions that have well-established strategies for their international activities. Here, the mayor closely monitors the international activities that are carried out by the service, and he is directly involved in the strategic decision-making process. The city administration, especially the different departments, have considerably more freedom in carrying out their own international contacts in the city-regions that have only recently or have not yet established strategies for their international activities. In those city-regions, the duties of the services for international activities, if they exist, are much broader, often including external intra-national relations or city development.

The city parliaments are only included in the decision-making procedures in two city-regions, and they have a moderating effect on the city's international contacts. The public is seldom involved in the city-regions' international activities. The decision-making process for the international activities of city-regions can therefore be described as top-down. The investigation of the seven city-regions' actual decision-making procedures supports the hypothesis derived from the pessimistic strand of the rescaling theory. Blatter *et al.* (2008: 485) determined, based on their analysis of the foreign policy of regions, that 'most partnerships feature a strong involvement of socio-economic organisations and cultural groupings, parliamentarian and lower-level bureaucrats'. This conclusion is not applicable to city-regions, except for its last aspect. The international activities on the city-region's scale are organised in a closed circle of only a small number of policy-makers.

In the seven city-regions under scrutiny here, there has been no public movement against the trend to globalise on the city-region scale or against the accompanying shift towards a competitiveness orientation in these international contacts. Boudreau's (2007: 2608) conclusion, based on her observations of social movements in Toronto's metropolitan governance, is true for urban foreign policy as well: 'But they [the social movements] are faced with serious barriers generated by the redefinition of the political process in this new city-regional political space.'[5] The city-regions that are most active on the international scale are also those in which politicians, most prominently the mayor, are engaged in obscuring their international activities from the public. Often, policy-makers are well aware that international activities are part of a larger turn towards neo-liberal policy-making at the urban scale. Because they are also aware that the public does not necessarily appreciate this policy shift, they try to organise their international activities behind closed doors.

Thus, there is a double tendency. On the one hand, traditional policy-making still occurs at the urban scale, where politicians see opportunities to gain votes by promoting social and ecological policies. On the other hand, politicians, especially mayors, increasingly engage in networking for the sake of the city's increased competitiveness. This engagement is rooted in a neo-liberal discourse on the need to adapt to globalisation logics. Groups that might oppose such a shift in urban policy-making are not (fully) aware of this aspect of increased international connectivity. This might explain the weak opposition towards city-regions' increasing

---

5   However, Boudreau's (2007: 2608) empirical finding that 'many social movements in Toronto work actively against the competitive regional imaginary pushed by economic elites' is not transferable to city-regions' international activities. I did not observe any substantial resistance against the international activities of city-regions. The same argument, i.e. that metropolitanisation is used to strengthen an international economic position, can be found in the Swiss context (see *Neue Zürcher Zeitung*, 2008, 31st May: 47). Here, economic leaders argue for joint policy-making in the metropolitan area of Zurich in order to 'stand in the international competition' (author's translation).

international activities. The other explanation, at least for most city-regions under scrutiny, is the limited intensity of the international activities.

The general conclusion offered by Cox (1991a: 337) is only partially true for the city-region's scale. Cox states that 'central agencies that act as transmission belts for the world economy [...] have become pre-eminent within governments over those agencies that deal with primarily internal affairs'. Although the importance of international activities has increased, especially for city-regions that emphasise competitiveness, this increase must be relativised. Almost all involved policy-makers note that local policy-making still prevails over international contacts.

Many mayors spend a considerable amount of their time abroad dedicated to international contacts. However, they do not accentuate these international contacts when presenting their goals and achievements to the public; usually, public statements underestimate the amount of time and resources devoted to the international arena. Only in Lyon and Stuttgart have there been small attempts to capitalise internally on international activities. Thus, there is a gap between the mayors' actual devotion to international activities and their presentation of these activities towards voters. As several policy-makers point out, this is linked to the fact that citizens (i.e. voters) care much more about local policy measures than international ones.

Policy-makers generally agree that citizens do not understand the importance of international activities for the city-region's economic well-being. The public does not recognise the goal of jumping scales through the city-regions' international activities and its accompanying economic importance. Kincaid (1989: 233), in the only study that actually investigates the public opinion on sub-national foreign policy, quotes one interview partner: 'These officials have time to visit London, Tokyo, and Beijing, but they never have time to visit my neighbourhood'.

There seems to be a double logic in city-regions' international activities. The involved policy-makers see the activities as extremely important, but they seldom try to publicise them because they fear the voters' non-acceptance of these activities. Their logic can thus be summarised by this representation of their perspective: 'We do it, because we know that it is important (i.e. backstage politics), but we do not speak about it, because the voters do not know that it is important' (i.e. front-stage politics; see van Tatenhove et al. 2006). Although the international activities have become increasingly important, in the view of local politicians and policy-makers, the actors still engage in a discourse on local policy-making for the benefit of the public because they know, as one interview partner exaggerated, that 'with international activities, there are no votes to gain'.

Still, Cappellin's (1993: 80) pessimistic conclusion that 'regional public institutions and collective organisations seem to be concerned only with local problems and not to be aware of the need for a strategy in external relations' is not confirmed by this analysis. Several of the seven city-regions under scrutiny have relatively clear-cut strategies for their international activities; others are currently engaged in developing them.[6]

---

6   See Lefèvre and d'Albergo (2007) on the notion of the 'prevailing strategy' in international activities.

An examination of the dichotomy between an output legitimacy and an input legitimacy (Scharpf 1998) reveals a link between the orientation and the democratic legitimacy of city-regions' international activities. As seen above, the activities are controlled by the mayor and the bureaucracy. These policy-makers usually argue within a competitiveness-oriented discourse, defending their involvement in international activities. They clearly focus on an output-oriented logic because the international activities must bring economic gains to the city-region. The involved policy-makers usually downplay the input side of democratic legitimacy because they fear that the public might not (fully) support their strategy of competitiveness.

Overall, the decision-making process in international activities is top-down. The mayor and the bureaucracy hold strong positions in it, and the parliaments and the public are seldom included, which corresponds with the international activities' competitiveness orientation.

HORIZONTAL GOVERNANCE: LONESOME CORE CITIES

After the analysis of the decision-making process at the city-region scale, interscalar changes will now be inspected. First, the interplay on the horizontal level between the core cities and the agglomeration communities will be analysed through two parts. First, the analysis will examine the direct contacts between the core city and the agglomeration communities. Second, it will address their indirect contacts through metropolitan governments (where they exist).

Core cities and agglomeration communities: independently global

The conclusion concerning the interplay between the core cities and the agglomeration communities is straightforward; there are no cooperation schemes between the two concerning their international activities, and core cities have no increased influence against the agglomeration communities due to their primary position in international activities (see Table 4.2). The fourth hypothesis predicted that core cities would use their precursory position in connecting the whole metropolitan area to the global sphere against the agglomeration communities; this was not supported by the empirical investigation.

The first and rather astonishing conclusion from the analysis of the agglomeration communities' international activities is their limitation to city partnerships. In all seven city-regions, the agglomeration communities are involved in city partnerships, but only in the two cases of Zurich and Stuttgart are there (very modest) engagements of these communities in interurban networking. In the agglomeration of Zurich, Dübendorf is a member of the Climate Alliance network. However, Dübendorf has not participated in the network's international meetings. Dübendorf has had no direct contacts with the city of Zurich in this respect except its regular contacts through the national section of the Climate Alliance network (the KBSS). The fact that Dübendorf belongs to the agglomeration of Zurich does not lead to a special cooperation between the core city and its agglomeration community within that network.

Table 4.2: Horizontal governance: gained influence for core cities

City-region	Metropolitan government	Contacts between the core city and the agglomeration communities on international activities	Gained influence for core city
Berne	–	–	–
Geneva	–	–	–
Lausanne	–	–	–
Lucerne	–	–	–
Zurich	–	–	–
Stuttgart	✓	✓ (through metropolitan government)	–
Lyon	✓	✓ (through metropolitan government)	–

In the case of Stuttgart, three of the five district cities belong to the Climate Alliance. Their membership, however, is primarily symbolic; none of the three district cities have ever participated in the network's international meetings. The member cities from the agglomeration of Stuttgart do cooperate in this area, however. Because only the city of Stuttgart is able to participate in the network's international meetings, the Climate Alliance's other member cities from the region delegate their voice to the city of Stuttgart. They informally coordinate their position on agenda items for the international meetings.

The city partnerships from the agglomeration communities are carried out in a traditional manner; almost all of them focus on political exchanges between the partner cities. Actors from civil society, mostly in the domains of sports and music, participate in these partnerships. Economic exchanges occur only very rarely. The core cities' partnerships can be divided into two groups: those that include economic aspects, and those from the agglomeration communities that are more social-political in their orientation. Policy-makers from the agglomeration communities all perceive the importance of the city partnerships to be rather modest, and these partnerships are seldom connected to an overall city-region strategy.

Among all seven city-regions under scrutiny, there is no contact between the core cities and the agglomeration communities concerning their partnerships. Such possible cooperation schemes are usually complete non-issues. Neither the policy-makers of the core city nor those of the agglomeration communities have ever considered such a strategic cooperation. Usually, each side is not even fully aware of the other side's international contacts. Agglomeration communities administer their own international partnerships but are unaware of the mushrooming international contacts of their respective core cities. The converse is also true; the core cities are unaware of the partnerships of their agglomeration communities.

This lack of awareness and cooperation is surprising because the distinct separation between the core cities and the agglomeration communities clearly leads to centrality burdens for the core cities, since the core cities must devote a considerable amount of money to their international contacts. The international engagement is increasingly aligned with financial costs, not only because of the need to travel abroad for international meetings but also because of the workforce required to manage the interurban networking activities.

Six of the seven core cities under scrutiny maintain services or at least subservices for external relations. In most of the agglomeration communities, there are no such services. The district towns in the region of Stuttgart are an exception; some of them have (usually part-time) employees who deal with the partnerships. In all other city-regions, the agglomeration communities attach their international partnerships to departments that deal with them on the side.

Core cities' centrality burdens[7] concerning their international contacts are unsurprising since there are many other policy fields in which the agglomeration communities profit from the core city's engagement. However, in many of these policy fields, there is at least a debate around these centrality burdens and a discussion of possible ways to overcome them, either by incorporating the agglomeration communities into a common policy-making scheme or by letting the communities contribute financially. However, in the area of international activities, there is no indication of such a debate in any of the seven city-regions under scrutiny.

In the two EU cases, at least, the inclusion of the metropolitan government has led to a certain equalisation of the core city's centrality burdens (see below). Even in the Swiss city-regions that have relatively long-standing traditions of international engagement (i.e. Geneva and Lucerne), there is no consideration of a possible inclusion or financial participation of the agglomeration communities. The involved policy-makers do not question the international contacts' restriction to the core city. Hubbard's (2007: 195) argument that the core cities are not dependent on the financial contributions of the agglomeration communities to their international activities is thus true. Hubbard (2007: 197) additionally states that policy-makers in the core cities perceive extra-regional linkages as more important than intra-regional ones. Connecting to the global market seems to be more important than connecting to the local hinterland. However, even if this argument is valid, it does not explain why the core cities never demand co-financing of their international activities from the agglomeration communities. Only in the case of Lyon, where a metropolitan government exists, has such an attempt succeeded (see below).

This finding partially contradicts the varieties of capitalism analysis presented above. Because the city-region composes one economic area, the logic of its perceived need to engage in international activities according to its economic outline should not be limited to the core city. The same logic should apply to the agglomeration communities as well, but they seem to be freeriders in this respect. Although they profit from the core city's function as the nodal point that links the local economy to the global market, they do not participate in any respective political connectivity. The communities profit from the core city's centrality trap

---

7   This should be relativised for the Swiss city-regions that are only reluctantly engaged in urban foreign policy. In these cases, centrality burdens are of course much lower.

as the only political entity that is able to engage politically beyond the national border. The link from the international activities to the broader phenomenon of urban entrepreneurialism is therefore also limited to the core city. Only within core cities do policy-makers link their international activities to the economic needs of the city-region as a whole.

Kübler and Piliutyte (2007: 364f.) explain the dominance of core cities in the international activities of city-regions by noting the positive effects of these international contacts for the core city. This analysis confirmed this idea insofar as the core cities are the uncontested leaders of the whole city-region's international connectivity. This creates a certain monopoly for the core cities. However, according to the varieties of capitalism approach as well as the assessments of several policy-makers, there are spillover effects into the whole city-region. In the agglomeration communities, although they belong to the same economic area, there is not (yet) any perceived need to support the core cities' international activities. Thus, the core cities do not gain influence against the agglomeration communities through their predominant position in linking the whole city-region to the global scale.

Metropolitan governments: added international activities
Within the analysis of the cooperation schemes between the core cities and the agglomeration communities, the issue of metropolitan governance needs further examination. Although the relations between the communities and the metropolitan government could be treated as issues of vertical governance,[8] they will be treated here as a special form of cooperation between the core city and the agglomeration communities. As seen in the case studies of Lyon and Stuttgart, both city-regions' metropolitan governments are very active on the international scale. Thus, it can be first concluded that the existence of a metropolitan government leads to an increase in the city-region's international activities. This additional layer of government forms another local scale that can engage in international activities, as the two EU case studies show.

The metropolitan government also helps to overcome the core city's centrality burdens since the agglomeration communities finance the metropolitan government and thereby help finance the metropolitan government's international activities. However, this has not led to increased cooperation between the core city and the agglomeration communities. The regions carry out their international activities independently from their member communities. Both regions are unaware of their communities' international activities. Thus, there is only cooperation (or competition, in the case of Stuttgart; see below) between the core city and the metropolitan government, but there is no additional inclusion or cooperation between the metropolitan government and the agglomeration communities. In international activities, the metropolitan governments act independently from their communal members but not independently from their respective core cities.

---

8   That is why the corresponding sections in the case studies can be found under 'vertical governance'.

Stuttgart and Lyon's respective relations between the metropolitan government and the core city are vastly different; the relations are cooperative in Lyon and competitive in Stuttgart. In the case of Stuttgart, there is a competition in international activities between the core city and the metropolitan government. The region of Stuttgart, as a newly-instituted metropolitan government, is under permanent pressure to justify its own existence. Its international contacts clearly enhance this justification. The region views itself as the ideal scale to establish international contacts in the policy domains in which it has some competences (e.g. spatial planning and public transport) or towards the EU. Hence, the region maintains its own office in Brussels (see below).

The general understanding between the region and the city of Stuttgart is traditionally conflictive. This manifests itself in their respective international contacts. Although the international activities of the city and the region address the same domains and are both coherent with the city-region's economic outline, they seldom cooperate in their respective international activities. This leads to a particular situation in which the city and the region of Stuttgart are sometimes both members of the same interurban network. Except for the standardised inclusion of the city as a member of the metropolitan government, there is no cooperation between the two scales on their international activities. The core city perceives itself as the leader in international contacts, whereas the region uses its own international contacts to justify its existence as an additional governmental layer. This leads to a conflict of predominance in the area of international contacts.

In the case of Lyon, both the general understanding between the core city and the metropolitan government and their collaboration concerning international activities are much more cooperative. This cooperation is prompted by the city's very strong position in the metropolitan government. The city of Lyon holds the majority of the seats in the regional parliament, and the mayor of Lyon is traditionally also the president of the region. The city of Lyon therefore controls the decision-making process on the regional scale as well. The current mayor initiated the amalgamation of the two scales' services for international contacts in 2006. He thereby managed to dissolve the centrality burdens of the city's international activities. Now, all the agglomeration communities indirectly co-finance the city's international activities through their affiliation with the metropolitan government.

Thus, the conclusion of the analysis of metropolitan governments' participation in the international activities of the city-regions is twofold. One the one hand, the existence of a metropolitan government clearly increases the number of international activities at the local scale. On the other hand, the relation between the core city and the metropolitan government is not necessarily cooperative concerning their respective international activities.

Stuttgart displays a conflictive relation between the two scales, which hinders a coherent international appearance. Lyon presents a much more coherent appearance and a close cooperation between its two scales concerning their international activities. This difference can be explained by the general climate between the core city and the metropolitan government and by their relative structure. When the core city is dominant in the decision-making process at the regional scale as well (as in the case of Lyon), close cooperation with the metropolitan government allows the core city to disperse the centrality burdens of its international activities. When the core city's position within the metropolitan government structure is weak (as in the case of Stuttgart), the agglomeration communities will block the core city's attempt to demand a financial contribution to its international activities. Stuttgart's metropolitan government uses its international contacts in the policy domains in which it has responsibility to legitimise its own existence. This leads to a competition of the two scales, which hampers a coherent international appearance.

In conclusion, the core cities are the uncontested leaders in connecting the whole city-region to the global scale. Currently, core cities are the only elements of city-regions that have developed urban foreign policies. There is almost no contact with the agglomeration communities concerning international activities, not even in the two cities that have metropolitan governments. Such cooperation seems to be a non-issue in six of the seven city-regions. Only in Lyon has the core city successfully managed to obtain co-financing for its international activities from its agglomeration communities.

VERTICAL GOVERNANCE: ONLY THE EU

The analysis of the upper-level governments' inclusion in the city-regions' international activities can be divided along the three different upper-level governments; the regional scale will be discussed first, then the national scale, and lastly the EU scale.

The fifth hypothesis, which was derived from the rescaling approach, was that city-regions would use their increased political steering capacity (resulting from their increased importance as nodal points in the globalised economy) to gain influence against upper-level governments. Table 4.3 summarises the empirical findings for this hypothesis. The first three columns note whether contacts with upper-level governments exist at all. The last column displays whether the city-region has gained increased influence through its intrascalar relations. This first overview clearly shows two things; contacts with upper-level governments are very limited, and even where they exist, they seldom strengthen the city-region's position. The empirical analysis of the seven city-regions under scrutiny thus has not confirmed the fifth hypothesis.

Relations with the first upper-level government

Although the regional government maintains its own service for international contacts in six of the seven city-regions under scrutiny, cooperation schemes are very rare. Lyon is the only case that displays a close cooperation between the two scales on their international contacts. In Lyon, the persons responsible for the international activities of the city-region and of the département meet regularly. In a rather limited sense, each also adjusts its international activities to those of the other scale. The département pursues some international partnerships that focus on development aid, whereas the city-region of Lyon recently developed a partnership with a city from the area that profits from the regional development aid. The

Table 4.3: Vertical governance: gained influence for the city-regions

City-Region	Contacts with the regional scale on international activities	Contacts with the national scale on international activities	Contacts with the EU on international activities	Gained influence for the city-region
Berne	–	–	–	–*
Geneva	–	–	–	✓ (Against the regional scale)
Lausanne	–	–	–	–
Lucerne	–	–	–	–
Zurich	–	–	–	–
Stuttgart	✓ (Only with metropolitan government)	–	✓	✓ (Together with EU scale)
Lyon	✓	–	✓	✓ (Against national scale / Together with EU scale)

* As seen (on pages 172ff.), one of the goals of the ECDP network (in which Berne, Lucerne, and Zurich were members) was to lobby at the national scale for a more liberal drug policy. Because ECDP has had no recent activity and because it is the only network explicitly set up against the national scale, I do not judge the overall international strategies of those three city-regions as focused against the national scale. On the contrary, Berne and Zurich indirectly pursue a good understanding with the national scale when engaging in international activities.

département was involved in Lyon's candidacy to become the European capital of culture in 2013. The relations between the département du Rhône and the city-region of Lyon are not conflictive, and the city-region of Lyon does not use its own very strong international presence against the regional scale. Rather, these international contacts are a response against a strong centralist state structure (see below).

The Stuttgart region sends its own delegate to the EU. The Land has not supported this decision because it maintains its own staff in Brussels. However, the EU office of the Stuttgart region was set up to justify its own existence, not to oppose any scale. There are no formally established contacts between the city, the region, and the Land concerning their respective international activities.

For the Swiss city-regions, there are only a few contacts between the city-regions and their respective cantonal governments concerning the city-regions' international activities. In Lausanne and Lucerne, there is no contact between the two scales, whereas in Geneva, Berne, and Zurich, there is limited cooperation. In Berne and Zurich, the cantonal governments initiated partnership programmes between their communities and Czech communities. In Berne, the canton stopped this engagement shortly after the initiation of the programme, whereas the canton of Zurich financed the programme's coordinator and partnership meetings for several years. Currently, in both cases, the canton only monitors the respective partnerships of its communities, without pursuing any further cooperation in this activity. Policy-makers, both on the cantonal and on the communal level, agree that these partnerships are not strategically important.

Geneva is the only city-region under scrutiny that shows a truly conflictive relation between the city and the cantonal scale concerning their international contacts. Contrary to many other Swiss cantons, the canton of Geneva is very active on the international scale, and cantonal policy-makers view their international engagement as important for the economic well-being of the area. The city also justifies its own strong commitment to international contacts by emphasising the city-region's economic needs. The general relations between the city and the canton are not harmonious, and this is manifested in their international activities. Although policy-makers from both scales agree that their international contacts primarily serve to promote Geneva globally as a city-region for international peace negotiations and as a worldwide headquarters for IGOs and NGOs, they still do not cooperate in this area. However, in the case of Geneva, there is no strategic use of the city-region's international contacts against the cantonal scale. Instead, the two scales carry out their international contacts independently from each other.

Several of the Swiss core cities under scrutiny used their international contacts within the ECDP network to lobby for a more moderate drug policy; this action was also oriented against their respective cantons, which supported a more restrictive drug policy. Since the primary target scale for a policy change of the ECDP member cities was the national one, this network will be examined in the following section, which presents an analysis of the relations between the city-regions' international activities and the national scale.

The general conclusion concerning the relations between the city-region and the regional scale is that the first does not strategically use its new role on the international level against the latter. There are only rare contacts between the two scales, and these contacts are not part of an (inter)scalar strategy.

Relations between the city-regions and the national scale
The same is true for the relations between the city-regions and the national scale concerning the city-regions' international activities; interscalar contacts are very rare. In general, the national and local scales carry out their foreign policies independently. However, the city-region's relations with the national scale are nevertheless important for its international activities, albeit indirectly.

Lyon is the only city-region in which conflictive relations with the national scale partially explain the city's international activities. The policy-makers of Lyon perceive their city-region as a secondary city within the centralistic state structure of France, which strongly focuses on Paris. These policy-makers have developed a strategy for increased international visibility because they feel neglected by the inner-state system. Feeling unable to compete with the national powerhouse, Paris, Lyon's policy-makers have redirected their scalar attention away from an inner-state competition towards an international (or at least a European) one. Their goal is to become one of the top fifteen economic areas in Europe. Their international activities are part of their strategy to increase the region's international visibility and to oppose the national scale.

Although policy-makers in Stuttgart also feel uneasy concerning the city-region's position within the German federal state, they do not orient themselves against the national scale through the city's international activities. In Stuttgart's rather special case, the city's outstanding economic situation within the German urban system causes this unease. Stuttgart is an economic powerhouse, whereas other, especially Eastern German, city-regions face severe unemployment and population loss. This leads to different needs in cooperation schemes for Stuttgart than for other German city-regions. Hence, the city-region seeks international cooperation schemes instead of inner-state ones. This urban policy is not purposefully oriented against the national scale, however, as in the case of Lyon.

The analysis of Lyon and Stuttgart thus reveals that the state's structure (i.e. federalism or centralism) does not necessarily influence the intensity or orientation of a city-region's international activities. Even in the highly centralistic country of France, Lyon has developed its own international strategy that is completely uncoupled from the national foreign policy. Nevertheless, the centralistic state structure has fostered Lyon's international engagement. This is quite contrary to the theoretical notion that a strong, national-centralistic state would hinder any sub-national foreign engagement. Stuttgart, although settled in a federal country, is also uneasy within its national setting. The causalities between the state structure and city-regions' international activities are thus more complex than expected by the theoretical argument. The relations between the city-regions' international activities and the national foreign policy regarding international contacts are much less developed in the literature than those between the national and regional scales (Blatter 2000; Sturny 1998).

Among the Swiss city-regions, only one international activity on the city-region scale has ever been set up as a strategy against the national scale.[9] Three of the five Swiss city-regions under scrutiny were among the first and most active members of ECDP. This network, which was built in the early 1990s, was a cooperation scheme that brought together cities facing severe centrality problems with drug users. The city scale faced the most problems with drug addicts at that time, and policy-makers at this scale felt neglected by upper-level governments regarding this specific issue. The ECDP network was highly appreciated as international backup for cities' demand for more liberal drug policies. Cities cooperated in the ECDP network not only to share best practices in dealing with drug-related centrality problems but also to lobby at the national scale for a policy change. However, this was the only international activity of Swiss city-regions in which a scalar conflict was the direct origin of international cooperation.

---

9   The ECDP network was also partially oriented against the regional scale; see page 171.

The empirical analysis therefore does not support the hypothesis of city-regions' gained influence against the national scale through the city-regions' international activities. In Berne, Zurich, and Geneva, in fact, a good understanding with the national scale is viewed as more important than the development of independent international activities. Berne, as the capital city that is thereby economically dependent on the national administration, pursues almost no international activities. This demonstrates the city's anticipatory obedience to the national foreign policy. Good relations with the national scale are seen as highly important for the economic well-being of the city-region, whereas international contacts are seen as much less important in economic terms. These two aspects together explain Berne's reluctance to participate in international activities.

For Zurich, a good understanding with the national scale is maintained indirectly. Because it depends on the national regulations of its important and globalised banking sector, Zurich does not offend the national scale with its own international activities but rather carefully preserves friendly external relations with other Swiss city-regions and within the Swiss federal system. Geneva also considers its relations with the federal scale when managing its own international contacts. Policy-makers in Geneva are aware of the need for a close collaboration between the national and local scales in order to preserve Geneva's image as an international city.

Therefore, contrary to the theoretical argument, the international activities of the three city-regions are never used against the national scale but are rather carried out in respect of the national foreign policy. Although Hobbs (1988, 1994) and Kirby *et al.* (1995: 276f.) state that the international activities of American cities have often served to contradict a national foreign policy, this is not true for the EU city-regions under scrutiny here. Lyon is the only examined city-region that orients its international strategy against the national state. However, this strategy does not directly oppose the state's foreign policy; rather, it enables Lyon to promote itself outside of the centralistic state structure, which predominantly focuses on Paris.

The importance of the national scale in city-regions' international activities can be observed not only when noting the missing strategic scalar use of these activities against the national scale but also when analysing the importance of national (and especially language) borders within interurban networking. The phenomenon of interurban networking is therefore not as global (or at least as European) as it is often considered. Language-borders and corresponding national borders still play an important role in interurban networking. This weakens the theoretical idea of bypassing of the national scale through interurban networking.

National policy-making systems also play an important role in interurban networking. The relevant issue here regards not the amount of political steering capacity that is admitted to the local scale but rather the wide variety of opportunities to act politically on the local scale among different countries. Conflicting understandings of the role of the state in a specific policy field create challenges for interurban cooperation across countries.

Overall, the analysis supports Lefèvre and d'Albergo's (2007: 324) analysis that the local-national relations concerning city-regions' international activities demonstrate reciprocal indifference. Although the three Swiss city-regions of Berne, Geneva, and Zurich reflect on their relations with the national scale when they go global, they do not conduct any formal contacts with the federal scale. Only Lyon's international strategy is oriented against the national scale, but it does not directly oppose the national foreign policy. City-regions generally carry out their international activities independently from the national foreign policy. This reveals interscalar neglect between the national and local scales rather than a close centre-local relation.

Relations between the city-regions and the EU

When examining the last scalar relation, between the city-region and the EU, concerning the city-region's international activities, an obvious distinction must be made between city-regions outside and within the EU. For those within the EU, relations to the EU are crucial to understanding the new movement of interurban networking; for those outside of it, the Swiss absence from the EU partially explains the Swiss city-regions' reluctance to engage in such networking activities.

However, the two EU city-regions' approaches towards the EU are quite different. For Stuttgart, the EU is the key target of both the city's and the region's international activities. Lyon's international activities, on the other hand, have an increasingly global scalar orientation and therefore reach beyond the European scale. However, through the presidency of Eurocities, Lyon's mayor is situated in a key position to access EU policy-making. Lyon therefore stresses uploading rather than downloading in its relations with the EU. Its primary goal is not to obtain co-financing for its international activities but rather to remain at the forefront as the EU launches new regulations that can affect the city-regions and to influence those decisions.

Stuttgart, conversely, invests increasing effort in the downloading function, seeking a co-financing of several of its international contacts by the EU. With the instalment of a contact person for EU relations in every department, the city clearly also considers the uploading function. The mayor's strategic goal is to ensure that Stuttgart is informed about upcoming decisions on the EU scale that might concern the city-region. The Stuttgart region even decided to open its own office in Brussels in order to gain easier access to the EU decision-making process.

Both the downloading and uploading functions of the relations between city-regions and the EU are only partially barred for Swiss city-regions. Membership in Eurocities, the interurban network that primarily lobbies at the EU scale for large urban areas and thereby secures the uploading function, is open to European cities from non-EU countries. Still, only two Swiss cities, Geneva and Zurich, have opted for such a membership. Geneva was a member of Eurocities in the 1990s but then resigned due to internal political conflicts over both the membership itself and the high membership fee. It is too early to determine whether any Swiss cities will use the Eurocities network to increase their linkages with the EU.

It is much more difficult for Swiss city-regions to achieve the downloading function, here perceived as a co-financing of urban policy-making by the EU, than the uploading function. Cooperation schemes in interurban networks, which are co-financed by the EU, do often not allow for the funding of non-EU city-regions.[10] Swiss city-regions then face two options: either they can pay for their own parts of the programme, or, in certain cases, they can ask the federal state to substitute for the missing EU funds. In any case, participation in interurban networking is more complex for city-regions that are not located in EU-member countries.

Additionally, several interurban networks have increased their scalar attention towards the EU and have shifted from policy-learning networks towards networks that coordinate city-regions' financial demands at the EU. Therefore there can only be partial agreement with Church and Reid's (1996: 1299) conclusion that 'European networks may well offer a potential route to EC resources, but there are wider political reasons for this growing involvement'. Access to EU resources is one of the main goals of interurban networking nowadays. Several networks have been formed for accessing EU funds or have changed their focus towards that goal. The city-regions that engage in these networks clearly target EU funding in their respective policy fields. Because EU-financing of urban projects often demands crossborder cooperation, international interurban networks are predestined to foster exactly the cooperation schemes that are necessary for obtaining EU funding. Since this aspect is much less promising for Swiss city-regions, several policy-specific interurban networks do not offer any specific benefit for Swiss city-regions.

The EU's strong influence in interurban networking has been demonstrated by several scholars (see Church and Reid 1996: 1297f.; Phelps *et al.* 2002: 211; Ward and Williams 1997). The absence of Swiss city-regions in this development strengthens the authors' argument for the EU's importance in this area, whereas Goldsmith's (2002: 110) notion that the EU 'commission's ability to control subnational governments is limited' can not be supported, at least regarding the subnational governments' international activities. There are increasing ties between urban areas and the supranational EU scale. Many city-regions' international activities are carried out in close collaboration with the EU and with its strong support.

Why is the EU so strongly engaged in interurban networking? The logic of 'glocalisation' helps to explain this scalar cooperation between the local and the supranational scale. The international activities of city-regions bypass the national state (see Friedmann 2001: 129). Leitner *et al.* (2002: 288, original emphasis) therefore state that 'the inter-urban networks of the EU were created by EU institutions in part to strengthen their power and authority *vis-à-vis* nation-states (and are contested by some nation-states for this reason)'. This argument of a strategy against the national state is convincing. Both the local and the supranational scale are intermingled in a scalar power-struggle against the national scale, which explains their cooperation in interurban networking (Keating 1999: 7). Harding (1997: 302, with reference to Jones and Keating 1995) correctly identifies 'links

---

10   In one exception to this rule, for certain cooperation schemes, the Swiss national state compensates for the missing financial contribution from the EU. The most prominent example of this is the Interreg programme.

between the European Commission and sub-national interests, both of which see advantage in trying to outmanoeuvre nation-states over policy directions and the use of resources'.

Because most of the analysed interurban networks have a European scalar orientation and because only few international activities of city-regions go beyond this scale, it might be better to speak of an Europeanisation instead of an internationalisation or globalisation of urban policy-making. Although the driving force behind the globalisation of city-regions might be economic issues, the political response is (so far) not global but rather limited to Europe. This is clearly linked to the importance of the EU in this area.

This analysis does not support Leitner and Sheppard's (1999: 241, see also 2002: 159) statement that 'cooperative networks that develop on their own initiative, from the bottom up, and particularly those sharing a common geographical identity, are more likely to result in successful long-term cooperative efforts than networks artificially constructed by Eurocrats'. The distinction between bottom-up and top-down networks is increasingly blurred. Hardly any interurban policy networks can be labelled as totally bottom-up, almost all of them have some connections to the EU. EU funding is an important factor in fostering interurban networking; hence, most networks are less oriented towards bottom-up procedures.

However, cooperation between the EU and the local scale also follows the theoretical argument of a rescaled statehood. According to that theory,[11] the reshuffling of the state scalar structure increases the possibilities for political steering capacity at the supranational and sub-national scales, whereas national states tend to lose ground. This follows from an economic logic in which large city-regions are nodal points of economic development. City-regions become the primary scale of both economic and political interest. By focusing on this scale and its interlinkage to other scales through interurban networking, the EU adapts to the logics of a 'glocalised' economic structure. Thus, upscaling and downscaling are much more closely intertwined than first expected, especially in interurban networking.

What is the nature of the cooperation between the two scales that theoretically possess political steering capacity in a globalised economy? The strategic cooperation of the supranational and sub-national scales is important for global competitiveness in a rescaled statehood, and this is the EU's reason for supporting interurban networking. However, it remains uncertain whether this goal can be achieved. Policy learning fostered through interurban cooperation is generally seen as a means for increasing the competitiveness of the European area as a whole, and it is encouraged by the EU as part of the Lisbon goals. However, the analysis of the actual policy-making processes of city-regions within these interurban networks shows that city-regions focus on their own competitiveness against other European city-regions (see also Begg 1999: 796). Therefore, the competitiveness of the European economic area as a whole may not be strengthened due to an increased connectivity of city-regions throughout Europe.

---

11   See pages 5ff.

The notion of a zero-sum inner-European competition, despite interurban networking, might seem more appropriate after an analysis of the city-regions' underlying motivations and mechanisms.[12] Jakoby and Schmolinsky (2005) note correctly that 'cities are extremely important for growth and employment, and thus for realisation of the Lisbon strategy'. The critical literature on the European integration process as a further development of the neo-liberal agenda (see Amin and Thrift 1995), as well as the literature on urban entrepreneurialism (Harvey 1989), should thus develop a common, more scalar sensitive approach to the shift towards neo-liberal policy-making.

Häupl's (2005, see also Esser 2005) demand that urban areas should try to change the EU's Lisbon goals will not be fulfilled. The hopes for a change against neo-liberal policy-making at the urban scale appear even less promising after the analysis of the EU's role in interurban networking. A multi-scalar and interscalar analysis of the content of interurban networking confirms its orientation towards increased competitiveness instead of an orientation towards social cohesion. This realisation strengthens the conclusion from the first section, which revealed a close relation of urban foreign policy and the shift towards urban entrepreneurialism.

INTRASCALAR AND INTERSCALAR ASPECTS OF URBAN FOREIGN POLICY

Clearly, Cremer *et al.'s* (2001: 393) conclusion regarding general interscalar co-operation schemes' importance in interurban networking is not supported by this analysis. Only the EU plays a crucial role in urban foreign policy; relations along the agglomeration communities (horizontal governance), the regional scale, and the national scale (vertical governance) are almost negligible. City-regions generally do not use their international activities strategically for their positioning in horizontal or vertical governance. Their close linkages with the EU, however, show a certain bypassing of the national scale (Leitner and Sheppard 2002: 159).

The two EU city-regions act more independently on the international level than the Swiss city-regions; in fact, policy-makers in three of the five Swiss city-regions (Berne, Geneva, and Zurich) explicitly consider the national scale when they go global. Therefore, Swiss city-regions are not only lagging behind in their international engagements but also are more settled in the traditional federal state structure, whereas their EU counterparts utilise the possibilities for bypassing the national scale much more frequently and strategically.

The Swiss absence from the EU explains the Swiss city-regions' reluctance to go global. It is an open question whether their strategic use of international activities will play a more significant role in the future. The case of Geneva, which has a long-standing and well-established urban foreign policy, does not support this expectation. Time does not seem to be a crucial factor in explaining the missing strategic use of urban foreign policy in horizontal and vertical governance.

---

12   Here, this contradicts Harvey (1989: 5), who sees it as a positive-sum game due to the increased interurban cooperation forms. Leitner and Sheppard (1999: 233), however, even speak of a negative-sum game due to increased competition among city-regions.

The examination of interscalar and intrascalar relations reveals some interesting links to the first part of the analysis (e.g. how to explain city-regions' international activities). The economic logic that was presented to explain the intensity and content of city-regions' international activities also drives the city-regions' relations with upper-level governments. The city-regions strategically incorporate their relations with upper-level governments into their international strategies, according to their economic needs. The interscalar relations that are most important for the city-regions' economic well-being are those that are most respected in the relevant international activities. The relations with other scales that are seen as less important in economic terms are neglected. Where good relations with the national scale are vital for the city-region's economic well-being, there is no bypassing of the national scale; instead, policy-makers endeavour to align their international activities with the national foreign policy. Where the national scale is seen as a hindrance to the city-region's economic well-being (e.g. Lyon), the international activities are carried out independently, sometimes even against the national scale.

The policy-making process at the city-region' scale is also aligned to this economically determined logic. Not only do city-regions strategically select their interscalar relations with upper-level governments according to their economic needs, they also structure their internal policy-making processes according to this goal of competitiveness. The strong roles of the mayor and the bureaucracy at the city-region scale accord with the city-regions' relations in horizontal and vertical governance, which pursue the goal of increased economic competitiveness.

The underlying competitiveness logic also explains why this analysis only affirmed the third hypothesis, which addressed the intrascalar change towards a more elitist policy-making process. Hypotheses four and five, regarding the strategic interscalar use of international activities, needed to be revised to consider the city-regions' economic needs more carefully. In their original outline, the empirical analysis did not confirm those hypotheses.

| conclusion

City-regions' international activities are mushrooming all over Europe. Traditional city partnerships have been followed by newly emerging city networks. These international activities do not fit the traditional understanding of the state structure since they bypass the national scale, which is notably the scale that traditionally (indeed, for centuries) has been responsible for foreign policy.

Among the seven city-regions under scrutiny, only one (Berne) has not increased its international contacts over the past two decades. All other city-regions follow the rescaling approach's prediction of an increase in international activities. Moreover, as revealed through incorporating the varieties of capitalism approach, they do so in coherence with their local economic settings.

The first research question, concerning the extent and orientation of city-regions' international activities, was answered through a combination of the rescaling approach and the varieties of capitalism approach. Only the incorporation of the local economic setting into the broader approach to state rescaling produced a satisfying explanation of city-regions' international activities. This detour was also necessary to reveal the competitive orientation of urban networking. However, the primary purpose of the city-regions' engagement in these networks is to make international political contacts that align with their economic outlines. The analysis of urban foreign policy through the combination of the two approaches also showed, contrary to the prediction of the rescaling theory, that city-regions display various responses to globalisation. The problem that many city-regions share (i.e. an increasing fear of international interurban competition) does not necessarily require a unitary solution. As the analysis shows, most city-regions develop strategies that consider their specific economic outlines when selecting international activities.

The analysis also disproved the theoretical idea of overcoming interurban competition through increased cooperation of city-regions as nodal points of the globalised economy. Although the interurban networks often deal with non-competitive issues, the underlying strategy of the involved city-regions reveals a different picture. Policy-makers view the international activities of city-regions as an integral part of their competitiveness-oriented strategies. It was therefore argued that because of these indirect but very strong linkages to the city-regions' economic profile and their underlying economic strategies, the city-regions' international activities are part of the neo-liberal shift in urban politics (Harvey 1989; Jessop *et al*. 2007; MacLeod and Goodwin 1999; McNeill 2005).

The pessimistic strand of the rescaling approach was thus correct that these international activities are part of the increasing interurban competition among large city-regions. This agrees with Brenner (2004: 17), who argues that

> new forms of interurban networking have addressed at least some of the disruptive effects of unfettered uneven spatial development – albeit still within

the parameters of an explicitly growth-driven, competitiveness-oriented model of state spatial regulation' and that 'interurban networking initiatives [...] have deepened rather than alleviated the political-economic dislocations, regulatory failures, and territorial inequalities that were generated through previous rounds or urban locational policy.

(Brenner 2004: 26)

Becker and Keller (2007: 9; author's translation) state provocatively but nevertheless correctly that 'international capital becomes the fetish of a network based (foreign) policy at the city scale [and that...] networking has become a standard and the thereof resulting advantage an illusion.' Many city-regions do not seek direct rewards from their international activities; rather, they desire to increase their global visibility, which is often the key goal of urban foreign policy. International activities provide opportunities for acquiring international publicity and are a strategic instrument in urban politics.

The goal of increasing competitiveness through interurban cooperation is inherently illogical; city-regions try to increase their relative competitiveness towards other city-regions by cooperating with them. City-regions' unwillingness to cooperate in the domain of locational politics, the policy area most closely linked to competitiveness, clearly reveals this illogicality. The less a policy domain is concerned with competitiveness, the more city-regions are willing to share their best practices in that domain. However, this still undermines the underlying strategy of increasing competitiveness through interurban networking (see also Parkinson and Harding 1995).

Still, the economic outline explains the intensity and orientation of a city-region's international activities. Where this outline is more national, city-regions focus their external relations on the national scale. Where the economy is globally oriented and policy-makers fear pressure from the global interurban competition for local workplaces, the city-regions will increase their international political connectivity. Here again, place-specific economic needs explain the scalar orientation of city-regions; this was only revealed by the applied combination of the rescaling and the varieties of capitalism approaches. Additionally, it was noted that city-regions' perceived vulnerability to globalisation explains their high engagement in urban foreign policy. The involved policy-makers view their economic positions as highly contested, and therefore they aggressively enhance their global visibility through international activities.

The second research question asked whether international activities transform city-regions' policy-making processes and their relations to other regional governments and to upper-level governments. The policy-making process was therefore investigated at the urban scale and interscalar changes examined, both horizontally between the core city and the agglomeration communities and vertically between the region and the upper-level governments. This investigation revealed that the positions of the mayor and the bureaucracy are strong in city-regions' international activities, whereas (direct) democratic control is very limited.

The analysis of the relations between the core city and the agglomeration communities showed that these interscalar relations are in almost all cases a non-issue.

Policy-makers do not reflect on the centrality burdens of their international contacts, which are primarily controlled by the core cities. Core cities do not use their nodal position in establishing the political contacts across borders against the agglomeration communities, although they are part of the same economic area, or against upper-level governments, except for the EU. However, core cities have a monopoly in connecting the whole city-region to the international sphere.

The city-regions' relations with the EU are essential to their international activities. The EU-urban relation has both an uploading and a downloading function. City-regions use interurban networks to lobby jointly at the EU for their benefit (i.e. uploading). Membership in the Eurocities network has become crucial in this respect. City-regions also obtain financial help for their interurban cooperation schemes from the EU (i.e. downloading). The logic hereby is that the EU has an incentive to strengthen urban areas and their interlinkages in order to bypass the national scale. City-regions are also nodal points of global competitiveness, and fostering interurban cooperation is seen as one possibility to achieve the Lisbon goals to increase the competitiveness of the European economy as a whole (Jakoby and Schmolinsky 2005). The aspects of state upscaling and downscaling are thus much more closely interlinked than theoretically expected. The bypassing of the national scale leads to a close cooperation between the sub-national and supranational scales. Those two scales still have political steering capacity in the age of globalisation, according to the rescaling theory. However, as the analysis has shown, the two scales cooperate for the sake of competitiveness, not social cohesion, through interurban networking.

The Swiss city-regions demonstrate a relative reluctance to pursue international contacts. They lag considerably behind the two EU city-regions under scrutiny regarding international connectivity and strategic reflections on this aspect of urban policy-making. Geneva and Lucerne are the only two Swiss city-regions under scrutiny that have long-standing and well-established international strategies, whereas Lausanne and Zurich only very recently began to reflect upon the need to go global. Berne is completely absent from this development. Switzerland's absence from the EU explains the Swiss city-regions' general reluctance towards international contacts. Because many networks exist to lobby at the EU scale and many existing networks have changed their focus towards the EU, joining such interurban networks is thus not very rewarding for Swiss city-regions. However, Swiss city-regions have also not used their own international contacts to oppose the Swiss national policy of not joining the EU.

The examination of the changes caused by city-regions' international activities proves the need for a scalarly open analysis. Whereas the questions of horizontal governance among the agglomeration communities and the horizontal relations within the regional scale are of little importance for city-regions' international activities, its relations with the EU are highly significant. Scale and interscalar relations thus matter, and previous research of city-regions' international activities has too simply (and often without discussion) assumed a scalar limitation of this phenomenon to core cities.

In the three Swiss city-regions of Berne, Geneva, and Zurich, policy-makers are careful not to contradict the national policy when they engage in international contacts because they are economically dependent on a good understanding with the national state. The increase of international activities at the city-region scale does thus not necessarily lead to a hollowing out of the national scale; on the contrary, the national scale is clearly, although indirectly, important in urban foreign policy. Lyon is the only city-region under scrutiny in which the international contacts are part of a strategy against the national state. However, Lyon's strategy contradicts the centralistic state structure rather than the national foreign policy. Except for the somewhat anti-centralism strategy of Lyon's international activities, no differences in intensity or orientation were discovered between the city-regions from federalist countries and those from centralistic countries.

The analysis' division into two steps, first treating the international activities of city-regions as the dependent variable and then treating them as the independent variable, proved to be a valuable guideline. However, as the analysis in the second section showed, all three elements presented as changes in the international activities of city-regions also influence these activities in three ways.

First, the international activities do grant the mayor a stronger position within the city-region, as was theoretically predicted. A proactive mayor can promote certain international activities as part of his/her political programme. Although the evidence for such proactive strategies here is less clear than in other studies of this phenomenon (see Martins and Rodriguez Alvarez 2007), it is clear that mayors strategically reflect upon and proactively steer their city-regions' international activities. Second, the analysis revealed the important role of metropolitan governments, which influence the intensity of the regions' international contacts. In both city-regions with metropolitan governments (Lyon and Stuttgart), these bodies are highly engaged in international activities. These two cases contrast in their relations between the core city and the metropolitan government; the two scales are harmonic in Lyon and conflictive in Stuttgart. This aligns with the respective city-regions' understandings between the core city and the metropolitan government. In both cases, however, the existence of a metropolitan government tends to increase the international activities. Third, the analysis of city-regions' relationships to upper-level governments revealed the importance of the supranational EU in this respect. The EU's support is partially responsible for the new movement of city-regions' international activities that began in the 1980s.

Clearly, the traditional understanding that international relations are dominated by national states must be revised after this analysis of urban foreign policy. The long-standing notion of external unity and internal diversity (Ehrenzeller *et al*. 2002: 55) as a characteristic element of national states must be replaced by a multi-scalar and interscalar conceptualisation of international activities. Duchacek (1990) is thus right when he states that the multi-level governance system of foreign policy is now a system of perforated sovereignty. City-regions as nodal points of a 'glocalised' economy become increasingly involved in independent international activities, often thereby bypassing the national state.

| bibliography

24 heures (1st April 2006) *Lausanne s'interdit tout jumelage en raison de son statut de capital olympique*. Online. Available <http://archives.24heures.ch/VQ/LAUSANNE/-/article-2006-04-112/des-collaborations-thtiques-ne-sont-pourtant-pas-exclues> (accessed 11 November 2008).

– (21st May 2008) *Lausanne est désormais ville gourmande du monde*. Online. Available <http://archives.24heures.ch/VQ/LAUSANNE/-/article-2008-05-638/lausanne-s8217en-leche-deja-les-babines> (accessed 11 November 2008).

Ache, P., Andersen, H. T., Maloutas, T., Raco, M. and Tasan-Kok, T. (eds) (2008) *Cities between Competitiveness and Cohesion*: New York: Springer.

Agnew, J. (1999) 'Mapping Political Power Beyond State Boundaries: Territory, Identity, and Movement in World Politics', *Millenium*, 28(3): 499–521.

Albo, G. (2005) 'Contesting the 'New Capitalism'', in D. Coates (ed.) *Varieties of Capitalism. Varieties of Approaches*. New York: Palgrave McMillan. 63–82.

Aldecoa, F. and Keating, M. (1999) 'Introduction', *Regional and Federal Studies*, 9(1): I–VIII.

Amable, B. (2003) *Diversity of Modern Capitalism*. Oxford: Oxford University Press.

Amin, A. (1994) 'Post-Fordism: Models, Fantasies and Phantoms of Transition', in A. Amin (ed.) *Post-Fordism. A Reader*. Oxford: Blackwell.

Amin, A. and Thrift, N. (1995) 'Institutional Issues for the European Regions: From Markets and Plans to Socioeconomics and Powers of Association', *Economy and Society*, 24(1): 41–66.

Amt für Gemeinden des Kantons Bern (1997) *Gemeindepartnerschaften Kanton Bern – Tschechische Republik / Umfrage Januar 1997*.

Aoki, M. (1994) 'The Contingent Governance of Teams: Analysis of Institutional Complementarity', *International Economic Review*, 35(3): 657–76.

Articus, S. (2005) 'Reposition or Lose – Municipalities' Reactions to European Integration', *Deutsche Zeitschrift für Kommunalwissenschaft*, 44(2).

Beaverstock, J. V., Smith, R. G. and Taylor, P. J. (1999) 'A Roster of World Cities', *Cities*, 16(6): 445–58.

Beck, U. (1997) *Was ist Globalisierung? Irrtümer des Globalismus – Antworten auf Globalisierung*. Frankfurt am Main: Suhrkamp.

Becker, J. and Keller, J. (2007) 'Netzwerkbasierte Stadtaussenpolitik', *Dérive. Zeitschrift für Stadtforschung*, 26: 5-10.

Begg, I. (1999) 'Cities and Competitiveness', *Urban Studies*, 36(5/6): 785–809.

Behringer, J. (2003) *Nationale und transnationale Städtenetzwerke in der Alpenregion. Discussion Paper SP IV 2003–104*. Wissenschaftszentrum Berlin für Sozialforschung.

Benington, J. and Harvey, J. (1999a) 'Networking in Europe', in G. Stoker (ed.) *The New Management of British Local Governance*. Basingstoke: Macmillan. 197–221.

– J. and Harvey, J. (1999b) 'Transnational Local Authority Networking within the European Union: Passing Fashion or New Paradigm?', in D. Marsh (ed.) *Comparing Policy Networks*. Buckingham: Open University Press. 149–66.

Berger, S. (1996) 'Introduction', in S. Berger and R. Dore (eds) *National Diversity and Global Capitalism*. New York: Cornell University Press. 1–25.

Berger, S. and Dore, R. (eds) (1996) *National Diversity and Global Capitalism*. New York: Cornell University Press.

Berry, F. S. and Berry, W. D. (1990) 'State Lottery Adoptions as Policy Innovations: An Event History Analysis', *The American Political Science Review*, 84(2): 395–415.

Betsill, M. M. and Bulkeley, H. (2004) 'Transnational Networks and Global Environmental Governance: The Cities for Climate Protection Program', *International Studies Quarterly*, 48(2): 471–93.

Blatter, J. (1997) 'Explaining Crossborder Cooperation: A Border-Focused and Border-External Approach', *Journal of Borderlands Studies*, XII (1&2): 151–74.

– (2000) *Entgrenzung der Staatenwelt? Politische Institutionenbildung in grenzüberschreitenden Regionen in Europa und Nordamerika*. Baden-Baden: Nomos.

– (2006) 'Geographic Scale and Funtional Scope in Metropolitan Governance Reform: Theory and Evidence from Germany', *Journal of Urban Affairs*, 28(2): 121–50.

Blatter, J., Kreutzer, M., Rentl, M. and Thiele, J. (2008) 'The Foreign Relations of European Regions: Competences and Strategies', *West European Politics*, 31(3): 464–90.

Blöchliger, H., Eichler, M., Grass, M., Koellreuter, C., Liechti, P. and Roth, U. (2004) *Innovation und Wachstum. Wo steht Zürich im internationalen Vergleich?* Zürich: Zürcher Kantonalbank.

Boudreau, J.-A. (2003) 'The Politics of Territorialization: Regionalism, Localism and other Isms. The Case of Montreal', *Journal of Urban Affairs*, 25(2): 179–99.

Boudreau, J.-A. (2007) 'Making New Political Spaces: Mobilizing Spatial Imaginaries, Instrumentalizing Spatial Practices, and Strategically Using Spatial Tools', *Environment and Planning A*, 39(11): 2593–611.

Boudreau, J.-A., Hamel, P., Jouve, B. and Keil, R. (2007) 'New State Spaces in Canada: Metropolitanization in Montreal and Toronto Compared', *Urban Geography*, 28(1): 30–53.

Boudreau, J.-A. and Keil, R. (2001) 'Seceding from Responsibility? Secession Movements in Los Angeles', *Urban Studies*, 38(10): 1701–31.

Boyer, R. (1986) *La théorie de la régulation: une analyse critique*. Paris: La Découverte.

– (1996) 'The Convergence Hypothesis Revisited: Globalization but Still the Century of Nations? ', in S. Berger and R. Dore (eds) *National Diversity and Global Capitalism*. Ithaca/London: Cornell University Press. 29–59.

– (1997) 'The Variety and Unequal Performance of Really Existing Markets: Farewell to Doctor Pangloss?', in J. R. Hollingsworth and R. Boyer (eds) *Contemporary Capitalism*. Cambridge, New York: Cambridge University Press. 55–93.

Boyer, R. and Hollingsworth, J. R. (1997) 'The Variety of Institutional Arrangements and Their Complementarity in Modern Economies', in J. R. Hollingsworth and R. Boyer (eds) *Contemporary Capitalism*. Cambridge, New York: Cambridge University Press. 49–54.

Braun, D. and Gilardi, F. (2006) 'Taking 'Galton's Problem' Seriously: Towards a Theory of Policy Diffusion', *Journal of Theoretical Politics*, 18(3): 298–322.

Brenner, N. (1998) 'Global Cities, Glocal States: Global City Formation and State Territorial Restructuring in Contemporary Europe', *Review of International Political Economy*, 5(1): 1–37.

– (1999) 'Globalisation as Reterritorialisation: The Re-scaling of Urban Governance in the European Union', *Urban Studies*, 36(3): 431–51.

– (2000a) 'Building 'Euro-Regions'', *European Urban and Regional Studies*, 7(4): 319–45.

– (2000b) 'The Urban Question as a Scale Question: Reflections on Henri Lefebvre, Urban Theory and the Politics of Scale', *International Journal of Urban and Regional Research*, 24(2): 361–78.

– (2003) 'Metropolitan Institutional Reform and the Rescaling of State Space in Contemporary Western Europe', *European Urban and Regional Studies*, 10(4): 297–324.

– (2004) *New State Spaces. Urban Governance and the Rescaling of Statehood*. Oxford: Oxford University Press.

Brenner, N., Jessop, B., Jones, M. and MacLeod, G. (2003) 'Introduction: State Space in Question', in N. Brenner, B. Jessop, M. Jones and G. MacLeod (eds) *State/Space. A Reader*. Oxford: Blackwell.

Brenner, N. and Theodore, N. (2002) 'Cities and the Geographies of 'Actually Existing Neoliberalism'', *Antipode*, 34(3): 341–7.

Buck, N., Gordon, I., Harding, A. and Turok, I. (2005) 'Moving Beyond the Conventional Wisdom', in N. Buck, I. Gordon, A. Harding and I. Turok (eds) *Changing Cities. Rethinking Urban Competitiveness, Cohesion and Governance*. Houndsmith/New York: Palgrave. 263–82.

Budd, L. (1998) 'Territorial Competition and Globalisation: Scylla and Charybdis of European Cities', *Urban Studies*, 35(4): 663–85.

Bühlmann, K. (ed.) (1998) *Kultur- und Kongresszentrum Luzern: die Geschichte seines Werdens, die Zukunft seiner Idee*. Rotkreuz: Zürcher Druck und Verlag.

Bulkeley, H. (2005) 'Reconfiguring Environmental Governance: Towards a Politics of Scales and Networks', *Political Geography*, 24(8): 875–902.

Bundesamt für Statistik (2008) *Agglomerationen und Metropolitanräume*. Online. Available <http://www.bfs.admin.ch/bfs/portal/de/index/regionen/11/geo/analyse_regionen/04.html> (accessed 8 May 2008).

– (2007) *Bevölkerungsstand und -struktur – Analysen*. Online. Available <http://www.bfs.admin.ch/bfs/portal/de/index/themen/01/02/blank/dos/result.Document.20561.xls> (accessed 18 March 2010).

– (2008a) *Agglomerationen und Metropolitanräume*. Online. Available <http://www.bfs.admin.ch/bfs/portal/de/index/regionen/11/geo/analyse_regionen/04.html> (accessed 18 March 2010).

– (2008b) *Eidgenössische Betriebszählung 2005*. Online. Available <http://www.bfs.admin.ch/bfs/portal/de/index/dienstleistungen/geostat/datenbeschreibung/betriebszaehlung05.html> (accessed 18 March 2010).

Camagni, R. (2007) 'City Networks as Tools for Competitiveness and Sustainability', in P. J. Taylor, B. Derudder, P. Saey and F. Witlox (eds) *Cities in Globalization. Practices, Policies and Theories*. London, New York: Routledge. 107–29.

Canton de Genève (2008) *Les membres du Groupe interdépartemental aux affaires internationales*. Online. Available <http://www.geneve.ch/internationale/les-organes-associes/les-membres-du-groupe/> (accessed 18 March 2010).

Canton de Vaud (2008) *Sport International*. Online. Available <http://www.vd.ch/no_cache/fr/themes/vie-privee/sports-et-loisirs/sport-international/?sword_list%5B0%5D=international> (accessed 26 July 2008).

Cappellin, R. (1992) 'Theories of Local Endogenous Development and International Cooperation', in M. Tykkylainen (ed.) *Development Issues and Strategies in the New Europe*. Avebury: Aldershot. 1–19.

– (1993) 'Interregional Cooperation and the Design of a Regional Foreign Policy', in R. Cappellin and P. W. J. Batey (eds) *Regional Networks, Border Regions and European Integration*. London: Pion. 70–88.

Castells, M. (1994) 'European Cities, the Informational Society, and the Global Economy', *New Left Review*, 204: 18–32.

– (1996) *The Rise of the Network Society*. Malden: Blackwell.

Cheshire, P. (1999) 'Cities in Competition: Articulating the Gains from Integration', *Urban Studies*, 36(5/6): 843–64.

Church, A. and Reid, P. J. (1996) 'Urban Power, International Networks, and Competition: The Example of Cross-Border Cooperation', *Urban Studies*, 36(7): 1297–318.

Cities for Mobility (2008) *Premium Partners*. Online. Available <http://www.cities-for-mobility.net/index.php?option=com_content&task=blogcategory&id=50&Itemid=172> (accessed 8 August 2008).

City Mayors (2008) *Largest French Cities*. Online. Available <http://www.citymayors.com/gratis/french_cities.html> (accessed 18 August 2008).

City Population (2007) *Die grössten Städte Deutschlands*. Online. Available <http://www.citypopulation.de/Deutschland-Cities_d.html#Stadt_gross> (accessed 18 March 2010).

Citynet (2008) *Members' Profiles*. Online. Available <http://www.citynet-ap.org/members/profiles/filter/20/> (accessed 18 March 2010).

Clement, S. and Erdmenger, C. (2003) *EU-Forschungsprojekt RELIEF. Potentialanalyse – Perspektiven umweltfreundlicher Beschaffung in Zürich*. Online. Available <http://www.stadt-zuerich.ch/internet/ugz/home/fachbereiche/umweltschutzfachstelle/relief-index/6a.ParagraphContainerList.ParagraphContainer0.ParagraphList.0002.File.pdf/PA_Zuerich_final.pdf> (accessed 22 July 2008).

Coates, D. (2005) 'Paradigms of Explanation', in D. Coates (ed.) *Varieties of Capitalism. Varieties of Approaches*. New York: Palgrave McMillan. 1–25.

Collinge, C. (1999) 'Self-Organization of Society by Scale: a Spatial Reworking of Regulation Theory', *Environment and Planning D*, 17(5): 557–74.

Collomb, G. (2005) 'An Enlarged Europe Needs Strong Urban Centres', *Deutsche Zeitschrift für Kommunalwissenschaft*, 44(2).

Cox, K. R. (1991a) 'The Global Political Economy and Social Choice', in D. Drache and M. S. Gertler (eds) *The New Era of Global Competition: State Policy and Market Power*. Montreal: McGill-Queen's University Press. 335–50.

Cox, K. R. (1991b) 'Questions of Abstraction in Studies in the New Urban Politics', *Journal of Urban Affairs*, 13(3): 267–80.
– (1993) 'The Local and the Global in the New Urban Politics: A Critical Review', *Environment and Planning D*, 11(4): 433–48.
– (1995) 'Globalisation, Competition and the Politics of Local Economic Development', *Urban Studies*, 32(2): 213–25.
– (1997) 'Introduction: Globalization and Its Politics in Question', in K. R. Cox (ed.) *Spaces of Globalization. Reasserting the Power of the Local*. New York: The Guilford Press. 1–18.
Cox, K. R. and Mair, A. (1991) 'From Localised Social Structures to Localities as Agents', *Environment and Planning A*, 23(2): 197–213.
Credit Suisse (2004) *Wirtschaftsstandort Zürich. Struktur und Perspektiven*. Online. Available <https://entry4.credit-suisse.ch/csfs/research/p/d/de/schweiz/regionen/media/pdf/reg_rst_zuerich_2004_de.pdf> (accessed 15 July 2008).
Cremer, R. D., De Bruin, A. and Dupuis, A. (2001) 'International Sister-Cities. Bridging the Global-Local Divide', *American Journal of Economics and Sociology*, 60(1): 377–401.
Crouch, C. and Schmitter, P. C. (eds) (1996) *Varieties of Capitalism*. London and Paris: Pinter.
Crouch, C. and Streeck, W. (1997) 'Introduction: The Future of Capitalist Diversity', in C. Crouch and W. Streeck (eds) *Political Economy of Modern Capitalism: Mapping Convergence and Diversity*. London: Sage. 1–18.
Cushman & Wakefield/Healey & Baker (1990–2009) *European Cities Monitor 1990–2009*. London: Cushman & Wakefield, Healey & Baker.
Dicken, P. (1994) 'Global-Local Tensions: Firms and States in the Global Space Economy', *Economic Geography*, 70(2): 101–28.
Duchacek, I. D. (1984) 'The International Dimension of Sub-National Self-Government', *Publius: The Journal of Federalism*, 14(4): 5–31.
– (1990) 'Perforated Sovereignties: Towards a Typology of New Actors in International Relations', in H. J. Michelmann and S. Panayotis (eds) *Federalism and International Relations: The Role of Subnational Units*. Oxford: Clarendon Press. 1–33.
ECDP (1990) *The Frankfurt Resolution*. Online. Available <http://www.cannabisculture.com/backissues/cc00/frankfurt_resolution.html> (accessed 18 March 2010).
Ehrenzeller, B., Hrbek, R., Malinverni, G. and Thürer, D. (2002) 'Federalism and Foreign Relations', in R. Blindenbacher, N. Aroney and L. Basta-Fleiner (eds) *Federalism in a Changing World: Learning from Each Other*. Montreal: McGill-Queen's University Press. 49–84.
Eisner, M. (1997) *Das Ende der zivilisierten Stadt? Die Auswirkungen von Modernisierung und urbaner Krise auf Gewaltdelinquenz*. Frankfurt a.M.: Campus.
Elam, M. (1994) 'Puzzling out the Post-Fordist Debate: Technology. Markets and Institutions', in A. Amin (ed.) *Post-Fordism. A Reader*. Oxford: Blackwell. 43–70.
Esser, J. (2005) 'Municipalities and Länder in the Wake of European Multilevel Governance', *Deutsche Zeitschrift für Kommunalwissenschaft*, 44(2).
Ewen, S. and Hebbert, M. (2007) 'European Cities in a Networked World During the Long 20th Century', *Environment and Planning C*, 25(3): 327–40.
Fainstein, S. S. (2001a) 'Competitiveness, Cohesion, and Governance: Their Implications for Social Justice', *International Journal of Urban and Regional Research*, 25(4): 884–8.
– (2001b) 'Inequality in Global City-Regions', in A. J. Scott (ed.) *Global City-regions: Trends, Theory, Policy*. Oxford: Oxford University Press. 285–98.
Feldman, M. M. A. (1997) 'Spatial Structures for Regulation and Urban Regimes', in M. Lauria (ed.) *Reconstructing Urban Regime Theory. Regulation Urban Politics in a Global Economy*. Thousand Oaks, London, New Delhi: Sage. 30–50.
FIPOI (2008) *The Financing of Building Construction*. Online. Available <http://www.fipoi.ch/eng/financing.html> (accessed 18 March 2010).
Frefel, S. (2005) *Luzerner Stadtmarketing anno dazumal. Die Schiller-Huldigung 1905*. Luzern: Stadtarchiv Luzern.
Frey, R. L. (2004) *Städtewachstum in die Breite oder in die Höhe? Überlegungen und Standpunkte der Stadt- und Regionalökonomie*. Schriftliche Fassung des Referats anlässlich des Symposiums Städtische Dichte in der Schweiz. Chancen und Potenziale einer wirtschaftlichen Ausnützung vom 5.12.2003.

Friedmann, J. (2001) 'Intercity Networks in a Globalizing Era', in A. J. Scott (ed.) *Global City-regions. Trends, Theory, Policy*. Oxford: Oxford University Press. 119–38.

Garegnani, P. (1983) 'The Classical Theory of Wages and the Role of Demand Schedules in the Determination of Relative Prices', *American Economic Review*, 73(2): 309–13.

Gemeinderat Zürich (1997) *Postulat von GPK und RPK. GR Nr. 97/425*. Online. Available <http://www.gemeinderat-zuerich.ch/DocumentLoader.aspx?ID=6acd438c-a247-44e9-9a60-15bd50dfb4a7.pdf&Title=1997_0425.pdf> (accessed 18 March 2010).

– (1998) *Postulat von Dr. Kathy Riklin (CVP) und 6 Mitunterzeichnenden. GR Nr. 98/388*. Online. Available <http://www.gemeinderat-zuerich.ch/DocumentLoader.aspx?ID=8dd83728-3c3f-40a1-922c-63425fd86fa8.pdf&Title=1998_0388.pdf > (accessed 22 July 2008).

– (2000a) *Postulat von Adrian Hug (CVP) und 7 Mitunterzeichnenden. GR Nr. 2000/335*. Online. Available <http://www.gemeinderat-zuerich.ch/DocumentLoader.aspx?ID=18b2d458-239a-4330-acc7-94da84f7f8df.pdf&Title=2000_0335.pdf> (accessed 18 March 2010).

– (2000b) *Postulat von Raphaela Ulcay-Hauser und Christian Mettler (beide SVP). GR Nr. 2000/6*. Online. Available <http://www.gemeinderat-zuerich.ch/DocumentLoader.aspx?ID=26c3c8cc-d1bb-4b93-9976-a1f0fc707029.pdf&Title=2000_0006.pdf> (accessed 18 March 2010).

– (2000c) *Protokoll der 105. Sitzung des Gemeinderates von Zürich. Mittwoch, 12. Juli 2000*.

Geneva Economic Development Office (2000) *Business-Friendly Environment for Optimum Financial Growth*. Online. Available <http://www.geneva.ch/WG1_Finance.htm> (accessed 30 July 2008).

– (2008a) *Geneva: Some Figures*. Online. Available <http://www.geneva.ch/geneva_figures.ht>m (accessed 30 July 2008).

– (2008b) *History of Geneva*. Online. Available <http://www.geneva.ch/history.htm> (accessed 30 July 2008).

– (2008c) *International Comparisons 2007/2008*. Online. Available <http://www.geneva.ch/Publications/ci07/en/ci07_en.pdf> (accessed 30 July 2008).

Geneva Welcome Centre (2008) *Goal of the Geneva Welcome Centre*. Online. Available <http://www.cagi.ch/en/but_du_cagi.htm> (accessed 18 March 2010).

Gestring, N., Glasauer, H., Hannemann, C., Pohlan, J. and Petrowski, W. (eds) (2005) *Jahrbuch StadtRegion 2004/2005. Schwerpunktthema: Schrumpfende Städte*. Wiesbaden: VS Verlag für Sozialwissenschaften.

Giddens, A. (1981) *A Contemporary Critique of Historical Materialism*. London: Stanford University Press.

Giezen, M. (2005) *Municipal Cooperation and Competition in a Globalising World. The Foreign Policies of London, Berlin and Amsterdam*. London: Masters Thesis.

Gill, S. (1995) 'Globalisation, Market Civilisation, and Disciplinary Neoliberalism', *Millenium*, 24(3): 399–423.

Goldsmith, M. (2002) 'Central Control over Local Government – a Western European Comparison', *Local Government Studies*, 28(3): 91–112.

Goodwin, M., Jones, M. and Jones, R. (2005) 'Devolution, Constitutional Change and Economic Development: Explaining and Understanding the New Institutional Geographies of the British State', *Regional Studies*, 39(4): 421–36.

– (2006) 'Devolution and Economic Governance in the UK: Rescaling Territories and Organizations', *European Planning Studies*, 14(7): 979–95.

Goodwin, M. and Painter, J. (1996) 'Local Governance, the Crisis of Fordism and the Changing Geographies of Regulation', *Transactions of the Institute of British Geographers*, 21(4): 635–348.

Gordon, I. (1999) 'Internationalisation and Urban Competition', *Urban Studies*, 36(5/6): 1001–16.

Grand Lyon (2005a) *Document stratégique de référence*. Online. Available <http://entreprendre.grandlyon.com/fileadmin/user_upload/pdf/fr/GLEE/DSR_GLEE_2005.pdf> (accessed 15 August 2008).

– (2005b) *Lyon Solidaire*. Lyon.

–   (2006a) *Lyon internationale. Rapport d'activité janvier 2005 – septembre 2006*. Lyon: Direction des Relations Internationales.
–   (2006b) *Stratégie de l'action internationale du Grand Lyon*. Lyon: Direction des relations internationales.
–   (2007) *Lyon, Economic Strength*. Online. Available <http://business.grandlyon.com/fileadmin/user_upload/pdf/en/OPALE/Lyon_key_figures_2007.pdf> (accessed 15 August 2008).
–   (2008a) *57 communes*. Online. Available <http://www.grandlyon.com/57-communes.570.0.html> (accessed 8 May 2008).
–   (2008b) *Un territoire d'exception*. Online. Available <http://www.grandlyon.com/Un-territoire-d-exception.18.0.html> (accessed 8 May 8 2008).
–   (undated) *Carnet de retours de voyages. Les résultats et les retombées pour Lyon, de ses missions internationales*. Lyon.
Granovetter, M. (1985) 'Economic Action and Social Structure: The Problem of Embeddedness', *American Journal of Sociology*, 91(3): 481–510.
Greater Zurich Area (2006) *Greater Zurich Area Insight 2/2006*. Online. Available <http://www.greaterzuricharea.ch/content/12/downloads/gza_insight022006de.pdf> (accessed 15 July 2008).
Habegger, U. (ed.) (1998) *Kapellbrücke und Wasserturm: der Wiederaufbau eines Wahrzeichens im Spiegel der Restaurierung und Forschung*. Luzern: Stadt Luzern.
Hall, P. A. (2001) 'Global City-Regions in the Twenty-First Century', in A. J. Scott (ed.) *Global City-Regions: Trends, Theory, Policy*. Oxford: Oxford University Press. 59–77.
Hall, P. A. and Soskice, D. W. (2001a) 'An Introduction to Varieties of Capitalism', in P. A. Hall and D. W. Soskice (eds) *Varieties of Capitalism. The Institutional Foundations of Comparative Advantage*. Oxford: Oxford University Press. 1–68.
–   (eds) (2001b) *Varieties of Capitalism. The Institutional Foundations of Comparative Advantage*. Oxford: Oxford University Press.
Hall, T. and Hubbart, P. (1996) 'The Entrepreneurial City: New Urban Politics, New Urban Geographies?', *Progress in Human Geography*, 20(2): 153–74.
–   (eds) (1998) *The Entrepreneurial City: Geographies of Politics, Regime and Representation*. Chichester: Wiley.
Hancké, B. (2003) 'Many Roads to Flexibility. How Large Firms Built Flexible Regional Production Systems in France', *International Journal of Urban and Regional Development*, 27(3): 510–26.
Hanser, C., Goetz, R. and Schmid, H. (2003) *Masterplan Stadt Luzern. Strategie für die wirtschaftliche Entwicklung*. Zürich: BHP Hanser und Partner AG.
Harding, A. (1995) 'Elite Theory and Growth Machines', in D. Judge, G. Stoker and H. Wolman (eds) *Theories of Urban Politics*. London: Sage. 35–53.
Harding, A. (1997) 'Urban Regimes in a Europe of the Cities?', *European Urban and Regional Studies*, 4(4): 291–314.
Harding, A., Wilks-Heeg, S. and Hutchins, M. (2000) 'Business, Government and the Business of Urban Governance', *Urban Studies*, 37(5–6): 975–94.
Harvey, D. (1985) *The Urbanization of Capital. Studies in the History and Theory of Capitalist Urbanization*. Baltimore: John Hopkins University Press.
–   (1989) 'From Managerialism to Entrepreneurialism: The Transformation in Urban Governance in Late Capitalism', *Geografiska Annaler. Series B, Human Geography*, 71(1): 3–17.
–   (1992) 'Social Justice, Postmodernism and the City', *International Journal of Urban and Regional Research*, 16(4): 558–601.
Häupl, M. (2005) 'Europa funktioniert nur mit den Gemeinden', *Deutsche Zeitschrift für Kommunalwissenschaft*, 44(2).
Heeg, S., Klagge, B. and Ossenbrügge, J. (2003) 'Metropolitan Cooperation in Europe: Theoretical Issues and Perspectives for Urban Networking', *European Planning Studies*, 11(2): 139–53.
Heinelt, H. and Kübler, D. (eds) (2005) *Metropolitan Governance: Capacity, Democracy and the Dynamics of Place*. London: Routledge.
Heinelt, H. and Niederhafner, S. (2008) 'Cities and Organized Interest Intermediation in the EU Multi-Level System', *European Urban and Regional Studies*, 15(2): 173–87.
Held, D. (1995) *Democracy and the Global Order*. Cambridge: Polity.

Hirst, P. and Thompson, G. (1996) *Globalization in Question: the International Economy and the Possibilities for Governance*. Cambridge: Polity Press.
– (1997) 'Globalization in Question: International Economic Relations and Forms of Public Governance', in J. R. Hollingsworth and R. Boyer (eds) *Contemporary Capitalism: the Embeddedness of Institutions*. New York: Cambridge University Press. 35–73.
Hirst, P. and Zeitlin, J. (1997) 'Flexible Specialization: Theory and Evidence in the Analysis of Industrial Change', in J. R. Hollingsworth and R. Boyer (eds) *Contemparary Capitalism. The Embeddedness of Institutions*. Oxford: Oxford University Press. 220–39.
Hitz, H., Schmid, C. and Wolff, R. (1994) 'Urbanization in Zurich: Headquarter Economy and City-Belt', *Environment and Planning D*, 12(2): 167–85.
Hobbs, H. (1988) *American Cities in International Perspective: Local Governments in Foreign Affairs*. Los Angeles: unpublished thesis.
– (1994) *City Hall Goes Abroad. The Foreign Policy of Local Politics*. Thousand Oaks: Sage.
Hocking, B. (1999) 'Patrolling the 'Frontier': Globalization, Localization and the 'Actorness' of Non-Central Governments', *Regional and Federal Studies*, 9(1): 17–39.
Hödl, H. (2004) *Europabewusstsein im Fußball – ein Produkt der Politik der 50er Jahre?* Online. Available <http://www-stud.uni-graz.at/~03hoedlh/europabewusstsein.html> (accessed 18 March 2010).
Hoggett, P. (1987) 'A Farewell to Mass Production? Decentralization as an Emergent Private and Public Sector Paradigm', in P. Hoggett and R. Hambleton (eds) *Decentralization and Democracy: Localizing Public Services*. Bristol: School for Advanced Urban Studies.
Hollenstein, R. (2000) *Architektur als Mutter aller Künste. Gesamteröffnung des Kunst- und Kongresszentrums Luzern*, in *Neue Zürcher Zeitung*. 25.03.2000. Page 65.
Hollingsworth, J. R. (1991) 'The Logic of Coordinating American Manufacturing Sectors', in J. L. Campbell, J. R. Hollingsworth and L. N. Lindberg (eds) *The Governance of the American Economy*. Cambridge and New York: Cambridge University Press. 35–73.
– (1997) 'Continuities and Changes in Social Systems of Production: The Cases of Japan, Germany, and the United States', in J. R. Hollingsworth and R. Boyer (eds) *Contemporary Capitalism*. Cambridge, New York: Cambridge University Press. 265–310.
– (1998) 'New Perspectives on the Spatial Dimensions of Economic Coordination: Tensions between Globalization and Social Systems of Production', *Review of International Political Economy*, 5(3): 482–507.
Hollingsworth, J. R. and Boyer, R. (1997) 'Coordination of Economic Actors and Social Systems of Production', in J. R. Hollingsworth and R. Boyer (eds) *Contemporary Capitalism*. Cambridge, New York: Cambridge University Press. 1–47.
Hollingsworth, J. R., Schmitter, P. C. and Streeck, W. (1994) 'Capitalism, Sectors, Institutions, and Performance', in J. R. Hollingsworth, P. C. Schmitter and W. Streeck (eds) *Governing Capitalist Economies. Performance and Control of Economic Sectors*. New York, Oxford: Oxford University Press. 3–16.
Hollingsworth, J. R. and Streeck, W. (1994) 'Countries and Sectors. Concluding Remarks on Performance, Convergence, and Competitiveness', in J. R. Hollingsworth, P. C. Schmitter and W. Streeck (eds) *Governing Capitalist Economies. Performance and Control of Economic Sectors*. New York, Oxford: Oxford University Press. 270–300.
Hubbard, P (2007) 'Positioning Cities in the World. Towards a Politics of Flow', in P. J. Taylor, B. Derudder, P. Saey and F. Witlox (eds) *Cities in Globalization: Practices, Policies and Theories*. London, New York: Routledge. 187–201.
IFGRA (2007) *About IFGRA*. Online. Available <http://www.ifgra.org/i_about.htm> (accessed 18 March 2010).
IFSports Guide (2008) *Lausanne, Olympic Capital*. Online. Available <http://www.ifsports-guide.ch/english/navigation/lausanne_en.html> (accessed 18 March 2010).
IHK Region Stuttgart (2008) *Strukturdaten Region Stuttgart*. Online. Available <http://www.stuttgart.ihk24.de/produktmarken/konjunktur/wirtschaftsstatistik/Wirtschaftsstruktur_Region/Wirtschaftsstruktur_Region_Stuttgart2.pdf> (accessed 16 October 2008).
Illi, K. (2006) 'Das Kreuz mit dem Schweizerkreuz', *Student Business Review*, Winter 2006: 6–9.

Initiativkreis Europäische Metropolregionen in Deutschland (2006) *Regionales Monitoring 2006. Daten und Karten zu den Europäischen Metropolregionen in Deutschland.*

Jakoby, H. and Schmolinsky, C. (2005) 'Economic Development Promotion in German Cities in the Light of New EU Regional Policy from 2006', *German Journal of Urban Studies*, 44(1).

Jessop, B. (1990) *State Theory: Putting Capitalist States in Their Place.* Cambridge: Polity Press.

– (1992a) 'Fordism and Post-Fordism: a Critical Reformulation', in M. Storper and A. J. Scott (eds) *Pathways to Industrialization and Regional Development.* London: Routledge. 46–69.

– (1992b) 'Post-Fordism and Flexible Specialisation: Incommensurable, Contradictory, Complemetary, or Just Plain Different Perspectives?', in H. Ernste and V. Meier (eds) *Regional Development and Contemporary Response: Extending Flexible Specialisation*, 25–44. London: Belhaven.

– (1994) 'Post-Fordism and the State', in A. Amin (ed.) *Post-Fordism: A Reader.* Cambridge: Blackwell. 251–79.

– (1997) 'A Neo-Gramscian Approach to the Regulation of Urban Regimes. Accumulation Strategies, Hegemonic Projects, and Governance', in M. Lauria (ed.) *Reconstructing Urban Regime Theory. Regulation Urban Politics in a Global Economy.* Thousand Oaks, London, New Delhi: Sage. 51–73.

– (1998) 'The Narrative of Enterprise and the Enterprise of Narrative: Place Marketing and the Entrepreneurial City', in T. Hall and P. Hubbart (eds) *The Entrepreneurial City.* Chichester: Wiley. 77–102.

– (2002) 'The Political Economy of Scale', in M. Perkmann and N.-L. Sum (eds) *Globalization, Regionalization and Cross-Border Regions.* London: Palgrave. 25–49.

– (2004) 'Hollowing out the 'Nation-State' and Multilevel Governance', in P. Kennett (ed.) *A Handbook Of Comparative Social Policy.* Cheltenham: Edward Elgar Publishing. 11–25.

Jessop, B., Peck, J. and Tickell, A. (2007) 'Retooling the Machine. Economic Crisis, State Restructuring, and Urban Politics', in A. E. G. Jonas and D. Wilson (eds) *The Urban Growth Machine: Critical Perspectives Two Decades Later.* New York: Suny Press. 141–60.

John, P. (2000) 'The Europeanisation of Sub-national Governance', *Urban Studies*, 37(5–6): 877–94.

Jonas, A. E. G. and Ward, K. (2007) 'Introduction to a Debate on City-Regions: New Geographies of Governance, Democracy and Social Reproduction', *International Journal of Urban and Regional Research*, 31(1): 169–78.

Jones, B. and Keating, M. (eds) (1995) *The European Union and the Regions.* Oxford: Clarendon.

Jones, M. and MacLeod, G. (1999) 'Towards a Regional Renaissance? Re-inventing and Re-scaling England's Economic Governance', *Transactions IBG*, 24: 295–313.

Jones, M. and Ward, K. (2004) 'Capitalist Development and Crisis Theory: Towards a "Fourth Cut"', *Antipode*, 36(3): 497–511.

Jouve, B. (2007) 'Urban Societies and Dominant Political Coalitions in the Internationalization of Cities', *Environment and Planning C*, 25(3): 374–90.

Justiz- Gemeinde- und Kirchendirektion des Kantons Bern (2004) *Zusammenarbeit Kanton Bern – Kreis Südböhmen CZ. Bericht der Arbeitsgruppe zum Projekt Zusammenarbeit Kanton Bern – Kreis Südböhmen.*

Kanton Bern (1998) *Partnerschaften zwischen bernischen und tschechischen Gemeinden: Weitere elf Gemeinden haben Partner gefunden. Medienmitteilung des Kantons Bern.* Online. Available <http://www.be.ch/web/print/kanton-mediencenter-mm-detail?id=2515&nozoom=true> (accessed 18 March 2010).

– (2001) *10 Jahre Partnerschaften zwischen bernischen und tschechischen Gemeinden. Medienmitteilung des Kantons Bern.* Online. Available <http://www.be.ch/web/index/kanton/kanton-mediencenter/kanton-mediencenter-mm/kanton-mediencenter-mm-detail.htm?id=4151&linkName=10%20Jahre%20Partnerschaften%20zwischen%20bernischen%20und%20tschechischen%20Gemeinden> (accessed 18 March 2010).

– (2002a) *Kurzinformationen aus dem Regierungsrat. 26.4.2001. Medienmitteilung des Kantons Bern.* Online. Available <http://www.be.ch/web/index/kanton/kanton-mediencenter/kanton-mediencenter-mm/kanton-mediencenter-mm-detail.htm?id=3852&linkName=Kurzinformation%20aus%20dem%20Regierungsrat> (accessed 18 March 2010).

–   (2002b) *Tschechische Region sucht den Kontakt zum Kanton Bern. Medienmitteilung des Kantons Bern*. Online. Available <http://www.be.ch/web/print/kanton-mediencenter-mm-detail?id=4370&nozoom=true> (accessed 18 March 2010).

–   (2004) *Kanton Bern will Beziehungen zur Region Südböhmen ausbauen. Medienmitteilung des Kantons Bern*. Online. Available <http://www.be.ch/web/ index/kanton/kanton-mediencenter/kanton-mediencenter-mm/kanton-mediencenter-mm-detail.htm?id=5637&linkName=Kanton%20Bern%20will%20Beziehungen%20 zur%20Region%20S%26uuml%3bdb%26ouml%3bhmen%20ausbauen> (accessed 18 March 2010).

Katzenstein, P. J. (1985) *Small States in World Markets: Industrial Policy in Europe*. Ithaca: Cornell University Press.

–   (2003) 'Small States and Small States Revisited', *New Political Economy*, 8(1): 9–30.

Keating, M. (1995) 'Size, Efficiency and Democracy: Consolidation, Fragmentation and Public Choice', in D. Judge, G. Stoker and H. Wolman (eds) *Theories of Urban Politics*. London, Thousand Oaks, New Delhi: Sage.

–   (1999) 'Regions and International Affairs: Motives, Opportunities and Strategies', *Regional and Federal Studies*, 9(1): 1–16.

Keating, M. (2001) 'Governing Cities and Regions: Territorial Restructuring in a Global Age', in A. J. Scott (ed.) *Global City-Regions: Trends, Theory, Policy*. Oxford: Oxford University Press. 371–90.

Keeling, D. J. (1995) 'Transport and the World City Paradigm', in P. L. Knox and P. J. Taylor (eds) *World Cities in a World-System*. Cambridge: Cambridge University Press. 115–31.

Keil, R. (2003) 'Globalization Makes States: Perspectives of Local Governance in the Age of the World City', in N. Brenner, B. Jessop, M. Jones and G. MacLeod (eds) *State/Space. A Reader*. Oxford: Blackwell. 278–95.

Keiner, M. and Kim, A. (2007) 'Transnational City Networks for Sustainability', *European Planning Studies*, 15(10): 1369–95.

Kincaid, J. (1989) 'Rain Clouds Over Municipal Diplomacy: Dimensions and Possible Sources of Negative Public Opinion', in E. H. Fry, L. H. Radebaugh and S. Panayotis (eds) *The New International Cities Era: The Global Activities of North American Municipal Governments*. Provo: David M. Kennedy Center for International Affairs, Brigham Young University. 223–49.

–   (2002) 'Constituent Diplomacy in Federal Systems', in R. Blindenbacher, N. Aroney and L. Basta-Fleiner (eds) *Federalism in a Changing World: Learning from Each Other*. Montreal: McGill-Queen's University Press. 85–119.

Kirby, A., Marston, S. A. and Seasholes, K. (1995) 'World Cities and Global Communities: The Municipal Foreign Policy Movement and New Roles for Cities', in P. L. Knox and P. J. Taylor (eds) *World Cities in a World-System*. Cambridge: Cambridge University Press. 267–89.

Kitschelt, H., Lange, P., Marks, G. and Stephens, J. D. (1999) 'Convergence and Divergence in Advanced Capitalist Economies', in H. Kitschelt, P. Lange, G. Marks and J. D. Stephens (eds) *Continuity and Change in Contemporary Capitalism*. Cambridge: Cambridge University Press. 427–60.

Klaus, P. (2006) 'Das Mass der Weltstadt. Zürichs Position im globalen Netz der Weltstädte', *Stadtblick*, 13(März 2006): 6–8.

Klöti, U., Hirschi, C., Serdült, U. and Widmer, T. (2005) *Verkannte Aussenpolitik: Entscheidungsprozesse in der Schweiz*. Chur/Zürich: Rüegger.

Knox, P. L. (1995) 'World Cities in a World-System', in P. L. Knox and P. J. Taylor (eds) *World Cities in a World-System*. Cambridge: Cambridge University Press. 3–20.

Krasner, S. D. (1988) 'Sovereignty: An Institutional Perspective', *Comparative Political Studies*, 21(1): 66–94.

Krätke, S. (2007) 'The Metropolization of the European Urban System in the Era of Globalization', in P. J. Taylor, B. Derudder, P. Saey and F. Witlox (eds) *Cities in Globalization. Practices, Policies and Theories*. London and New York: Routledge. 157–83.

Kreher, A. (2006) 'Resümee und Ausblick', in Landeshauptstadt Stuttgart (ed.) *Dokumentation IV. Stuttgarter Städtepartnerschaftstreffen. Seminar für Städtepartnerschaftsverantwortliche*. Stuttgart: Landeshauptstadt Stuttgart. 264–7.

Krugman, P. R. (1996) 'Making Sense of the Competitiveness Debate', *Oxford Review of Economic Policy*, 12: 17–25.

Kübler, D. (2003) '"Metropolitan Governance" oder: Die unendliche Geschichte der

Institutionenbildung in Stadtregionen', *Informationen zur Raumentwicklung*, 8/9: 1–7.

Kübler, D. and Piliutyte, J. (2007) 'Intergovernmental Relations and International Urban Strategies: Constraints and Opportunities in Multilevel Polities', *Environment and Planning C*, 25(3): 357–73.

Kübler, D., van der Heiden, N. and Koch, P. *'Denationalisation from Below. Globalisation and Its Impacts on Governance in Metropolitan Areas'*, paper presented at the Jahreskongress SVPW Balsthal, 22–23 November 2007.

Kübler, D. and Wälti, S. (2001) 'Drug Policy-Making in Metropolitan Areas: Urban Conflicts and Governance', *International Journal of Urban and Regional Research*, 25(1): 35–54.

Kunzmann, K. R. (2002) 'Zur transnationalen Zusammenarbeit europäischer Metropolregionen', *Informationen zur Raumentwicklung*, 6/7: 341–4.

Kvale, S. (1996) *InterViews: An Introduction to Qualitative Research Interviewing*. London, Thousand Oaks: Sage.

Lachat, R. (2008) 'Switzerland: Another Case of Transformation Driven by an Established Party', in H. Kriesi, E. Grande, R. Lachat, M. Dolezal, S. Bornschier and T. Frey (eds) *West European Politics in the Age of Globalization*. Cambridge: Cambridge University Press. 130–53.

Landeshauptstadt Stuttgart (2003a) *Europa in Stuttgart*.

–   (2003b) *URB-AL (Urbs América Latina). Steuerung der urbanen Mobilität. Europäisch-lateinamerikanisches Kompetenzzentrum "Urbane Mobilität" Stuttgart*. Online. Available <http://www.stuttgart.de/sde/menu/frame/top.php?seite=http%3A// www.stuttgart.de/sde/item/gen/16726.htm> (accessed 8 August 2008).

–   (2003c) *Vierter Bericht des Koordinators für europäische und internationale Angelegenheiten/Städtepartnerschaften*. GRDrs 699/2003.

–   (2006a) *Candidacy of the City of Stuttgart for the Creation and Presidency of the Committee on Urban Mobility of United Cities and Local Governments*.

–   (2006b) *Cities for Mobility*. The World Wide Network for Mobility.

–   (2006c) *EU-Projekte 1998–2005 unter städtischer Beteiligung und Förderung aus Mitteln des Europäischen Sozialfonds*. GRDrs 595/2006.

–   (2006d) *Städtepartnerschaften: Konzeption und Aktivitäten 2005*. GRDrs 98/2006.

–   (2006e) *Stuttgart Pact for Integration*. Visions for Our International City.

–   (2006f) *Stuttgarter Partnerschaft Eine Welt*. Idee, Grundlagen, Ziele, Mitglieder, Netzwerke.

–   (2007) *Delegation aus Georgien besuchte Stuttgarter Rathaus*. Online. Available <http://www.stuttgart.de/sde/menu/frame/top.php?seite=http%3A//www.stuttgart.de/ sde/presse/detail/223805 > (accessed 16 October 2008).

–   (2008) *Stuttgarts Oberbürgermeister Schuster in den "Rat der Weisen" zur Zukunft der EU gewählt*. Online. Available <http://www.stuttgart.de/sde/menu/frame/ ns_top_11021.htm> (accessed 11 November 2008).

Lash, S. and Urry, J. (1987) *The End of Organized Capitalism*. Cambridge: Polity Press.

–   (1993) *Economies of Signs and Space: After Organised Capitalism*. London: Sage.

Lausanne Tourisme (2008) *Assemblée générale 2008 de Lausanne Tourisme*. Online. Available <http://www.lausanne.ch/view.asp?DocID=29327&Language=F> (accessed 18 March 2010).

Le Galès, P. (1998) 'Conclusion: Government or Governance?', in P. Le Galès and C. Lequesne (eds) *Regions in Europe*. London, New York: Routledge. 239–67.

–   (2002) *European Cities. Social Conflicts and Governance*. Oxford: Oxford University Press.

–   (2003) *Le retour des villes européennes: sociétés urbaines, mondialisation, gouvernement et gouvernance*. Paris: Presses de Sciences Po.

Ledergerber, E. (2007) *Wo Städte Zusammenarbeit suchen und wohin sie ihre Fühler ausstrecken. Die verschiedenen Ebenen der Stadtzürcher Aussenpolitik*, in *Neue Zürcher Zeitung*. 06.11.2007, p. 19.

Lefebvre, H. (1974) *The Production of Space*. Cambridge MA: Blackwell.

Lefèvre, C. (1998) 'Metropolitan Government and Governance in Western Countries: A Critical Review', *International Journal of Urban and Regional Research*, 22(1): 9–25.

Lefèvre, C. and d'Albergo, E. (2007) 'Why Cities Are Looking Abroad and How They Go About It', *Environment and Planning C*, 25(3): 317–26.

Leitner, H. (2004) 'The Politics of Scale and Networks of Spatial Connectivity: Transnational

Interurban Networks and the Rescaling of Political Governance in Europe', in E. Sheppard and R. McMaster (eds) *Scale and Geographic Inquiry*. Oxford: Blackwell. 236–55.

Leitner, H., Pavlik, C. and Sheppard, E. (2002) 'Networks, Governance and the Politics of Scale: Inter-Urban Networks and the European Union', in A. Herod and M. Wright (eds) *Geographies of Power: Placing Scale*. Oxford: Blackwell. 274–303.

Leitner, H. and Sheppard, E. (1998) 'Economic Uncertainty, Inter-Urban Competition and the Efficacy of Entrepreneurialism', in T. Hall and P. Hubbart (eds) *The Entrepreneurial City. Geographies of Politics, Regime and Representation*. Chichester: John Wiley & Sons. 285–307.

– (1999) 'Transcending Interurban Competition: Conceptual Issues and Policy Alternatives in the European Union', in A. E. G. Jonas and D. Wilson (eds) *The Urban Growth Machine. Critical Perspectives Two Decades Later*. Albany: State University of New York Press. 227–43.

– (2002) '"The City is Dead, Long Live the Net': Harnessing European Interurban Networks for a Neoliberal Agenda', in N. Brenner and N. Theodore (eds) *Spaces of Neoliberalism*. Oxford: Blackwell. 148–71.

– (2003) 'Unbounding Critical Geographic Research on Cities: The 1990s and Beyond', *Urban Geography*, 24(6): 510–28.

Lever, W. F. (1999) 'Competitive Cities in Europe', *Urban Studies*, 36(5/6): 1029–44.

Lezzi, M. (2000) *Porträts von Schweizer EuroRegionen: grenzüberschreitende Ansätze zu einem europäischen Föderalismus*. Basel: Helbing & Lichtenhahn.

Liepitz, A. (1977) *Le Capital et son espace*. Paris: F. Maspéro.

– (1994a) 'The National and the Regional: Their Autonomy vis-à-vis the Capitalist World Crisis', in R. Palan and B. Gills (eds) *Transcending the State-Global Divide*. Boulder: Lynne Rienner. 23–44.

– (1994b) 'Post-Fordism and Democracy', in A. Amin (ed.) *Post-Fordism. A Reader*. Oxford: Blackwell. 338–57.

Linder, W. (2003) 'Direct Democracy', in U. Klöti, P. Knoepfel, H. Kriesi, W. Linder and Y. Papadopoulos (eds) *Handbook of Swiss Politics*. Zürich: Verlag Neue Zürcher Zeitung.

Lipset, S. M. and Rokkan, S. (eds) (1967) *Party Systems and Voter Alignments*. New York: Free Press.

Logan, J. R. and Molotch, H. L. (1987) *Urban Fortunes: The Political Economy of Place*. Berkeley/Los Angeles: University of California Press.

– (2002) 'The City as a Growth Machine', in S. S. Fainstein and S. Campbell (eds) *Readings in Urban Theory*. Oxford: Blackwell. 199–238.

Luzern Hotels (2008) *Logiernächte 2007 mit Vergleich 2006*. Online. Available <http://www.luzern-hotels.ch/webautor-data/22/LN_alle-Betriebe_2007.pdf> (accessed 18 March 2010).

Luzern Tourismus AG (2008a) *Aktionäre*. Online. Available <http://www.luzern.org/de/PDF/pdf_nav_item_cfm_deFactsLULTAGLU72907.pdf> (accessed 18 March 2010).

– (2008b) *Geschichtszahlen*. Online. Available <http://www.luzern.org/files/?id=1689> (accessed 18 March 2010).

– (undated) *Luzern: Geschichte, Tourismus, Wissenswertes*. Online. Available <http://www.luzern.org/files/?id=1692> (accessed 18 March 2010).

Lyon Business (2008) *Gastronomy*. Online. Available <http://www.lyon-business.org/ccm/en/cible/professionnel-tourisme/agence-voyage/lyon/accueil-hebergement/cuisine-lyonnaise/> (accessed 15 August 2008).

LyonPhiladelphia (2006) *Rhone-Alpes Region. Commonwealth of Pennsylvania. Newsletter nr. 3*. Lyon.

Mabrouk, T. B. and Jouve, B. (2002) 'Building a New Territory: The Urban Region of Lyons', in B. Jouve and C. Lefèvre (eds) *Local Power, Territory and Institutions in European Metropolitan Regions*. London: Frank Cass. 82–108.

MacLeod, G. (1999) 'Place, Politics and "Scale Dependence". Exploring the Structuration of Euro-Regionalism', *European Urban and Regional Studies*, 6(3): 231–53.

– (2001) 'New Regionalism Reconsidered: Globalization and the Remaking of Political Economic Space', *International Journal of Urban and Regional Research*, 25(4): 804–29.

MacLeod, G. and Goodwin, M. (1999) 'Reconstructing an Urban and Regional Political

Economy: On the State, Politics, Scale, and Explanation', *Political Geography*, 18(6): 697–730.

Marshall, A. (2005) 'Europeanization at the Urban Level: Local Actors, Institutions and the Dynamics of Multi-level Interaction', *Journal of European Public Policy*, 12(4): 668–86.

Marston, S. A. (2000) 'The Social Construction of Scale', *Progress in Human Geography*, 24(2): 219-42.

Martins, L. and Rodriguez Alvarez, J. M. (2007) 'Towards Glocal Leadership: Taking up the Challenge of New Local Governance', *Environment and Planning C*, 25(3): 391–409.

Massey, D. (2007) *World City*. Cambridge: Polity.

Mayer, M. (1992) 'The Shifting Local Political System in European Cities', in M. Dunford and G. Kafkalas (eds) *Cities and Regions in the New Europe: The Global-Local Interplay and Spatial Development Strategies*. London: Belhaven. 255–78.

Mayer, M. (1994) 'Post-Fordist City Politics', in A. Amin (ed.) *Post-Fordism. A Reader*. Oxford: Blackwell. 316–37.

McGuirk, P. M. (2004) 'State, Strategy, and Scale in the Competitive City: a Neo-Gramscian Analysis of the Governance of "Global Sydney"', *Environment and Planning A*, 36(6): 1019–43.

McNeill, D. (2005) 'Narrating Neoliberalism', *Geographical Research*, 43(1): 113–5.

Mercer Human Resource Consulting (2009) *Quality of Living Survey*. Online. Available <http://www.mercer.com/summary.jhtml?idContent=1128060> (accessed 18 March 2010).

Metrex (2000) *The Metrex Report. Position Statement for the First Five Years of Metrex 1996–2000. Prospectus for the Period 2001–2006*. Online. Available <http://www.eurometrex.org/Docs/About/enreport2000.pdf> (accessed 18 March 2010).

Meuser, M. and Nagel, U. (1991) 'Experteninterviews – vielfach erprobt, wenig beachtet: Ein Beitrag zur qualitativen Methodendiskussion', in D. Garz and K. Kraimer (eds) *Qualitativ-empirische Sozialforschung: Konzepte, Methoden, Analysen*. Opladen: Westdeutscher Verlag. 441–71.

Morgan, K. and Roberts, E. (1993) 'The Democratic Deficit: A Guide to Quangoland', *Papers in Planning Research*, 44: Department of City and Regional Planning, University of Wales, Cardiff.

Moss, M. L. and Townsend, A. M. (2004) 'Moving Information in the Twenty-First Century City', in R. Hanley (ed.) *Moving People, Goods and Information in the 21st Century*. New York: Routledge. 63–78.

Moulaert, F., Martinelli, F., Gonzalez, S. and Swyngedouw, E. (2007) 'Introduction: Social Innovation and Governance in European Cities. Urban Development between Path Dependency and Radical Innovation', *European Urban and Regional Studies*, 14(3): 195–209.

Moulaert, F., Rodriguez, A. and Swyngedouw, E. (eds) (2003a) *The Globalized City. Economic Restructuring and Social Polarization in European Cities*. Oxford: Oxford University Press.

–––   (2003b) 'Large-Scale Urban Development Projects, Urban Dynamics, and Social Polarization: A Methodological Reflection', in F. Moulaert, A. Rodriguez and E. Swyngedouw (eds) *The Globalized City. Economic Restructuring and Social Polarization in European Cities*. Oxford: Oxford University Press. 47–64.

Neue Luzerner Zeitung (25 October 2005) *Luzerner Stadtrat will Subventionen für Tourismus erhöhen*. Page unavailable online.

–––   (7 April 2006) *Luzerns Partnerstadt ertrinkt*, p. 24.

–––   (17 July 2007) *SVP kritisiert Künstleratelier in Chicago*. Page unavailable online.

–––   (20 July 1994) *Präferenz für Genf als WTO-Sitz. Weitere Etappe im Entscheidungsverfahren*, p. 19.

–––   (6 June 1995) *WTO-Sitz-Abkommen unterzeichnet*, p. 14.

–––   (9 December 1999) *Ratsberichterstattung Zürcher Gemeinderat*, p. 51.

–––   (21 November 2002) *Ratsberichterstattung Zürcher Gemeinderat*. Page unavailable.

–––   (29 and 30 May 2004) *Zürcher Tram und Künstler in San Francisco. Erste Auswirkungen der Städteinitiative*, p. 52.

–––   (15 June 2004) *Gratulation zum Jubiläum. 50 Jahre UEFA*, p. 62.

–––   (3 November 2004) *Transatlantische Schulreise. Städteinitiative ermöglicht Austausch mit San Francisco*, p. 49.

–   (25 January 2005) *Ein erster Besuch aus Zürichs Schwesterstadt. San Franciscos Bürgermeister Gavin Newsom trifft Elmar Ledergerber,* p. 49.
–   (8 July 2005) *Die Visionen des Stadtpräsidenten,* p. 51.
–   (21 July 2005) *Karriere trotz Kindern. Stuttgarter Pläne für Vereinbarkeit von Familie und Beruf,* p. 17.
–   (31 May 2006) *Jetzt hat auch Microsoft einen Sitz in Zürich,* p. 47.
–   (5 October 2006) *Ledergerber wirbt in New York für Zürich,* p. 55.
–   (18 January 2007) *Internet-Suchdienst Google baut Standort in Zürich aus,* p. 55.
–   (24 January 2007) *Zürich soll Erfahrungen aus den Strassen von San Francisco nutzen. Die Verwaltungen der beiden "verschwisterten" Städte tauschen künftig ihr Wissen aus,* p. 57.
–   (6 February 2007) *Das internationale Genf prägt eine Region. Grenzüberschreitende Politik im Standortwettbewerb,* p. 15.
–   (2 May 2007) *WTO fordert von der Schweiz ein Millionengeschenk,* p. 13.
–   (10 May 2007) *WTO-Chef droht erneut mit Wegzug aus Genf,* p. 16.
–   (20 September 2007) *Ausbau des WTO-Sitzes. Feilschen um kostengünstige Lösung,* p. 16.
–   (30 November 2007) *Stadt Zürich Mitglied in Städtenetzwerk,* p. 56.
–   (29 December 2007) *Maximal 130 Millionen für WTO-Gebäude in Genf,* p. 16.
–   (31 May 2008) *Unternehmer für "Metropolitanregion Zürich". Name soll nicht auf Zürich fokussieren,* p. 47.
–   (11 August 2008) *Fernbeziehungen auf Zeit. Rund die Hälfte der Gemeindepartnerschaften mit Osteuropa existiert nur noch auf dem Papier,* p. 9.
–   (15 September 2008) *"Geschenk" für die Welthandelsorganisation. Der Nationalrat unterstützt das internationale Genf,* p. 16.
–   (20 September 2008) *Die Stadt Zürich will den Club of Rome an die Limmat locken,* p. 55.
–   (24 September 2008) *Das Zürcher Kunming-Engagement beflügelt die Wirtschaft. Alt Stadtpräsident Thomas Wagner über den Erfolg der Städtepartnerschaft,* p. 54.
–   (25 September 2008) *Kunming will den Weg Zürichs gehen. 25 Jahre Städtepartnerschaft zum beidseitigen Nutzen,* p. 55.
Neue Zürcher Zeitung am Sonntag (16 September 2007) *Über 100 Millionen für WTO. Bundesrat beschliesst Verhandlungsmandat und Kostendach,* p. 17.
Nijkamp, P. (1993) 'Towards a Network of Regions: The United States of Europe', *European Planning Studies,* 1(2): 149–68.
Norris, D. F. (2001) 'Prospects for Regional Governance under the New Regionalism: Economic Imperative versus Political Impediments', *Journal of Urban Affairs,* 23(5): 557–71.
O'Toole, K. (2001) 'Kokusaka and Internationalization: Australian and Japanese Sister City Type Relationships', *Australian Journal of International Affairs,* 55(3): 403–19.
Ohmae, K. (2001) 'How to Invite Prosperity from the Global Economy Into a Region', in A. J. Scott (ed.) *Global City-Regions: Trends, Theory, Policy.* Oxford: Oxford University Press. 33–43.
Ostrom, E. (1972) 'Metropolitan Reform: Propositions Derived from Two Traditions', *Social Science Quarterly,* 53(4): 474–93.
Oswalt, P. and Rienits, T. (eds) (2006) *Atlas of Shrinking Cities.* Ostfildern: Hatje Cantz.
Parkinson, M. and Harding, A. (1995) 'European Cities Toward 2000: Entrepreneurialsm, Competition and Social Exclusion', in M. Rhodes (ed.) *The Regions and The New Europe. Patterns in Core and Periphery Development.* Manchester and New York: Manchester University Press. 53–77.
Peck, J. (2002) 'Political Economies of Scale: Fast Policy, Interscalar Relations, and Neoliberal Workfare', *Economic Geography,* 78(3): 331–60.
Peck, J. and Theodore, N. (2007) 'Variegated Capitalism', *Progress in Human Geography,* 31(6): 731–72.
Peck, J. and Tickell, A. (1994) 'Searching for a New Institutional Fix', in A. Amin (ed.) *Post-Fordism: A Reader.* Cambridge: Blackwell. 280–315.
Neue Zürcher Zeitung (1995) 'Business Goes Local – Dissecting the Business Agenda in Manchester', *Journal of Urban and Regional Research,* 19(1): 55–78.
Pendras, M. (2002) 'From Local Consciousness to Global Change: Asserting Power at the Local Scale', *International Journal of Urban and Regional Research,* 26(4): 823–33.
Perkmann, M. (2003) 'Cross-Border Regions in Europe. Significance and Drivers of Regional

Cross-Border Co-Operation', *European Urban and Regional Studies*, 10(2): 153–69.

Peterson, P. E. (1981) *City Limits*. Chicago: The University of Chicago Press.

Phelps, N. A., McNeill, D. and Parsons, N. (2002) 'In Search of a European Edge Urban Identity. Trans-European Networking among Edge Urban Municipalities', *European Urban and Regional Studies*, 9(3): 211–24.

Pickvance, C. and Preteceille, E. (1991) *State Restructuring and Local Power: A Comparative Perspective*. London: Pinter.

Porter, M. E. (1990) *The Competitive Advantage of Nations*. Basingstoke: Macmillan.

Präsidialdepartement der Stadt Zürich (2003) *Geschäftsbericht 2003*. Online. Available <http://www.stadt-zuerich.ch/internet/str/home/geschberichte/gesch_03. ParagraphContainerList.ParagraphContainer0.ParagraphList.0008.File.pdf/ praesidialdepartement.pdf> (accessed 25 July 2008).

Präsidialdepartement der Stadt Zürich (2004) *Zukunft der Städtepartnerschaft Zürich – Kunming*. Online. Available <http://www.stadt-zuerich.ch/internet/mm/home/mm_04/09_04/ mm_44.ParagraphContainerList.ParagraphContainer0.ParagraphList.0010.File. pdf/040928_Zukunft%20Kunming.pd>f (accessed 15 July 2008).

Präsidialdepartement der Stadt Zürich (2007) *San Francisco und Zürich stärken ihre Beziehung*. Online. Available <http://www.stadt-zuerich.ch/internet/mm/home/ mm_07/01_07/070123c.html> (accessed 18 March 2010).

Proact Asia Urbs (2005) *Enhancing the City-to-City Euro-Asian Dialogue: Towards Sustainable Urban Development*. Online. Available <http://www.proact-cooperation.org/ fileadmin/user_upload/pdf/BookletPROACT.pdf> (accessed 18 March 2010).

Purcell, M. (2006) 'Urban Democracy and the Local Trap', *Urban Studies*, 43(11): 1921–41.

– (2007) 'City-Regions, Neoliberal Globalization and Democracy: A Research Agenda', *International Journal of Urban and Regional Research*, 31(1): 197–206.

Ramasamy, B. and Cremer, R. D. (1998) 'Cities, Commerce and Culture. The Economic Role of International Sister-City Relationships between New Zealand and Asia', *Journal of the Asian Pacific Economy*, 3(3): 446–61.

Rees, N. (1997) 'Inter-Regional Cooperation in the EU and Beyond', *European Planning Studies*, 5(3): pages online not available.

Regierungsrat des Kantons Bern (2007) *Bericht des Regierungsrats an den Grossen Rat vom 21. März 2007 über die Aussenbeziehungen des Kantons Bern*. Online. Available <http:// www.sta.be.ch/site/bericht_aussenbeziehungen_de_2007.pdf> (accessed 18 March 2010).

Regierungsrat des Kantons Zürich (2006) *Zürich und Europa. Materialien für eine europapolitische Standortbestimmung des Kantons Zürich*. Zürich, Basel, Genf: Schulthess Juristische Medien.

Reinicke, W. H. and Deng, F. (2000) *Critical Choices. The United Nations, Networks, and the Future of Global Governance*. Toronto: International Development Research Centre.

Ricardo, D. (1817) *The Principles of Political Economy and Taxation*. London: John Murray.

Risse, T. (2006) 'Transnational Governance and Legitimacy', in A. Benz and Y. Papadopoulos (eds) *Governance and Democracy. Comparing National, European and International Experiences*. London: Routledge. 179–99.

Robertson, R. (1998) 'Glokalisierung: Homogenität und Heterogenität in Raum und Zeit', in U. Beck (ed.) *Perspektiven der Weltgesellschaft*. Frankfurt a.M.: Suhrkamp. 192–220.

Rüdiger, R. (2005) 'Municipalities and Business: Global Players', *Deutsche Zeitschrift für Kommunalwissenschaft*, 44(2).

RZU (2005) *Jahresbericht 2005*. RZU: Zürich.

Sabel, C. F. (1997) 'Constitutional Orders: Trust Building and Response to Change', in J. R. Hollingsworth and R. Boyer (eds) *Contemporary Capitalism. The Embeddedness of Institutions*. Cambridge: Cambridge University Press. 154–88.

Sager, F. (2002) *Vom Verwalten des urbanen Raums. Institutionelle Bedingungen von Politikkoordination am Beispiel der Raum- und Verkehrsplanung in städtischen Gebieten*. Bern, Stuttgart, Wien: Paul Haupt.

San Francisco – Zurich Initiative (2008) *Organization & Contacts*. Online. Available <http:// www.sfzhinitiative.com/en/abu_orgsetup.php> (accessed 25 July 2008).

Sanofi-aventis (2005) *Die Unternehmensgeschichte von sanofi-aventis*. Online. Available <http://www.sanofi-aventis.de/live/de/de/layout.jsp?scat=471A84AC-C8D6-481F-9F53-11BB8039A9DC> (accessed 18 March 2010).

Sassen, S. (1991) *The Global City*. Princeton, New Jersey: Princeton University Press.

–   (2001) 'Global Cities and Global City-Regions: A Comparison', in A. J. Scott (ed.) *Global City-Regions: Trends, Theory, Policy*. Oxford: Oxford University Press. 78–95.

Saunier, P.-Y. (2002) 'Taking Up the Bet on Connections: a Municipal Contribution', *Contemporary European History*, 11(4): 507–27.

Savitch, H. V. and Kantor, P. (2002) *Cities in the International Marketplace*. Princeton and Oxford: Princeton University Press.

Scharpf, F. (1998) 'Demokratie in der transnationalen Politik', in U. Beck (ed.) *Politik der Globalisierung*. Frankfurt a. M.: Suhrkamp. 228–53.

Schiffmann, O. (2005) *Top Noten für die Stadt Zürich. Online Publications Credit Suisse*. Online. Available <http://emagazine.credit-suisse.com/app/article/index.cfm?fuseaction=OpenArticle&aoid=96729&lang=de> (accessed 18 March 2010).

Schilt, J.-J. (2000) 'Lausanne. Centre de formation et de culture sur les bords du Léman', *DISP*, 142: 30–2.

Schmid, W. A., Keiner, M. and Kim, A. (2007) *Networking Cities and Regions for Sustainability. Final Report*. Zurich: Institute for Landscape and Spatial Planning.

Schreiber, S. (2007) 'Antenne der Region in Brüssel', *Region Stuttgart*: 7.

Schumacher, E. (1998) 'Common Cause Switzerland. Promotion of Peace, Local Democracy and Human Rights through Partnerships between Local Authorities', in C. Wellmann (ed.) *From Town to Town: Local Authorities as Transnational Actors*. Hamburg: LIT Verlag. 219–26.

Schuster, W. (2006) 'Begrüssung', in Landeshauptstadt Stuttgart (ed.) *Dokumentation IV. Stuttgarter Städteparnterschaftstreffen. Seminar für Städtepartnerschaftsverantwortliche*. Stuttgart: Landeshauptstadt Stuttgart. 1–5.

Schweizerischer Bundesrat (2008) *Botschaft über die Gewährung eines A-fonds-perdu-Beitrags an die Immobilienstiftung für die internationalen Organisationen (FIPOI) zur Finanzierung der Renovation des SItzgebäudes der Welthandelsorganisation (WTO) in Genf. Vorläufige Online-Fassung*. Online. Available <http://www.news-service.admin.ch/NSBSubscriber/message/attachments/12198.pdf> (accessed 18 March 2010).

Scott, A. J. (1996) 'Regional Motors of the Global Economy', *Futures*, 28(5): 391–411.

–   (2001) 'Introduction', in A. J. Scott (ed.) *Global City-Regions: Trends, Theory, Policy*. Oxford: Oxford University Press. 1–30.

Scott, A. J., Agnew, J., Soja, E. W. and Storper, M. (2001) 'Global City-Regions', in A. J. Scott (ed.) *Global City-Regions: Trends, Theory, Policy*. Oxford: Oxford University Press. 11–30.

SEGRE Lausanne (2008) *Lausanne dans ses relations exterieures*. Online. Available <http://www.lausanne.ch/view.asp?docId=24735&domId=61719&Language=F> (accessed 18 March 2010).

SEPAL (1988) 'Lyon 2010: un projet d'agglomération pour une métropole européenne', *Lyon*, Agence d'Urbanisme de la Communauté Urbaine de Lyon.

SESEC (2007) *SESEC VI Symposium*. Online. Available <http://www.sesec.org/>SESEC VI (accessed 26 July 2008).

Sevcik, T. (2007) *Wieso Zürich? Wohin sich Zürich entwickeln könnte – und was geschehen müsste*, in *Neue Zürcher Zeitung*. 22 January 2007, p. 31.

Simeon, R. (1991) 'Globalization and the Canadian Nation-State', in G. B. Doern and B. B. Purchase (eds) *Canada at Risk: Canadian Public Policy in the 1990's*. Ottawa: C. D. Howe Institute. 46–58.

Smith, N. (1995) 'Remaking Scale: Competition and Cooperation in Prenational and Postnational Europe', in H. Eskelinen and F. Snickars (eds) *Competitive European Peripheries*. Berlin: Springer. 59–74.

–   (2002) 'New Globalism, New Urbanism: Gentrification as Global Urban Strategy', in N. Brenner and N. Theodore (eds) *Spaces of Neoliberalism. Urban Restructuring in North America and Western Europe*. Oxford: Blackwell. 80–103.

Smith, N. and Dennis, W. (1987) 'The Restructuring of Geographical Scale: Coalescence and Fragmentation of the Northern Cor Region', *Economic Geography*, 63(2): 160–82.

Stadtrat Luzern (1992) *Frankfurter Resolution. Zustimmung zum Statut der ECDP*. Beschluss: 1673.

–   (2001a) *Mitgliedschaft Europäisches Klima-Bündnis. Beitritt*. Auszug aus dem

Verhandlungsprotokoll: StB 572.

–   (2001b) *Städtepartnerschaften: Konzept für die Fortführung internationaler Beziehungen.* Bericht und Antrag an den Grossen Stadtrat von Luzern vom 6 Dezember 2000: B+A 45/2000.

–   (2003) *Städtepartnerschaften, Rahmenkredit 2004–2006.* Bericht und Antrag an den Grossen Stadtrat von Luzern vom 13 August 2003: B+A 23/2003.

–   (2004) *Protokoll Nr: 2 über die Verhandlungen des Grossen Stadtrates von Luzern.* Grosser Stadtrat. Donnerstag, 30 September 2004.

–   (2007) *Auszug aus dem Verhandlungsprotokoll StB 251.* Grosser Stadtrat. 30. Ratssitzung vom 8 März 2007.

Stadtrat Zürich (2000a) *Auszug aus dem Protokoll des Stadtrates von Zürich. Antwort auf die Interpellation von Bruno Sidler und Monika Erfigen (beide SVP) GR Nr. 2000/310.* Online. Available <http://www.gemeinderat-zuerich.ch/DocumentLoader. aspx?ID=b1d169b4-5e7c-46f4-864d-3a2b51ea70a7.pdf&Title=2000_0310.pdf> (accessed 18 March 2010).

–   (2000b) *Auszug aus dem Protokoll des Stadtrates von Zürich. Antwort auf die Interpellation von Markus Schwyn und Mauro Tuena (beide SVP) GR Nr. 2000/290.* Online. Available <http://www.gemeinderat-zuerich.ch/DocumentLoader. aspx?ID=50a32c32-ab64-4725-ae8f-98a2df17c12a.pdf&Title=2000_0290.pdf> (accessed 18 March 2010).

–   (2001) *Medienmitteilung vom 15. November 2001. Erfolgreiche Einsätze in Kunming.* Online. Available no longer available online (accessed 18 March 2010).

–   (2002) *Medienmitteilung vom 28. August 2002. Letzte Etappe in der technischen Zusammenarbeit Zürich-Kunming eingeläutet.* Online. Available <http://www.stadt-zuerich.ch/str/Bulletinsausdemstadtrat/august_2002/28august2002.htm> (accessed 18 March 2010).

–   (2003) *Medienmitteilung vom 27. August 2003. Zusammenarbeit mit San Francisco.* Online. Available <http://www.stadt-zuerich.ch/internet/mm/home/0_mm_str/home/ mm_03/aug_03/tag_2/mm_1.html> (accessed 18 March 2010).

–   (2004) *Auszug aus dem Protokoll des Stadtrates von Zürich. Antwort auf die Interpellation von Susi Gut und Markus Schwyn (beide SVP) GR Nr. 2003/444.* Online. Available <http://www.gemeinderat-zuerich.ch/DocumentLoader.aspx?ID=dff35d5a-f5d3-45c1-a176-80445d41ea47.pdf&Title=2003_0444.pdf> (accessed 18 March 2010).

–   (2006) *Legislaturschwerpunkte 2006 – 2010. Ziele und Strategien für die laufende Legislatur.* Online. Available <http://www.stadt-zuerich.ch/content/dam/stzh/ portal/Deutsch/Politik%20der%20Stadt%20Zuerich/Publikationen%20und%20 Broschueren/060927_LSP_2006_2010.pdf> (accessed 18 March 2010).

Standortförderung Kanton Zürich (2004) *Schlüsselbranche Finanzdienstleistungen.* Online. Available <http://www.standort.zh.ch/internet/vd/awa/standort/de/wirtschaft/ branchen/finanz.html> (accessed 18 March 2010).

Statistikdienste der Stadt Bern (2007) *Eidgenössische Betriebszählung 2005 – Ergebnisse für die Stadt Bern.* Online. Available <www.bern.ch/leben_in_bern/stadt/statistik/bz2005/ mm042007> (accessed 18 March 2010).

Steinacher, B. (2006) *Aktivitäten und Vernetzung der Metropolregionen in Deutschland und Europa.* Online. Available <http://www.region-stuttgart.org/vrsuploads/ SteinacherIKM-Stuttgart.pdf> (accessed 8 August 2008).

Stone, C. (1993) 'Urban Regimes and the Capacity to Govern: A Political Economy Approach', *Journal of Urban Affairs*, 15(1): 1–28.

Storper, M. (1997) *The Regional World. Territorial Development in a Global Economy.* New York/London: Guilford Press.

Strange, S. (1997) 'The Future of Global Capitalism; Or, Will Divergence Persist Forever?', in C. Crouch and W. Streeck (eds) *Political Economy of Modern Capitalism. Mapping Convergence & Diversity.* London, Thousand Oaks, New Delhi: Sage. 182–91.

Straubhaar, T. (2006) 'Glokalisierung und die Zukunft der Städte', *Stadtblick*, 13(März 2006): 11–3.

–   (2006) 'Der kleine Gigant: Der Aufstieg Zürichs zu einem internationalen Finanzplatz', *Bankhistorisches Archiv*, Beiheft 45: Europäische Finanzplätze im Wettbewerb: 139–69.

Streeck, W. (1997) 'Beneficial Constraints: On the Economic Limits of Rational Voluntarism', in J. R. Hollingsworth and R. Boyer (eds) *Contemporary Capitalism. The Embeddedness of Institutions*. Cambridge: Cambridge University Press. 197–219.

Sturny, T. (1998) *Mitwirkungsrechte der Kantone an der Aussenpolitik des Bundes*. Freiburg: Universitäts Verlag.

Stuttgarter Zeitung (18 July 2005) *Stuttgart und Cardiff beenden "wilde Ehe". Delegation mit OB Schuster zu Gast in der Hauptstadt von Wales – Noch engere Kooperation*. Page unavailable online.

– (4 August 2005) *Stuttgart stellt sich der Übermacht der Europäischen Union. Bis zu 80 Prozent aller EU-Richtlinien haben Einfluss auf die Kommune – Die Landeshauptstadt mischt deshalb in Brüssel kräftig mit*, p. 22.

– (9 September 2005) *In politischer Mission bei Kofi Annan. OB Schuster stellt dem UN-Generalsekretär das Konzept "Stuttgarter Partnerschaft Eine Welt" vor*. Page unavailable online.

– (16 October 2008) *EU setzt "Rat der Weisen" ein. Stuttgarts OB Schuster dabei*. Online. Available <http://www.stuttgarter-zeitung.de/stz/page/1847891_0_2147_eusetzt-rat-der-weisen-ein-ob-schuster-ist-dabei.html> (accessed 18 March 2010).

Sutcliffe, A. (1983) 'In Search of the Urban Variable: Britain in the Later Nineteenth Century', in D. Fraser and A. Sutcliffe (eds) *The Pursuit of Urban History*. London: Edwards Arnold. 234–63.

Swissinfo (13 September 2008) *Berner Altstadt seit 25 Jahren Unesco -Weltkulturgut*. Online. Available <http://www.swissinfo.ch/ger/news/newsticker/Berner_Altstadt_seit_25_Jahren_Unesco_Weltkulturgut.html?siteSect=146&sid=9713717&cKey=122133127 5000&ty=ti&positionT=1> (accessed 13 September 2008).

SWX (2008) *Kennzahlen*. Online. Available <http://www.swx.com/swx/publications/annual_report_de.html> (accessed 15 July 2008).

Swyngedouw, E. (1992) 'The Mammon Quest. 'Glocalisation', Interspatial Competition and the Monetary Order: the Construction of New Scales', in M. Dunford and G. Kafkalas (eds) *Cities and Regions in the New Europe*. London: Belhaven. 39–67.

– (1996) 'Reconstructing Citizenship, the Re-scaling of the State and the New Authoritarianism: Closing the Belgian Mines', *Urban Studies*, 33(8): 1499–521.

– (1997) 'Neither Global nor Local: "Glocalisation" and the Politics of Scale', in K. R. Cox (ed.) *Spaces of Globalization*. New York: Guilford Press. 137–66.

– (1998) 'Homing in and Spacing Out: Re-configuring Scale', in H. Gebhardt, G. Heinritz and R. Weissner (eds) *Europa im Globalisierungsprozess von Wirtschaft und Gesellschaft*. Stuttgart: Franz Steiner. 81–100.

– (2000a) 'Authoritarian Governance, Power, and the Politics or Rescaling', *Environment and Planning D*, 18(1): 63–76.

– (2000b) 'Elite Power, Global Forces, and the Political Economy of 'Glocal' Development', in M. P. Feldman and M. S. Gertler (eds) *The Oxford Handbook of Economic Geography*. Oxford: Oxford University Press. 541–58.

Swyngedouw, E., Moulaert, F. and Rodriguez, A. (2002) 'Neoliberal Urbanization in Europe: Large-Scale Urban Development Projects and the New Urban Policy', in N. Brenner and N. Theodore (eds) *Spaces of Neoliberalism. Urban Restructuring in North America and Eastern Europe*. Oxford: Oxford University Press. 195–229.

– (2003) 'The World in a Grain of Sand: Large-Scale Urban Development Projects and the New Urban Policy.', in E. Swyngedouw, F. Moulaert and A. Rodriguez (eds) *The Globalized City. Economic Restructuring and Social Polarization in European Cities*. Oxford: Blackwell. 9–28.

Syrett, S. and Baldock, R. (2003) 'Reshaping London's economic governance', *European Urban and Regional Studies*, 10(1): 69–86.

Tagesanzeiger (9 July 2008) *Zusätzliches Personal für die Sozialhilfe*, p. 12.

Taylor, P. J. (1990) *Britain and the Cold War*. London: Pinter.

– (1995) 'World Cities and Territorial States: the Rise and Fall of Their Mutuality', in P. L. Knox and P. J. Taylor (eds) *World Cities in a World System*. Cambridge: Cambridge University Press. 48–62.

– (2004) *World City Network. A Global Urban Analysis*. London: Routledge.

– (2007) 'Prologue: A Lineage for Contemporary Inter-City Studies', in P. J. Taylor, B. Derudder, P. Saey and F. Witlox (eds) *Cities in Globalization. Practices, Policies and*

Theories. London, New York: Routledge. 1–12.

Taylor, P. J., Derudder, B., Saey, P. and Witlox, F. (eds) (2007a) *Cities in Globalization. Practices, Policies and Theories*. London, New York: Routledge.

–   (2007b) 'Introduction: Cities in Globalization', in P. J. Taylor, B. Derudder, P. Saey and F. Witlox (eds) *Cities in Globalization. Practices, Policies and Theories*. London, New York: Routledge. 13–8.

Thornley, A. (2003) 'London: Institutional Turbulence but Enduring Nation-State Control', in W. Salet, A. Thornley and A. Kreukels (eds) *Metropolitan Governance and Spatial Planning*. London: Sage. 203–33.

Tripartite Arbeitsgruppe Bundesstadtstatus (2003) *Bundesstadtstatus der Stadt Bern*. Online. Available < http://www.tinyurls.co.uk/P5417 > (accessed 18 March 2010).

Tussie, D. (2006) 'Globalization and World Trade: From Multilateralism to Regionalism', *Oxford Development Studies*, 26(1): 33–46.

Uitermark, J. (2005) 'The Genesis and Evolution of Urban Policy: A Confrontation of Regulationist and Governmentality Approaches', *Political Geography*, 24(2): 137–63.

Umweltschutzfachstelle der Stadt Zürich (1995) *Umweltpolitik der Stadt Zürich. Lokale Agenda 21*. Online. Available <http://www.stadt-zuerich.ch/internet/ugz/home/dokumente/ berichte.ParagraphContainerList.ParagraphContainer0.ParagraphList.0022.File.pdf/ us_umweltpolitik.pdf> (accessed 20 July 2008).

US Census Bureau (2006) *Principal Combined Metropolitan Areas*. Online. Available <http:// www.citypopulation.de/USA-CombMetro.html> (accessed 18 March 2010).

Vaissade, A. (2000) 'Genève, Ville internationale', *DISP*, 142: 26–9.

van der Heiden, N. and Terhorst, P. (2007) 'Varieties of Glocalisation: International Urban Economic Strategies Compared', *Environment and Planning C*, 25(3): 341–56.

van der Wusten, H. (2004) 'The Distribution of Political Centrality in the European State System', *Political Geography*, 23(6): 677–700.

–   (2007) 'Political World Cities. Where Flows Through Entwined Multi-State and Transnational Networks Meet Places', in P. J. Taylor, B. Derudder, P. Saey and F. Witlox (eds) *Cities in Globalization. Practices, Policies and Theories*. London, New York: Routledge. 202–17.

van Tatenhove, J., Mak, J. and Liefferink, D. (2006) 'The Inter-play between Formal and Informal Practices', *Perspectives on European Politics and Society*, 7(1): 8–24.

Verband Region Stuttgart (2000) *Auszug aus: "Die Region Stuttgart in Europa. Präsenz und Handlungsfelder auf europäischer Ebene"*.

–   (2001) *Die Region Stuttgart in Europa. Präsenz und Handlungsfelder auf europäischer Ebene*. Sitzungsvorlage Nr. 62/2001. Regionalversammlung am 11.07.2001.

–   (2007) *Facts & Figures*. Online. Available <http://www.region-stuttgart.org/ vrsuploads/ZDF_englisch2007.pdf> (accessed 8 August 2008).

–   (2008) *Wirtschaftsstruktur*. Online. Available <http://www.region-stuttgart.de/sixcms/ detail.php/167111> (accessed 18 March 2010).

Ville de Genève (2007) *Les relations extérieures de la ville de Genève. Législature 2003–2007*. Online. Available <http://www.ville-ge.ch/en/media/pdf/sre_rapport_0307.pdf> (accessed 18 March 2010).

Ville de Lausanne (2008a) *Lausanne, olympische Hauptstadt. Das weltweite Zentrum der sportlichen Institutionen*. Online. Available <http://www.lausanne.ch/view.asp?docId =20332&domId=30301&language=D> (accessed 18 March 2010).

– (2008b) *Le point sur le i. Promotion de l'image + city management*. Online. Available <http://www.lausanne-tourisme.ch/DataDir/LinkedDocsObjDir/7363.pdf> (accessed 18 March 2010).

– (2008c) *Politique culturelle*. Online. Available <http://www.lausanne.ch/view. asp?DomId=64560> (accessed 18 March 2010).

– (2008d) *Solidarité internationale*. Online. Available <http://www.lausanne.ch/view. asp?DomId=62300&Language=F> (accessed 26 July 2008).

Ville de Lyon (2002) *Cadidacy of Lyon. Eurocities. Executive Committee*. Lyon.

– (2006) *Dossier de Presse. Lyon 2013 – Capitale européenne de la culture. Ville candidate*. Lyon.

– (2007) *Lyon 2013 – Capitale européenne de la culture. Ville candidate*. Lyon.

– (2008a) *Partner Cities*. Online. Available <http://www.lyon.fr/vdl/sections/en/ villes_partenaires/villes_partenaires_2/?aIndex=1> (accessed 15 August 2008).

– (2008b) *A Quick Look at the Festival of Lights*. Online. Available <http://www. lumieres.lyon.fr/fetedeslumieres/sections/en/lyon_and_light/a_quick_look_at_the_ festival_of_lig> (accessed 15 August 2008).

Wagner, T. (2000) *Mediencommuniqué von Stadtrat Dr. Thomas Wagner. Städtepartnerschaft Zürich – Kunming*. 9. Juni 2000.

Ward, K. (1996) 'Rereading Urban Regime Theory: a Sympathetic Critique', *Geoforum*, 27: 427–38.

Ward, K. and Jonas, A. E. G. (2004) 'Competitive City-Regionalism as a Politics of Space: a Critical Reinterpretation of the New Regionalism', *Environment and Planning A*, 36(12): 2119–39.

Ward, S. and Williams, R. (1997) 'From Hierarchy to Networks? Sub-central Government and EU Urban Environment Policy', *Journal of Common Market Studies*, 35(3): 439–64.

Wehrli-Schindler, B. (2006) *Zürich soll zur Kongressstadt werden. Mangelnde Infrastruktur als Nachteil im Standortwettbewerb*, in *Neue Zürcher Zeitung*. 22 March 2006, p. 51.

Wellmann, C. (1998) 'Introduction', in C. Wellmann (ed.) *From Town to Town: Local Authorities as Transnational Actors*. Hamburg: LIT Verlag. 9–12.

Wirtschaftsförderung Region Bern (2008) *Wirtschaftsraum Bern: Allgemeines*. Online. Available <http://www.promotion.bern.ch/cgi/wirtschaftsraum/allgemeines.asp> (accessed 18 March 2010).

Wirtschaftsförderung Region Stuttgart GmbH (2001) *Die Region Stuttgart in Europa. Präsenz und Handlungsfelder auf europäischer Ebene*. Sitzungsvorlage Nr. 62/2001. Regionalversammlung am 11.07.2001.

Wood, A. (2005) 'Comparative Urban Politics and the Question of Scale', *Space and Polity*, 9(3): 201–15.

| index

www.ingramcontent.com/pod-product-compliance
Lightning Source LLC
Chambersburg PA
CBHW072122020426
42334CB00018B/1679